Defining New Christian/Jewish Dialogue

Defining New Christian/Jewish Dialogue

Edited by Irvin J. Borowsky

Sponsored by a generous grant from
Ed Satell and Family

A Crossroad Book
The Crossroad Publishing Company
New York

The Crossroad Publishing Company
16 Penn Plaza, 481 Eighth Avenue
New York, NY 10001

This book is typeset in 10.5/13 Palatino. The display type is Tiepolo.

Printed in the United States of America

Library of Congress Cataloging-in-Publication Data

Defining new Christian/Jewish dialogue / edited by Irvin J. Borowsky.
    p. cm.
  Includes bibliographical references and index.
  ISBN 0-8245-2288-5 (hardcover)
  1. Judaism – Relations – Christianity – 1945- 2. Christianity and other religions – 1945- 3. Jews in the New Testament. I. Borowsky, Irvin J.
  BM535.D43 2004
  261.2'6 – dc22

                                                    2004017769

1   2   3   4   5   6   7   8   9   10   10   09   08   07   06   05   04

Contents

Introduction

Defining New Christian/Jewish Dialogue

Irvin J. Borowsky

Although the New Testament represents only 22 percent of the Christian Bible, its teachings and influence are the cornerstone of a great compassionate and principled religion.

Regrettably, the poetry and reasoning that describe first-century events in the New Testament are diminished by inaccurate interpretations and translations that blame Jews for the crucifixion of Jesus two thousand years ago. It is this historical untruth, repeated in almost every edition of the New Testament since its inception, that is the foundation for most of the anti-Semitism that has led to the murder of Jews throughout Europe. It is time to stop teaching each new generation to distrust and hate Jews, based on misinterpretations of events of the first century.

This bigotry is as absurd as teaching hatred of all Germans because of Hitler's atrocities, or hatred of all Japanese because of the attack on Pearl Harbor, or hatred of all Muslims because of 9/11, or hatred of all descendants of Romans for nailing Jesus to the cross.

The chapters in this book represent an update to the work of the American Interfaith Institute, which was founded in 1982 to rebuild broken bridges between Christians and Jews by removing anti-Jewish references from the New Testament.

There are basic historical facts, well researched and acknowledged worldwide, that are catalysts for editions of the New Testament being developed by Bible scholars:

1. The Romans employed citizens of their conquered nations to administer the government, just as the Nazis did in Europe. Religious leaders, including the Sanhedrin, tax collectors, and

7

others, had power, but it was limited. If the instructions of the Roman overlords were not adhered to, their lackeys were either removed from their position, imprisoned, or even crucified.

2. Crucifixion was an exclusively Roman form of execution.

3. Because Jesus had a significant and devoted following, Pontius Pilate believed Jesus was a threat who had to be removed. When Pilate's troops crucified him, they ridiculed him publicly as "King of the Jews." The Romans wanted no competition: Caesar was the one and only king.

4. The first Christians were of Jewish background. Jesus and his earliest followers never heard the words "Christian" or "New Testament."

5. The inaccurate references to Jewish involvement in Jesus' death in the New Testament texts are the principal foundation for Christian anti-Semitism.

Today, Christians and Jews find themselves allies in a struggle for the soul and survival of our civilization. It is time to bury old suspicions and fears, time for people of the book to unite in a new movement of solidarity. Our connections are revealed as never before: the ethical teachings of Jews and Christians are grounded in respect for the sanctity of life, the pursuit of justice, and the call for peace.

Clearly, this is the moment to explore and celebrate the bridges that connect. That is why, now, more than ever before, it is vital that Bible publishers remove misinformation from their publications and publish new editions that are sensitive to the issues that divide.

It is appropriate, in light of contemporary research and truth, to re-examine the scriptures. The American Bible Society, the largest Bible society in the world, has taken the lead by publishing a historically more accurate translation of the New Testament, the Contemporary English Version (CEV), which the Vatican has approved. The research and production of this vast project extended over a ten-year period, and I was privileged to be involved in the process. The CEV has set the stage by translating the virulent references to Jews in light of the sociolinguistic setting of various New Testament writings. It is vital that anti-Jewish references in all other New Testament editions be critically examined within the sociological context of first-century events and the realities of current research.

Note John 7:1 and John 19:14–15 in the CEV as compared to three other editions:

John 7:1

Contemporary
English Version

Jesus decided to leave Judea and to start going through Galilee because *the leaders of the people* wanted to kill him.

King James Version

After these things Jesus walked in Galilee, for he would not walk in Jewry, because *the Jews* sought to kill him.

New International
Version

After this Jesus went around in Galilee, purposely staying away from Judea because *the Jews* there were waiting to take his life.

New Revised
Standard Version

After this Jesus went about in Galilee. He did not wish to go about in Judea because *the Jews* were looking for an opportunity to kill him.

John 19:14–15

Contemporary
English Version

Pilate said to *the crowd,* "Look at your king!" "Kill him! Kill him!" They yelled. "Nail him to a cross!"

King James Version

He [Pilate] saith unto *the Jews,* "Behold your king!" But they cried out, "Away with him, away with him, crucify him."

New International
Version

"Here is your king," Pilate said to *the Jews.* But they shouted, "Take him away! Take him away! Crucify him!"

New Revised
Standard Version

He [Pilate] said to *the Jews,* "Here is your king!" They cried out, "Away with him! Away with him! Crucify him!"

The CEV, KJV, NIV, and NRSV represent about 90 percent of all Bibles sold in America. There are no translations that are identical. Bible scholars have taken many liberties in translating the ancient Greek. It is unacceptable that their translations continue to indict the Jews when editors know the historical truth.

Throughout the world, Catholic and Protestant scholars, professors of religion, ministers, priests, and other Christians who are working to rid Christianity of its anti-Jewish references are urging that Bible publishers remove these hateful references to Jews. It is now well understood at every level of church administration and education that these distorted references to Jewish involvement in Jesus' death have been the principal foundation for Christian anti-Semitism. Re-examining historical texts in the light of new data is an accepted practice in every field of research.

Thoughtful Christians recognize that the Nazis could not have succeeded in the murder of six million Jews without assistance from Christian citizens. The Holocaust was a continuation of centuries of hostility toward Jews in Europe fed by inaccurate references to first-century events. The systematic teaching of contempt has led to expulsion or murder of Jews in every nation of Europe. The murder of six million innocent Jewish men, women, and children is an abomination.

It was this factor that desensitized apparently normal human beings, that encouraged participation in heinous acts, that enabled people to assist in rounding up their Jewish neighbors to be sent to death camps. That is why Christian leadership is now insisting that the Bible be rendered without hatred toward the Jewish community.

Today, "the Jews" means the whole Jewish people. But as used in John's Gospel, the term refers to a small group of Jewish leaders who were collaborating with the Roman invaders by serving on their ruling council. They were similar to the Quislings of Norway and the Vichy collaborators of France. It is imperative that Christian teachings acknowledge that Jesus was crucified by the Romans.

Many scholars believe that if the efforts of Vatican and Protestant leadership, plus those of the American Interfaith Institute and other like-minded organizations, had been started at the end of the nineteenth century rather than the end of the twentieth, the horrendous scope of the Holocaust would have been mitigated.

Had this initiative been implemented centuries ago, anti-Semitism would have been so diminished that Hitler and other purveyors of hate would not have succeeded. The Holocaust was a continuation of the atrocities that began with the First Crusade in the eleventh century. In just five short years from 1940 to 1945, more than 1,500,000 children were murdered because they had a Jewish mother.

Children's Bibles are particularly susceptible to nefarious interpretations because they often paraphrase scripture. The fact that children

Country	Estimated Number of Jews prior to World War II	Estimated Number[a] Murdered	Percentages of all Jews Murdered in Each Nation
Protectorate (*now Czech Republic*)	94,000	90,600	95%
Poland[b]	3,300,000	3,000,000	91%
Baltic Countries	264,500	215,000	81%
Slovakia	89,000	71,000	80%
Greece	77,000	60,000	78%
Yugoslavia	78,000	60,000	77%
The Netherlands	140,000	105,000	75%
Germany/Austria	215,000	141,000	66%
Belarus[c]	375,000	245,000[c]	65%
Ukraine[c]	1,500,000	900,000	60%
Hungary	850,000	450,000	53%
Norway	1,700	900	50%
Romania	750,000	330,000	44%
Luxembourg	3,500	1,500	43%
Belgium	90,000	32,000	36%
France	350,000	90,000	26%
Bulgaria	50,000	12,000	24%
Italy[d]	44,500	8,000	18%
Russia[c]	975,000	107,000	11%

a. Dr. Steven Hochberg and Dr. Peter Black, historians at the United States Holocaust Memorial Museum, graciously authenticated all information contained in the chart above.

b. While the Nazis were efficient in killing 91 percent of the Jews in Poland, twenty thousand or more were hidden by a Christian network and survived.

c. The combined total of the Soviet Union was 1,302,000, including Belarus and Ukraine.

d. Italy had one of the lowest percentages of its Jewish citizens killed. Prior to the German invasion of the nation, Italy refused to send any of its Jewish citizens to concentration camps. Thousands of Jews who escaped from adjoining nations also found safe harbor in Italy. They were hidden in convents and other religious buildings.

cannot easily comprehend the New Testament in terms of its own historical context makes this matter all the more urgent. These Bibles often do not make clear that Jesus himself was a Jew and that the ethical controversies in the Gospels are between Jesus' early Jewish followers and other Jews, such as some members of the Pharisees and Sadducees sects.

Christian youth must be taught historical truth. The American Interfaith Institute has reviewed and consulted with the publishers of 110 Bibles written for young people five to ten years of age. We are pleased to report that all but six editions have removed the inaccurate passages we identified. What follows is a small sample of what can be found in these six children's Bibles. *Note how recently they were copyrighted.*

Kids Study Bible
Edited by Jean E. Syswerda. Copyright 1996.

> *He knew that the Jews there were waiting to kill him* (p. 1523).
>
> *Again the Jews picked up stones to kill him* (p. 1530).

Youth Walk Devotional Bible
Edited by Jean E. Syswerda. Copyright 1992.

> *But no one would say anything publicly about him for fear of the Jews* (p. 1139).

Kids Study Bible and *Youth Walk Devotional Bible* are published by Zondervan Publishing, a division of HarperCollins, a Rupert Murdoch Company. 5300 Patterson Avenue S.W., Grand Rapids, MI 49512
Phone: 616-698-6900; fax: 616-698-3439; Web: www.zondervan.com

The Bedtime Bible Story Book
Edited by Daniel Partner. Copyright 1995.

> *The Jews saw the crowds and became jealous* (p. 331).
>
> *That's why the Jews tried to kill me* (p. 357).

Published by Paradise Press, Inc.
1575 N. Park Drive, Suite 100, Weston, FL 33326-3230
Telephone: 954-349-9474; fax: 954-349-7217

International Children's Story Bible
Edited by Mary Hollingsworth. Copyright 1990.

> *Finally, Pilate turned Jesus over to the Jews to be killed* (see John 18:28–19:16)

Published by Word Publishing, a division of Thomas Nelson, Inc.
PO Box 141000, Nashville, TN 37214
Phone: 615-902-1300; fax: 615-883-6353; Web: www.thomasnelson.com

The Treasure Study Bible
Edited by Daryl Lucas. Copyright 1997.

> *After this, Jesus went around Galilee, purposely staying away from Judea because the Jews there were waiting to take his life* (p. 1471).

Published by Kirkbride Bible Company
335 W. 9th Street, Indianapolis, IN 46206
Phone: 800-428-4385; fax: 317-633-1444; Web: www.kirkbride.com

365 Read to Me Bedtime Bible Stories
Edited by Melanie M. Burnette. Copyright 1989.

Judas knew the Jewish people and Pharisees wanted to lay a trap for Jesus (p. 255).

Published by Broadman & Holman
127 Ninth Avenue North, Nashville, TN 37234
Phone: 800-448-8032; fax: 800-296-4036; Web: www.broadmanholman.com

To avoid teaching each new generation of Christians to distrust and hate Jewish people, why not recognize and use two editions of the Bible? Historians may wish to continue their studies of the Greek text and numerous translations. For church services, Christian education, and personal study, the CEV edition incorporates a clarified translation based on historical truth.

Defining New Christian/Jewish Dialogue is a call to action, a call for respect. It is vital that Christian leadership the world over contact religious publishers to urge the removal of all Bibles from distribution that publish misleading information about the events of the first century. It is time to decry and deny untruths and to embrace the roots of faith that link us all . . . one to the other.

Chapter 1

Appropriate Christian Responses to the "Teaching of Contempt" for Jews in the New Testament

Norman A. Beck

The Significance of the Problem

As a pastor and professor of theology and classical languages in one of the excellent liberal arts universities of the Evangelical Lutheran Church in America, I have become painfully aware that my Christian religion, although it is a religion in which so much emphasis is placed on love and on God's love and grace, includes in its tradition a hateful "teaching of contempt"[1] for Jews. For many centuries Jews have noted the anomaly of this teaching within Christianity. They have suffered greatly, largely because of it, especially during the Christian Crusades and Inquisition and during countless pogroms and the Holocaust in lands dominated by Christians. Most Christians, however, including myself during the first forty years of my life, did not seem to notice this striking polarity between love and hate. Prior to the end of World War II, if Jews tried to bring this contradiction to the attention of Christians, they were in almost all instances ignored and often subjected to even more condemnation. Within a few decades after the end of World War II, however, Jewish religious leaders and writers[2] began to articulate the problem publicly and in books that were read by Christians, and some Christians began to acknowledge it as well.[3]

During the past few decades, with a major impetus given by the Second Vatican Council, many Roman Catholic, Lutheran, Episcopal, United Church of Christ, Disciples of Christ, Methodist, Presbyterian, and a few other Christian groups within the United States, Canada, Western Europe, and to some extent worldwide have rejected and renounced this teaching of contempt for Jews that was previously promulgated in the writings of their leaders. These Christian

15

groups, with increasing sensitivity, have removed the most hateful statements from their worship, educational, and promotional materials, especially from the materials they had been using on Good Friday and other days of the Christian Holy Week. Productive inter-religious dialogue with Jews has replaced their earlier attempts to convert Jews to Christianity. While such efforts are not embraced by all Christians within those groups and are opposed or ignored by most of the people within many other Christian groups, as a result of these efforts the Christian teaching of contempt for Jews has been reduced significantly.

Significant rejection and repudiation of the hateful Christian teaching of contempt for Jews that exists *in the New Testament itself,* however, has not occurred. We have, at best, been able only to scratch the surface of this problem. It has been much more difficult to address the problem in our sacred scriptures than in our worship, educational, and promotional materials that are largely derived from and influenced by these sacred scriptures. I am firmly convinced, however, that until we are able significantly to reject and to repudiate the hateful teaching of contempt for Jews that exists in the New Testament itself, difficult as that may be, we shall never be able to eliminate this teaching of contempt for Jews from our Christian tradition. It will always resurface from its source in the New Testament.

Denial that the Christian teaching of contempt exists in the New Testament itself is prevalent within Christianity today. It is most obvious among the large numbers of Christians who are basically biblical literalists. For these Christians, if the Bible "says it," God says it. That settles it! No more questions can be asked. For them, the Bible is a book of facts. If it is stated in the New Testament that all of the Jews killed Jesus and that the Jews are the offspring of Satan, not of Abraham, then all the Jews must have killed Jesus and the Jews must be the offspring of Satan, not of Abraham.

While most Christian biblical literalists deny that there is a teaching of contempt for Jews in the New Testament, there is another, much smaller but very influential group of Christians who also deny that the New Testament includes a significant teaching of contempt for Jews. Included in this group are Christian scholars, many of whom are among my close friends and are deeply committed to our productive Jewish-Christian dialogue, who insist that the vicious, name-calling statements directed against Pharisees and Jews collectively in the New Testament accounts are not *anti*-Jewish polemic (war with words). Instead, these scholars argue, these statements are *intra*-Jewish heated arguments.[4] They contend that such statements are the result of a "family feud." They provide evidence of the variety of "Judaisms" of the time of Jesus and of his earliest followers, a point well taken. They say that Jews enjoy using strong language, heated and passionate, in their discussions about scriptures, the way to live one's life in response to God's will, dietary limitations, etc., that Jews talked that way during the time of Jesus and still do today. They speak about the audience, the readers and hearers of the Gospel According to Matthew, for example, as Jewish, Jews contending with other Jews.[5]

These arguments of my scholarly Christian friends, whom I greatly respect, are nevertheless a form of denial, even though they, like most of the Christian biblical literalists, do not consider it to be such. It is a serious form of "blaming the other" rather than of "blaming one's self." It is a serious form of "blaming the victims," since the Jews tragically have been and remain the victims of this polemic. It makes our task of repudiation of the teaching of contempt for Jews in the New Testament far more difficult than it otherwise would be, because of the great respect with which these scholars, my colleagues, are held.

Before I turn in the next section to the issue of overcoming this denial, I shall briefly make a necessary distinction between the Christian teaching of contempt for Jews and other anti-Jewish polemic in the New Testament, cite a few examples of the most virulent polemic, and list a series of interrelated reasons for the Christian teaching of contempt within the sacred texts.

First, the anti-Jewish polemic of the New Testament documents should be classified into three major categories. The first type is *Christological*. It is present throughout the New Testament and can be summarized in the statement that "in the past Adonai was Lord, but now Jesus as the Risen Christ is Lord." This type of polemic should be handled with great sensitivity, but it should not be rejected nor repudiated. It is essential to the existence of Christianity. A religious community can designate anyone it chooses as its Lord, even when that designation is made against the backdrop of other designations by other communities of faith.

This first category of anti-Jewish polemic, however, led to the second category, the *supersessionistic* anti-Jewish polemic, expressed in statements that the Christian religion is the "New Israel," that it has superseded and replaced the Jewish religion as God's chosen people. This polemic, with its claims that the Jewish religion is no longer valid, that Christianity is the "only way" to God, begins the Christian teaching of contempt for Jews and paves the way for the third category of anti-Jewish polemic, the *defamatory* name-calling anti-Jewish polemic in the New Testament texts.[6]

The *supersessionistic* and the *defamatory* name-calling teaching of contempt for Jews in the New Testament documents is most prevalent in the Acts of the Apostles and in the four Gospels. In the letters of the Apostle Paul and in the epistles attributed to him it is present in only four verses, 1 Thessalonians 2:13–16, which are almost certainly an interpolation into his letter three decades after Paul had been executed by zealous advocates of Roman civil religion.[7] In the Acts of the Apostles, it is most pronounced in the major speeches written by the Lukan playwright for the characters Peter, Stephen, and Paul in that drama. In the four Gospels it is expressed in the Passion accounts,[8] in the conflict stories in Mark, Matthew, and Luke, and in accounts of serious conflicts between the Johannine Jesus and "the Jews" in John 5–12. It is in these texts that the Jews are condemned as "Christ-killers," "offspring of poisonous snakes," "descendants of the Devil, not of Abraham," etc. In the Passion account in Matthew 27:25, the Jews are given the line to speak that no Jew would ever say, "May the guilt for his [Jesus'] blood be upon us and upon our children!"[9]

While it is not possible fully to understand the reasons that leaders and writers in the early church expressed such hateful invective against the Jews, we can identify as many as seven interrelated factors. By identifying these factors, I am confident that we can address them and in doing so be enabled to reject and to repudiate this teaching of contempt. The most basic factor is what we may call

1. human perversity.

It is followed by:

2. the arrogance of religious exclusivists,
3. the frustrations of exclusivistic Christians because of their inability to convert Jews to their own Christian beliefs and practices,
4. the failure of exclusivistic Christians to understand that theists perceive God and the activity of God in human history in similar but not identical ways,
5. jealousy over the mature ethical monotheism of the Jews and their tenacity in maintaining their traditions even when subjected to horrendous persecution,
6. scapegoating the Jews by attempting to deflect Roman persecution away from Christians, and

7. the adolescent immaturity of much of Christianity at the time
   of the composition of many of the New Testament documents.[10]

Having considered the significance of the problem, we turn now
to suggestions of how the denial that the teaching of contempt exists
in the New Testament documents can be overcome.

Overcoming Denial

The denial by Christian biblical literalists that anything can or
should be done about the teaching of contempt for Jews in the New
Testament documents is a very substantial obstacle to appropriate
Christian responses to this problem. It makes the task of "rebuilding
the broken bridges between Christians and Jews" formidable. Our
greatest hope is that these our fellow Christians will eventually realize that the Bible is primarily a book of *faith*, not primarily a book of
facts. It is a book of Bible stories. It includes a great variety of genres
in which faith is expressed. It is not so much a history book as it is
a book of faith that should be understood in its historical context.
The Bible is not God. It is instead the inspired, revealed, and authoritative "Word of God" for us. Only God is our Absolute Authority.
The Bible, the church and its sacraments, and inspired individuals
are very significant secondary authorities for us. These are excellent
"means of grace" by which faith in God is expressed, communicated,
and encouraged and the grace of God comes to us. Many Christian
biblical literalists become aware of this while attending one of the
excellent liberal arts universities of the church.

The liberal arts universities of the church are also where Christian scholars committed to productive Jewish-Christian dialogue but
denying that the teaching of contempt occurs in the New Testament
itself—by their interpretation of the vicious, defamatory anti-Jewish
statements as *intra*-Jewish heated arguments — can best be addressed.
These scholars are already committed to the task of "rebuilding the
broken bridges between Christians and Jews." Within the academic
freedom of the liberal arts universities of the church, these scholars
can see that although the Apostle Paul and most of the other writers
of the New Testament documents were of Jewish background, they
were no longer Jews when they believed and declared that "Jesus as
the Risen Christ [not Adonai] is Lord!" that "to Jesus as the Risen
Christ [not to Adonai nor to Caesar] every knee in heaven, on earth,
and under the earth shall bow and every tongue confess that Jesus
Christ is Lord!" They were no longer Jews when they announced

that "all authority in heaven and on earth has been given to the Risen Christ. Go therefore and make disciples of all nations, baptizing them in the name of the Father and of the Son and of the Holy Spirit. . . . " These were statements made by Christians. No Jews would write such things. The New Testament documents were written by committed Christians, primarily for the edification of their fellow Christians, in attempts to attract non–Jewish background people to the Christian communities of faith, and, as was the situation especially for the writer of the Epistle to the Hebrews, to try to persuade Christians of Jewish background to remain within Christianity and not return to the Jewish faith and communities.

Denial is a natural human response, an initial defense mechanism to give the mind time to adjust to reports of tragedy and loss of someone or something held dear. Denial, of whatever sort, must be overcome, however, before we can make appropriate responses to the teaching of contempt in the New Testament or to reports of any other tragedy or loss. Once this denial has been overcome, we can move on to appropriate responses, which we shall now consider.

Avoiding Use of the Most Supersessionistic and Defamatory Texts

The first and least intrusive appropriate Christian response to the teaching of contempt is to avoid using the most defamatory texts in our private devotions and in our community worship experiences. To do this, it is helpful to use new translations of the Greek New Testament, such as Today's English Version (Good News Bible, 2nd ed., 1992), or, preferably, the Contemporary English Version (1995), both works by American Bible Society translators who have become sensitive to this issue, or my own *The New Testament: A New Translation and Redaction.*[11] In the most recent of these translations, the texts in which the supersessionistic and defamatory anti-Jewish segments occur (as well as the segments in which all women are relegated to a secondary and subordinate status within the church) are placed into small-print status. This makes it much easier to avoid the use of these segments in private and public devotions and worship.

Directly related to the above, the most effective way to avoid use of the Christian teaching of contempt texts in public worship is to remove such selections from our lectionaries, our lists of selections from the scriptures to be read during the annual church year cycles, or better yet, to prepare new lectionaries in which such texts are not included. These lectionary selections have a very significant impact on Christian worshipers in the confessional denominations in which they are used. In these congregations, currently involving approximately 85–90 percent of all Christians, the selections from the lectionaries are read orally and are the primary texts upon which sermons and homilies are constructed. Therefore, lectionary revision and the preparation of new lectionaries in which there is sensitivity to this issue should have a very high priority among us as responsible, mature Christians. I have prepared a new Four Year Lectionary that avoids all of the texts that defame Jews and relegate women to a subordinate position in the church. It is published as an Appendix in *The New Testament: A New Translation and Redaction* (2001) cited above. To my knowledge, it is the only lectionary of the church, at least in the English language, that avoids the texts in which the Christian teaching of contempt is expressed.[12]

Fortunately, most Christian priests, pastors, and ministers in this post-Holocaust era avoid, at least to some extent, the most defamatory texts in their sermons and homilies, whether their messages are topical or based on the lectionaries.

Sensitizing and Educating All Christians about the Problem

The largest and probably the most important appropriate Christian response to the teaching of contempt in the New Testament is the task of sensitizing and educating all Christians about the problem. It is an enormous task, to reach nearly two billion Christians, who speak hundreds of languages and most of whom do not want to be sensitized and educated about an issue in which something within the Christian scriptures is repudiated.

Nevertheless, this important task is in process. Again, it is proceeding most effectively within the excellent liberal arts universities of the church. It is reaching many of those who are the present and future leaders of the church, both lay and clergy. It is proceeding in many seminaries, in spite of objections made by some people within the church who do not want their priests, pastors, and ministers to be encouraged to be critical of anything that is in the Bible. This process of sensitization and education is occurring in significant ways in some congregations of the church.

The role of the top leadership of the church is crucial in this task. The Roman Catholic Church structure of authority gives that church a distinct advantage in this respect. In the Roman Catholic Church papal encyclicals can be written and issued that can impact this process in very positive ways. Courageous leaders in the denominations of Christianity that function in more democratic ways can be helpful by voicing their approval of this sensitization and education and by engaging in it themselves. This is not an action that should be subjected to a vote within an ecclesial assembly in "win-lose" situations that polarize the church.

Sensitizing and Educating Those Who Make Translations of the Texts

The process of sensitization and education of all two billion Christians is greatly facilitated when the relatively small number who make new translations of the Greek New Testament into modern languages are sensitive to this issue. Tremendous progress has been made in this respect within the past two decades. Translators in the American Bible Society demonstrated very significant sensitivity in the second edition (1992) of their Today's English Version (Good News Bible) and in their production of the Contemporary English Version (1995), especially with regard to their translations of the Gospel According to John.[13] The fact that most translations of the Bible are prepared by groups of translators, often in Bible societies and within associations such as the United Bible Societies, and are collaborative efforts makes the task of communication with translators easier. It also in some instances makes change and innovation more difficult, because of the almost inevitable compromises that must be accepted when decisions are made by committees.

Even individuals, however, can make a difference. For example, Lydie Huynh, a translator working with the United Bible Societies in Abidjan, Ivory Coast, wrote in a brief article, "The Next 2,000 Years...," that after reading an article by Roger Omanson, "Anti-Jewish Bias in the NT," and my book *Mature Christianity in the 21st Century*, she made changes in 128 places in the next edition of her translation of the Greek New Testament into a basic level of French, a translation that serves as a reference for translations into native African languages in as many as seventeen countries in sub-Saharan Africa.[14]

In my own work, *The New Testament: A New Translation and Redaction* (2001), for which *Mature Christianity* (1985) and *Mature Christianity in the 21st Century* (1994) provide the rationale and the design, I have been able to provide a consistency of sensitivity to the defamatory anti-Jewish polemic in translating the entire New Testament that has not otherwise been apparent in other translations of the Greek New Testament into modern English, in spite of very commendable efforts.

In this area, as in many others, the best changes are made, not by coercion applied by other people (even by votes taken within democratic assemblies), but by free choice made when individuals and groups select which materials they will purchase and use.

Maintaining Original Manuscripts as Historical Witnesses of the Problem

Appropriate Christian responses to the teaching of contempt, a process of "rebuilding the broken bridges between Christians and Jews," will always incorporate the original manuscripts of the Greek New Testament, now more than five thousand extant handwritten copies of extensive as well as fragmentary Greek New Testament texts, lectionaries, and quotations in other works that are preserved in museums and libraries throughout the world. No attempts to change any of these witnesses to the texts that were prepared prior to the introduction of movable print in the West are appropriate. We should never change or modify historical records. The handwritten Greek texts are our historical records of the New Testament. We can neither reject nor repudiate our history. We must maintain it and learn from it, even from its most undesirable elements.

A question that can be raised, however, is whether it may be an appropriate Christian response to make notations about our rejection and repudiation of the segments of the texts that defame Jews and degrade women in the modern editions of the Greek New Testament. These modern editions of the Greek New testament are not our primary historical records of the text. They are dynamic editions, updated dozens of times within the past decades. They are provided with very extensive editorial comments and notations as aids to readers and to translators who use these editions as the basis for their translations into modern languages. Perhaps additional notations that reflect the sensitivities of the editors of these editions to the subject of defaming Jews and degrading women could be very helpful as a means of sharing these sensitivities to potentially large numbers of Christians in the future. Smaller print or a different type of print could be used for these segments, with clearly written explanations provided for the readers and translators.

We must oppose any changes at the origins end of the spectrum, in the historical past. We should be open, however, to necessary changes in the dynamic present and future. We can say this because, for us, the "Word of God is living and active, sharper than the sharpest two-edged sword," as the writer of the Epistle to the Hebrews (4:12) put it during the early decades of the church, and as most Jews and most Christians would most likely agree.

New translations, new Bible story books for use by our children, new presentations of the Bible in audio and video form today and in whatever form communications of the Bible will take in the future all provide opportunities for us and for our descendants to "sharpen this sword," this dynamic "living and active Word of God" for us. The past is fixed, static, rigid; we are not responsible for the past, for the times before our birth. We are eminently responsible for the present and for the future, for what we do with the gifts that we believe that we receive from God. The Bible is indeed the Word of God in our hands! May it also be a means that we may use in "rebuilding the broken bridges between Christians and Jews"!

Notes

1. The term "teaching of contempt" for Jews is generally attributed to Jules Isaac and his book *The Teaching of Contempt: Christian Roots of Anti-Semitism* (New York: Holt, Rinehart & Winston, 1964).

2. Among these Jewish writers, Jules Isaac, cited in the previous note, and Samuel Sandmel, *Anti-Semitism in the New Testament?* (Philadelphia: Fortress Press, 1978), are probably the best known.

3. Rosemary R. Ruether, *Faith and Fratricide: The Theological Roots of Anti-Semitism* (New York: Seabury, 1974); Norman A. Beck, *Mature Christianity: The Recognition and Repudiation of the Anti-Jewish Polemic of the New Testament* (Selinsgrove, Pa.: Susquehanna University Press, 1985); George M. Smiga, *Pain and Polemic: Anti-Judaism in the Gospels* (Mahwah, N.J.: Paulist Press, 1992); Norman A. Beck, *Mature Christianity in the 21st Century,* expanded and rev. ed. (New York: Crossroad and the American Interfaith Institute/World Alliance, 1994), are among the most significant here.

4. The list of Christian scholars who present these arguments as *intra*-Jewish is extensive. Here I cite only one, Dennis McManus, Associate Director, Secretariat for the Liturgy, National Conference of Catholic Bishops, in a brief article, "A Christian Commentary on Matthew 23:12–33," published in *The Word Set Free: Deconstructing the Christian Understanding of Judaism from the New Testament* (New York: Anti-Defamation League, 2000), 7. According to McManus, in Matthew 23:13–33, "In effect, we are watching a very Jewish fight take shape.... It is important for us, therefore, to keep in mind that this passage was originally written for a Jewish audience whose reactions would have been quite different from our own, some 2,000 years later."

5. For my fellow Christians who have removed the most hateful anti-Jewish statements from their worship, educational, and promotional materials but are not willing to address the problem in the New Testament itself, the Christian teaching of contempt for Jews is a result not of what is stated in the New Testament, but of *interpretations* of the New Testament. Pope John Paul II articulated this position in a presentation in Rome, October 31, 1998, to a symposium on the topic, "The Roots of Anti-Judaism in the Christian Milieu." As quoted in *The Word Set Free*, 4, translated from the original French, John Paul II said there that "in the Christian world — I am not saying on the part of the church as such — erroneous and unjust interpretations of the New Testament relative to Jewish people and their presumed guilt circulated for too long, engendering sentiments of hostility toward this people."

6. For more detailed explanations of this, please see Beck, *Mature Christianity*, 283–86 and 321–24.

7. These four verses contradict what Paul himself wrote about Jews in Romans 9–11 and elsewhere within his seven basic letters. They do not fit well into the literary structure of his letter, and they have a close affinity with the thought patterns of the Acts of the Apostles drama, written three decades after the death of Paul.

8. For a brief, but excellent, discussion of this, see Raymond E. Brown, "The Narratives of Jesus' Passion and Anti-Judaism," *Explorations* 10, no. 3 (1996): 6–8.

9. The Christian "teaching of contempt" for Jews in the New Testament documents is depicted in detail most fully in *Mature Christianity*.

10. This is expressed in much greater detail in ibid., 325–28.

11. Norman A. Beck, *The New Testament: A New Translation and Redaction* (Lima, Ohio: Fairway Press, 2001).

12. For more about this, see my articles, "The Importance of Lectionary Revisions in the Repudiation of the Defamatory Anti-Jewish Polemic in the New Testament," *Explorations* 11, no. 3 (1997): 4, and "Removing Anti-Jewish Polemic from Our Christian Lectionaries: A Proposal," http://jcrelations.net/articl1/beck.htm (2001).

13. See explanations of this in David G. Burke, "Translating *Hoi Ioudaioi* in the New Testament," *Explorations* 9, no. 2 (1995): 1–7; Barclay M. Newman, "Making Peace Between Jews and Gentiles," *Explorations* 10, no. 1 (1996): 7–8; Irvin J. Borowsky, "The Need for Two Translations of the Bible, One for Scholars and a Second 'Hate-Free' Edition for the Public," *Explorations* 11, no. 2 (1997): 3; Barclay M. Newman, "Removing the Anti-Judaism from the New Testament," *Explorations* 12, no. 1 (1998): 1; James A. Sanders, "The Hermeneutics of Translation," *Explorations* 12, no. 2 (1998): 1; David G. Burke, "How the Contemporary English Edition Avoids Anti-Judaism," *Explorations* 12, no. 2 (1998): 8; Joseph Bailey, "A Plea for Paraphrase," *Explorations* 13, no. 1 (1999): 6; various articles in *Removing the Anti-Judaism from the New Testament*, ed. Howard Clark Kee and Irvin J. Borowsky (Philadelphia: American Interfaith Institute/World Alliance, 1998); and the comparisons of translations of Romans 11:11–32 provided in Beck, *Mature Christianity in the 21st Century*, 111–14.

14. See Lydie Huynh, "The Next 2,000 Years . . . ," *Explorations* 9, no. 3 (1995): 5; Roger Omanson, "Anti-Jewish Bias in the NT," *The Bible Translator* (July 1992); and Beck, *Mature Christianity in the 21st Century*.

Chapter 2

Recent Developments in Catholic-Jewish Relations

Edward Idris Cardinal Cassidy

Two Symbolic Events

On March 12, 2000, Pope John Paul II called for and presided over a special service in St. Peter's Basilica during which, in the name of the Catholic Church throughout the world, the following prayer was offered:

> God of our Fathers, you chose Abraham and his descendants to bring your name to the nations: we are deeply saddened by the behavior of those who in the course of history have caused these children of yours to suffer, and asking your forgiveness we wish to commit ourselves to genuine brotherhood with the people of the covenant.

On March 26, 2000, just two weeks later, Pope John Paul II placed this prayer seeking pardon for the suffering caused to the Jews in the course of history, with his signature on it, in the Western Wall of the Temple in Jerusalem. Three days earlier, His Holiness had laid a wreath on the tomb in the mausoleum of Yad Vashem and rekindled the flame that recalls the six million victims of the *Shoah*. In continuation, as it were, of the prayer offered in St. Peter's, the pope stated during that moving ceremony in Jerusalem:

> Here as at Auschwitz and many other places in Europe, we are overcome by the echo of the heartrending laments of so many. Men, women and children cry out to us from the depths of the horror that they knew. How can we fail to hear their cry? No one can forget or ignore what happened. No one can diminish its scale. We wish to remember. But we wish to remember for a purpose — namely, to ensure that never again will evil prevail, as it did for the millions of innocent victims of Nazism.

These events symbolize the new relationship that has been forged over the past thirty-six years, since the Second Vatican Council, between Catholics and Jews. Pope John Paul II, looking back at the many outstanding events of the Holy Year, did not hesitate to judge the visit to Jerusalem as one of the most significant. For those of us who were privileged to stand with him at the Western Wall of the Temple, it seemed that all the efforts made over the previous thirty-odd years to mend the broken and bloodstained fences between Jews and Christians had received the seal of God's blessing and could never be again undone. A well-known Dominican biblical scholar and long-time resident of Jerusalem, Rev. Father Jerome Murphy-O'Connor, commenting on Pope John Paul's visit to the Western Wall of the Temple, stated:

> By standing there [at the Western Wall], he transformed the relationship of Christianity towards Judaism. It is a complete reversal of history.

Three Important Recent Developments

In the past there has been a notable reluctance on the part of the Jewish partner to discuss questions concerning our faith understanding. This is of course very understandable in view of the past experiences of the Jewish people. Recently, however, to my delight, I am hearing more and more Jewish voices making the request that we enter into genuine dialogue or discussions on theological questions. Rabbi Eric H. Yoffie, the president of the Union of American Hebrew Congregations, which unites 1.5 million Reform Jews in 895 synagogues in North America, in a lecture called for Catholics and Jews to reflect together on faith questions and has urged the Catholic Church and his organization to undertake a joint campaign about the two religions. "This means," he said, "that the Catholics need to educate Catholics about Jews, and the Jews to educate Jews about Catholics."[1] While the Holocaust remains for him, as for Catholics, a deep concern, he believes that "a dialogue of grievance can no longer dominate our relations." We must — both Jews and Christians — bring the great news of Jewish-Christian reconciliation to the members of our communities if we wish to ensure that we are building on a solid foundation.

Three recent documents have come to confirm the great progress that has been made in Christian-Jewish relations and to look forward to a new era of cooperation. Moreover, they seem to me to open the way for more intense dialogue on questions that, so far, we have not dared to approach.

Dabru Emet

The first was an initiative from the Jewish partner in our dialogue, namely, the publication in September 2000 of the *Jewish Statement on Christians and Christianity: Dabru Emet* (Proclaim the Truth). The document opens with these words: "In recent years, there has been a dramatic and unprecedented shift in Jewish and Christian relations," and considers that the changes made by Christians "merit a thoughtful Jewish response." It then offers eight brief statements about how Jews and Christians might relate to one another:

- *Jews and Christians worship the same God.* "While Christian worship is not a viable religious choice for Jews, as Jewish theologians we rejoice that, through Christianity, hundreds of millions of people have entered into relationship with the God of Israel."

- *Jews and Christians seek authority from the same book — the Bible (what Jews call "Tanakh" and Christians call the "Old Testament").* While noting that Jews and Christians interpret the Bible differently on many points, the statement insists that such differences must always be respected.

- *Christians can respect the claim of the Jewish people upon the land of Israel.*

- *Jews and Christians respect the moral principles of Torah.* "Central to the moral principles of Torah is the inalienable sanctity and dignity of every human being. All of us were created in the image of God. This shared moral emphasis can be the basis of an improved relationship between our two communities. It can also be the basis of a powerful witness to all humanity for improving the lives of our fellow human beings and for standing up against the immoralities and idolatries that harm and degrade us."

- *Nazism was not a Christian phenomenon.* "Without the long history of Christian anti-Judaism and Christian violence against Jews, Nazi ideology could not have taken hold nor could it have been carried out. Too many Christians participated in, or were sympathetic to, Nazi atrocities against Jews. Other Christians did not protest sufficiently against these atrocities. But Nazism itself was not an inevitable consequence of Christianity. If the Nazi extermination of the Jews had been fully successful, it would have

turned its murderous rage more directly to Christians. We recognize with gratitude those Christians who risked or sacrificed
their lives to save Jews during the Nazi regime. With that in mind,
we encourage the continuation of recent efforts in Christian theology to repudiate unequivocally contempt of Judaism and the
Jewish people."

- *The humanly irreconcilable difference between Jews and Christians will
  not be settled until God redeems the entire world as promised in scripture.*

- *A new relationship between Jews and Christians will not weaken Jewish
  practice.*

- *Jews and Christians must work together for justice and peace.*[2]

Dabru Emet goes further than any other Jewish document in ac-
knowledging the close links that bind Jews and Christians together
and in calling for closer collaboration in favor of justice, peace, and
the preservation of the moral order. The statement on Christianity
and Nazism is particularly welcome, while the acknowledgment that
"the humanly irreconcilable difference between Jews and Christians
will not be settled until God redeems the entire world as promised in
scripture" is a timely reminder that, as we look to the future, Catholics and Jews must not dialogue with the expectation that they will
agree on everything. It would be naive of us to think so. We are two
distinct faith communities with common roots and a great deal in
common, yet with essential differences that must be respected. The
process of dialogue requires both a clear understanding of one's own
faith tradition and openness to the experience of others. We must not
be surprised or disturbed when, on one or other matter that touches
our faith or history, we have different opinions or understandings.
Neither should sincere criticism upset us, provided that it is objec-
tive and framed in a way that does not offend our mutual esteem and
respect for one another. Such criticism can be good for us. It helps
us to reflect more deeply on our positions or initiatives. This is, of
course, very different from certain aggressive criticism with its own
agenda, from the activity of pressure groups.

Abraham's Heritage — A Christmas Gift

The document *Dabru Emet* was followed by a short article by Cardinal
Joseph Ratzinger, published on the front page of *L'Osservatore Romano*
on December 29, 2000, entitled "Abraham's Heritage — A Christmas
Gift." Referring to the very negative Jewish reaction to the document

from the Congregation for the Doctrine of the Faith *Dominus Iesus,* published in September 2000, His Eminence affirms:

> It is evident that, as Christians, our dialogue with the Jews is situated on a different level than that in which we engage with other religions. The faith witnessed to by the Jewish Bible is not merely another religion to us, but is the foundation of our own faith.

The cardinal then gives what has been called "a new vision of the relationship with the Jews."[3] After tracing briefly the history of God's dealings with the Jewish people, the cardinal expresses "our gratitude to our Jewish brothers and sisters who, despite the hardness of their own history, have held on to faith in this God right up to the present and who witness to it in the sight of those peoples who, lacking knowledge of the one God, 'dwell in darkness and the shadow of death'" (Luke 1:79).

The article then has the following interesting comment on relations between Christians and Jews down through the centuries:

> Certainly from the beginning relations between the infant church and Israel were often marked by conflict. The Church was considered to be a degenerate daughter, while Christians considered their mother to be blind and obstinate. Down through the history of Christianity, already-strained relations deteriorated further, even giving birth to anti-Jewish attitudes that throughout history have led to deplorable acts of violence. Even if the most recent, loathsome experience of the *Shoah* was prepared in the name of an anti-Christian ideology that tried to strike the Christian faith at its Abrahamic roots in the people of Israel, it cannot be denied that a certain insufficient resistance to this atrocity on the part of Christians can be explained by the inherited anti-Judaism in the hearts of not a few Christians.

For the cardinal, it is perhaps this latest tragedy that has resulted in a new relationship between the church and Israel, which he defines as "a sincere willingness to overcome every kind of anti-Judaism and to initiate a constructive dialogue based on knowledge of each other and reconciliation." If such a dialogue is to be fruitful, the cardinal suggests that "it must begin with a prayer to our God first of all that he might grant to us Christians a greater esteem and love for that people, the people of Israel, to whom belong *the adoptions as sons, the glory, the covenants, the giving of the law, the worship and the promises; theirs the patriarchs, and from them, according to the flesh, is the Messiah*

(Rom. 9:4–5), and this not only in the past, but still today, *for the gifts and the call of God are irrevocable* (Rom. 11:29)." Cardinal Ratzinger goes on to propose to Christians that they in their turn might pray to God "that he grant also to the children of Israel a deeper knowledge of Jesus of Nazareth, who is their son and the gift they have made to us." His final conclusion reminds us of the sixth statement in *Dabru Emet:* "Since we are both waiting the final redemption, let us pray that the paths we follow may converge."

Reflections on Covenant and Mission

Reflections on Covenant and Mission is quite a remarkable statement "issued by the Ecumenical and Interreligious Affairs Committee of the United States Conference of Catholic Bishops and the National Council of Synagogues USA." It is the result of discussions between leaders of Jewish and Roman Catholic communities in the United States, who have been meeting twice a year over a period of two decades, and was published on August 12, 2002.

For several years, I have been advocating a study of this kind on the relationship between the two Covenants that basically describe the nature of the two religious communities. The document *Reflections on Covenant and Mission* is an encouraging response, that — in the words of the U.S. Bishops' moderator for Catholic-Jewish Relations, "marks a significant step forward in the dialogue between the Catholic Church and the Jewish community" in this country.

The Jewish and Catholic reflections are presented separately in the document, but affirm together important conclusions. The Catholic reflections describe the growing respect for the Jewish tradition that has unfolded since the Second Vatican Council, and state:

> A deepening Catholic appreciation of the eternal covenant between God and the Jewish people, together with the divinely-given mission to Jews to witness to God's faithful love, lead to the conclusion that campaigns that target Jews for conversion to Christianity are no longer theologically acceptable in the Catholic Church.

The document stresses that evangelization, or mission, in the church's work cannot be separated from its faith in Jesus Christ in whom Christians find the kingdom present and fulfilled. But it points out that this evangelizing mission goes far beyond "the invitation to a commitment to faith in Jesus Christ and to entry through baptism into the community of believers that is the church. It includes the church's activities of presence and witness; commitment to social development and human liberation; Christian worship, prayer, and contemplation; interreligious dialogue; and proclamation and catechesis."

But given the "utterly unique relationship of Christianity with Judaism" and the many aspects of this spiritual linkage, "the Catholic Church has come to recognize that its mission of preparing for the coming of the kingdom is one that is shared with the Jewish people, even if Jews do not conceive of this task Christologically as the Church does." In view of this, the document quotes Prof. Tommaso Federici and Cardinal Walter Kasper to state that there should not be in the church any organization dedicated to the conversion of the Jews. From the Catholic point of view, Judaism is a religion that springs from divine revelation. Cardinal Kasper notes:

> God's grace, which is the grace of Jesus Christ according to our faith, is available to all. Therefore, the Church believes that Judaism, i.e., the faithful response of the Jewish people to God's irrevocable covenant, is salvific for them, because God is faithful to his promises.

According to Roman Catholic teaching, the document states, both the church and the Jewish people abide in covenant with God. They both therefore have missions before God to undertake in the world. The church believes that the mission of the Jewish people is not restricted to their historical role as the people of whom Jesus was born "according to the flesh" (Rom. 9:5) and from whom the church's apostles came. It quotes Cardinal Ratzinger, who wrote, "God's providence... has obviously given Israel a particular mission in this 'time of the Gentiles.'" However, only the Jewish people themselves can articulate their mission, "in the light of their own religious experience."

The Catholic section of the document concludes with this profound statement:

> With the Jewish people, the Catholic Church, in the words of *Nostra Aetate*, "awaits the day, known to God alone, when all peoples will call on God with one voice and serve him shoulder to shoulder."

The Jewish reflections are given the title: "The Mission of the Jews and the Perfection of the World." This mission is described as threefold, rooted in scripture and developed in later Jewish sources:

There is, first, the mission of covenant — the ever-formative impetus to Jewish life that results from the covenant between God and the Jews. Second, the mission of witness, whereby the Jews see themselves "and are frequently seen by others" as God's eternal witnesses to his existence and to his redeeming power in the world. And third, the mission of humanity, a mission that understands the Biblical history of the Jews as containing a message to more than the Jews alone. It presupposes a message and a mission addressed to all human beings.

The document describes the mission of covenant and witness, before dealing more at length with the mission of humanity, stating that the message of the Bible is a message and a vision not only to Israel but to all of humanity. It then reminds the reader that Isaiah speaks twice of the Jews as a light to peoples and quotes the experience of Jonah to illustrate that it is a mistake to think that God is concerned only with the Jews. "The God of the Bible is the God of the world. His visions are visions for all of humanity. His love is a love that extends to every creature.... Adam and Eve were His first creations and they are created long before the first Jews. They are created in 'the image of God,' as are all of their children to eternity. Only the human creation is in the divine image:" *Tikun ha-olam,* perfection or repairing of the world, is a joint task of the Jews and all humanity. Though Jews see themselves as living in a world that is as yet unredeemed, God wills His creatures to participate in the world's repair.

Finally, the Jewish reflections point out certain practical conclusions that follow from the threefold "mission" in classical Judaism, and that suggest a joint agenda for Christians and Jews. The reflection begins with the following statement:

Although Christians and Jews understand the messianic hope involved in that perfection quite differently, still, whether we are waiting for the messiah — as Jews believe — or for the messiah's second coming — as Christians believe — we share the belief that we live in an unredeemed world that longs for repair.

Then it asks: "Why not articulate a common agenda? Why not join together our spiritual forces to state and to act upon the values we share in common and that lead to the repair of the unredeemed world?" It then outlines what Jews and Christians have already done together: advancing the cause of social justice, marching together for civil rights, championing the cause of labor and farm workers, petitioning the government to address the needs of the

poor and homeless; calling on the country's leaders to seek nuclear
disarmament.

Looking then to the Talmud, the document draws from that source
thoughts about repairing the world, giving details of charity directed
to the poor and deeds of kindness to all, the poor and the rich, the living and the dead; creating an economy where people are encouraged
to help one another financially as an expression of their common
fellowship; obligations to the sick and mourners; preserving the dignity of the aged. While Jewish law is of course directed at Jews and its
primary concern is to encourage the expression of love to the members of the community, it points out that many of these actions are
mandatory toward all people, and quotes the Talmud as saying:

> One must provide for the needs of the gentile poor with the
> Jewish poor. One must visit the gentile sick with the Jewish sick.
> One must care for the burial of a gentile, just as one must care
> for the burial of a Jew. [These obligations are universal] because
> these are the ways of peace.

Our Common Mission

Not everyone in our two communities will agree with all that is stated
in this document. Yet I believe the challenge it poses can be, and
should be, fully shared by Christians and Jews. At the conclusion of
the historic meeting, on March 23, 2000, between the two chief rabbis
of Israel and Pope John Paul II at the Heichal Shlomo, the pope did
not hesitate to affirm:

> There is much that we have in common. There is much that we
> can do together for peace, for justice, for a more human and
> fraternal world. May the Lord of heaven and earth lead us to a
> new and fruitful era of mutual respect and co-operation, for the
> benefit of all.[4]

If we examine both the Jewish and Christian relationship to God,
it is clear that both have been given a common mission: to be a light
to the nations. Pope John Paul II has stated:

> As Christians and Jews, following the example of the faith of
> Abraham, we are called to be a blessing to the world. This is
> a common task awaiting us. It is therefore necessary for us,
> Christians and Jews, to be first a blessing to one another.[5]

Our world today urgently needs our common witness to the truths that God has entrusted to us, Jews and Christians. Already in Prague, in 1990, the International Liaison Commission pledged its members to seek Common Goals. We are faced with a growing secularization worldwide, a deep crisis of faith that either denies or simply ignores the very existence of God. The extraordinary advances in technology and the enormous effects on commerce and life of globalization tend to make the creature once again arrogant and self-sufficient, as at the time that men set out to build a tower "with its top reaching heaven," which has been named Babel (Gen. 11:4–9). The events of September 11 and the aftermath have shown us just how much evil there is in our world today and what terrible resources are available to those who set out on the path of evil. In the days following the attack on New York, Pope John Paul II, on his visit to Kazakstan, appealed "to everyone, Christians and the followers of other religions, that we work together to build a world without violence, a world that loves life, and grows in justice and solidarity. . . . May people everywhere, strengthened by divine wisdom, work for a civilization of love, in which there is no room for hatred, discrimination or violence."

Can we make now the great change that this calls for in our relationship, by moving away further from the old mistrust and suspicion to a partnership in the cause of "peace, justice, and a more human, fraternal world"? That I believe is the challenge that we face. While preserving past gains, I would hope that we, Catholics and Jews, might move toward a closer *partnership*. I would wish to see our dialogue as the work of two equal partners seeking together to build a better world. We began our discussions in order to solve our problems and promote a new relationship. It seems to me that we need now to go further and move our gaze from the bilateral relations of Jews and Christians to a wider world.

The Jewish section of the document *Reflections on Covenant and Mission* challenges all Christians and Jews to take up such a path:

> Does not humanity need a common path that seeks the ways of peace? Does not humanity need a common vision of the sacred nature of our human existence that we can teach our children and that we can foster in our communities in order to further the ways of peace? Does not humanity need a commitment of its religious leadership, within each faith and beyond each faith, to join hands and create bonds that will inspire and guide humanity to reach toward its sacred promise? For Jews and Christians who have heard the call of God to be a blessing and a light to the

world, the challenge and mission are clear. Nothing less should be our challenge — and that is the true meaning of mission that we all need to share.

Notes

1. "Joseph Klein Lecture on Judaic Affairs," Assumption College, March 23, 2000, 25.

2. The Institute for Christian and Jewish Studies, National Jewish Scholars Project *Dabru Emet*, 13.09.00, www.icjs.org/what/njps/dabruemet.htm.

3. *CNS Documentary Service*, 30–35 (February 15, 2000), 565–66. My quotations are to be found there.

4. *L'Osservatore Romano*, March 30, 2000, vii.

5. John Paul II, *On the Fiftieth Anniversary of the Warsaw Ghetto Uprising*, April 6, 1993, Information Service PCPUC 84 (1001), 157.

Chapter 3 _____

From God's Perspective
We Are All Minorities

Krister Stendahl _____

I have found from experience that there is something special about multilateral dialogue, one in which we are all minorities, for the simple reason that in so much of religious history the relation among religions has usually been defined in terms of differences — one's identity being defined by that which is different from the other. This is so natural to our whole habit of thinking that it is hard for us to conceive a way of defining our identity by that which makes us glad. Multicultural dialogue nurtures that vision: that in the eyes of God we are all minorities. In this plural and diverse situation and the increased consciousness of that being so, the attempt at a common denominator approach has proved increasingly hard to work. When it has succeeded, it has just created one new religion — as if we needed another one. Nor is tolerance quite the solution. It usually has an elitist lining, either an elitist lining in the sense that you can be tolerant because for you it is not that important, or an elitist lining of *noblesse oblige* — I know, but I cannot expect the other to know as much as I do.

These approaches do not work very well, once one wakes up to radical pluralism. Nor does the model in which one anticipates the victory of one over the many work either. Many of you have heard me use as symbolic of this attitude the fact that ninety years ago in the United States, we got a journal called the *Christian Century*. It's a very enlightened journal. It even switched from Gothic print to Latin letters in its masthead some twenty years ago. But it is sort of cute to think that at the beginning of this century Americans really believed that with American know-how and a little help from God we would end up by the year 2000 in a christianized world. What

This text is based on a lecture delivered on February 27, 1992, at the Center for the Study of World Religions, Harvard University, as edited by Arvind Sharma and Jennifer Baichwal.

actually happened was an enormous renewal of the major religions of the world: great meetings, in Rangoon I think, in the 1930s and 1940s revivifying the Buddhist canon; the end of the classical form of Jewish assimilation after the *Shoah* and the establishment of the state of Israel; Hinduism in its various shapes and forms becoming a reality in practically all parts of the Western world. And Muslims outnumbering Jews in many parts of the West. That's what happened — what happened was that Gandhi became the rejuvenator of the social consciousness of Martin Luther King. What happened was quite different from what was expected. So the only alternative is a plural alternative, and so I ask myself: How to sing my song to Jesus with abandon without telling negative stories about others? Or, if you want to sound more academic: "toward a Christian theology of religions."

I want to deal with that subject very seriously, and I want to do it as a biblical scholar or at least as a reader of the Bible that I love. I want to deal with questions of how one, as a Bible-tutored Christian, can come to think about God's whole menagerie and the place of the Christian church and the Christian religion in the midst of it. How, in the wider *missio dei*, are we to define the *missio christi* and the *missio ecclesiae*, to use terms that Catholic theologians have used to cope with this problem? How to define the wider mission of God, the specific mission of Christ, and the way in which the mission of the church fits into God's total plan?

Three Texts in Context

It seems that there are clear words against any such enterprise of radical pluralism. I will start by lifting up three famous scriptural passages that seem to close the matter before we have opened it:

1. Acts 4:12: "For there is no other name under heaven given among human beings, whereby we must be saved."

2. John 14:6: "I am the way, the truth, and the life: no one comes to the Father except through me."

3. Matthew 28:19: "Go therefore and make disciples of all the nations, baptizing them in the name of the Father, and of the Son, and of the Holy Spirit."

1. I have an old exegetical rule that says that when you apply the right answer to the wrong question, it will always be wrong, even if — or especially if — the answer is God's word. Now what was the question to which Peter gave that answer in Acts?

The question was the accusation that Peter had performed the miracle of a magician in his own name, and he answers with the exclamation: "Heavens no, in no other name is there salvation but Jesus." This does not relate to the problem of Christianity and Buddhism — at least not on the conscious level. But words like that grow legs and walk out of their context. And even when that is legitimate we must also remind ourselves of the very nature of confessional language. As Eastern Christianity has always known better than the West, confessional language is doxological. It is a way of praising God. It is the primary language of faith. The home language of the church is the language of prayer, worship, and doxology, giving praise out of the fullness of one's heart. Actually, confessional and liturgical and doxological language is a kind of caressing language by which we express our devotion with abandon and joy. Raymond Brown, the outstanding Roman Catholic exegete, in writing about the development of biblical studies in the Roman Catholic Church, hails Pius XII's encyclical of 1943, long before Vatican II, as the milestone in setting biblical scholarship free in Catholic studies. This the encyclical did when it admitted or even hailed the fact that in studying scriptures you have to study the genre, the style, the nature of the language it has, so that you don't read it in the wrong key. I think this is apropos to Acts 4:12. I can preach wonderful sermons on this but I have to restrict myself.

2.   The Johannine passage (John 14:6) is found in the beginning of what is called the farewell speech of Jesus. The setting is this: "Do not be upset in your hearts, believe in God, believe also in me. I'm going to leave you, but in this world there are many ways — many ways — for you to stay. If there were not I would take you with me right now, but you can stay here. Don't worry.... And you know the way to where I am going." Then Thomas asks: "But we don't know where you are going. How can we then know the way?" Thomas is always pretty smart, good questions, good logic. Jesus said to him: "I am the way, the truth and the life. Nobody comes to the Father except through me."

It strikes me very odd to take a passage from the most intimate and tender conversation with the most intimate and closest circle of disciples, from a context in which their hearts are full of foreboding with the imminent fear of relations about to be severed, to lift a word from *that* conversation, and use it in answering the question of Christianity's relation to other religions. It is just not apropos. It is odd that one of the few passages that are used by those who have closed the doors on a theology of religions in Christianity should be a passage that is dealing not with the question of the periphery or the margins or exclusion, but that, on the contrary, lies at the very heart of the mystery of what came to be the Trinity: the relation between the Father and the Son.

3. Anyone who reads Matthew's Gospel finds this a rather stunning statement toward the end, because Matthew's Gospel is totally built on the theory that during the ministry of Jesus, neither Jesus nor the disciples were to move outside Israel. Matthew has rather striking statements: "Do not go to any Gentiles.... You will not lack cities in Israel before the Son of Man appears" (10:5, 23). This concentration on the mission to Israel has its contrast in the announcement of the Gentile mission in the last verses of the gospel — "all the nation" refers to "all the Gentiles." But what kind of mission is this? How did Matthew — if we start on that level — think of this mission? Did he think of it as a saturation mission, did he think of it as the christianization of the world, the cosmos?

I think we can be very clear that Matthew thinks of the mission of the church on a minority model, as did Paul. You will remember that in Romans 15 Paul says, "I have a principle: never run a mission where anybody else has preached the gospel before. And now I have run out of space, there is no place for me to go in the East. So I have to go to Spain, I have to go West." That's an odd way of looking at things. What matters to Paul seems to be establishing a presence, a small minority in these centers of the East. It is a minority image; it is the establishment, as I like to say of Laboratory II. Israel was Laboratory I, and when God felt that some good things had been achieved in Laboratory I, God said, "Let's now try it out on a somewhat broader basis...on a Gentile basis" — but still a laboratory, with Christians as the guinea pigs, Christian as another "peculiar people."

The images in the Gospel of Matthew are minority images. "You are the salt of the earth." Nobody wants the world to be a salt mine. "You are the light of the world and let your light so shine before the people that they see your good deeds and become Christians." *That's not what it says.* It says: that they see your good deeds and praise your Father who is in Heaven, have some reason for joy. That's what it says. And think of the magi — the Ayatollahs from Iran. They did not start the church when they got home. We might in retrospect think that was sad; anyway they didn't, and it doesn't seem to bother Matthew. Because for Matthew they got the experience of their life, and they had touched the holiness of God's kingdom. Matthew's perspective is centered in what we refer to as the Kingdom. I'll come back to that.

So these three pivotal passages from Acts, John, and Matthew are not as simple as one might think. They are opening up perspectives. Let us take the special case of Matthew. Matthew operates with what I call the biblical model, the Jewish model (of Isaiah 49 and many other texts), the understanding that Israel is to be a light to the Gentiles, a theme Luke picks up in the Song of Simeon, a theme recited in large parts of Christendom every evening, "a light to lighten the Gentiles and the glory of thy people of Israel" (Luke 2:32). This is a peculiar view. Judaism is a revelatory religion, a religion of the book, a religion of salvation — a revelatory religion, however, that at the same time doesn't think that everybody has to be a Jew in order to be acceptable to God. Now once that structure of religion came into the hands of Christianity and Islam, it was coupled with universalism in such a manner that no one could be acceptable to God who did not think and believe as Christians and Muslims think and believe.

That is why, in the world of pluralism, it is not so strange that Christians who wake up to the fact that they are not any more a self-evident majority should find their way to the Jews and ask them: "You have lived for a pretty long time as a minority. Do you have a secret to share with us?" And the secret is quite simply this, that universalism is the ultimate arrogance in the realm of religion. It is by definition and unavoidably spiritual colonialism, spiritual imperialism. The Crusades can be more civilized, but they will still be Crusades, by definition. And the insight of a revelatory non-universalism is this: to be a particular, even a peculiar people, somehow needed by God as a witness, faithful, doing what God has told them to do, but not claiming to be the whole.

But particularism has been so ridiculed, especially after the Enlightenment. Have you ever read Voltaire's anti-Jewish statements? They are all based on the alleged tribal primitiveness and particularity of Judaism. But I would suggest revelatory religion without such a particularism instead of a universalism is lethal. That's my lesson, and I am very intrigued as a student of the Gospel of Matthew that Matthean thinking constructed that same model: the church being another peculiar people, willed by God to have a function (what I earlier called Laboratory II), now built on a Gentile base, *panta ta ethne*, disciples of all the Gentile nations, yet still a minority. This is beautifully expressed in the sublime eschatological vision of Micah 4:5: Thus God will judge among the many peoples and arbitrate for the multitude of nations, however distant, and they shall beat their swords into ploughshares, spears into pruning hooks, nation shall not take up sword against nation, they shall never again know war or learn war. But every man shall sit under his grapevine or fig tree with no one to disturb him. For it was the Lord of Hosts who spoke: *for all people will walk, each in the names of their Gods, and we will walk in the name of the Lord our God for ever and ever.* It's quite a stunning vision. I have used rabbinic scholar E. E. Urbach's translation with an *and* rather than a *but* in the last sentence: *and* we will walk. . . . Urbach, in his discussion about similar matters in one of the famous volumes on Jewish and Christian self-definition, says: "In their relations with other nations, most of the sages (i.e., Rabbis) would have satisfied themselves with the declaration of Micah 4:5."[1]

Matthew suggests to me that he thought of the church as a church of such a peculiar people in a new key. Universalism comes with power, Constantinian or otherwise. I think there are two alternatives to thinking what it is all about from a Christian perspective; and if I want to use drastic images I would say: What is the first thing that God asks when God comes to the oval office in the morning? Is it for a printout of the latest salvation statistics of the Christian churches? Or is it a question like: Has there been any progress toward the Kingdom and, by the way, what has the role of the Christians been in that? Or is it totally an accident that in the very last vision on the very last pages of the Christian Bible there is, for us theologians, priests and ministers, that shocking statement: "And I saw no temple in that city." There is something rather striking about a religious tradition that envisions the consummation not as the cathedral of cathedrals, but as a city in which there is no temple.

Two Model Texts

I want to lift up two other texts, "model texts" as I call them. These are intimations, models of attitude, which I find important toward building theology, which I cannot do. I am not a systematic theologian. I am just a Bible scholar — providing a little biblical encouragement to the theologian's models. One would of course expect that the first person, the first theologian — the first Christian theologian — who saw the specter of Christian anti-Semitism and anti-Judaism coming was the apostle Paul. He detected, in his Gentile followers, an attitude of superiority toward Israel, not only toward Judaism but also toward Israel, the people, the Jews. And his missionary strategy is contained in Romans, chapters 9–11. The Calvinists thought it was a tractate on predestination because they were interested in that, but it's actually Paul's ruminations on how his mission to the Gentiles fits into God's plans and how it relates to the people of Israel. Paul ends with a scathing critique of Gentile Christians and their attitude of superiority toward Israel (11:11ff.). He uses a lot of images of olive trees and grafting, and he gets so upset he mixes up what grafting actually does to a tree. But we have to ascribe that to his intensity of feeling — or to his lack of knowledge about horticulture. He was a city boy. I feel for him. He is trying to come to grips with this fact that there is this feeling of superiority, and he doesn't like it. And he ultimately says: I'll tell you a mystery, lest you be conceited. And that is that the whole of Israel will in due time be saved, and that's none of your business because God won't go back on His promises. And he doesn't actually say this is going to happen because they are going to accept Jesus as the Messiah. And the doxology he ends with, the only one he wrote, is straight God-language without any Christological twist.

When I speak about this, theologians get very upset and they say, "You teach two ways to salvation: one for Israel and one for the rest of humankind." And I say, "No, I say with Paul that it is a mystery — if I taught two ways it would be a traffic plan." But Paul is trying to set in various ways a kind of limit to missionary zeal. And why? I know why: He had been burnt once. It was out of religious zeal that he committed the only thing that he ever confesses as a sin: having persecuted the church of Jesus Christ. So he was aware of the risk of such zeal.

The other text is of another nature. It is Paul's reflection on pluralism when he is up against it in Corinth, in 1 Corinthians. Paul was not a great ecumenist through most of his ministry. And in Galatians it seems that he really thought that if he stamped his foot enough they would really go with him. And he says: "Even if an angel from heaven comes and teaches otherwise than I taught you, let that angel be accursed!" That's chutzpah! But in Corinth he is low on the totem pole, and he is almost going to be read out of the church, so he has to settle for ecumenism. He is in minority status and that's perhaps why it is in that epistle that his basic thinking about love, as the elasticity that makes it possible to have diversity, is born. The ode to love in 1 Corinthians is not speaking about love in general but is Paul's solution to the problem of how diversity can be an asset instead of a liability. Now, what is so interesting to me in this context is how Paul presents the problem, and the ensuing insight. To deal with different theologies as if they were competing philosophies — on the model of Stoicism and Epicureanism, etc. — is wrong and shows no understanding of the nature of the church. Paul gropes for other metaphors. He speaks about the garden, he speaks about the house, and he speaks about the temple. The diversity of theologies is not like philosophical schools arguing with one another; that's a fleshly way of thinking — or, as we would say, it is a secular way of thinking about religious diversity (1 Cor. 3).

Matters of religion do not represent a zero-sum problem. That's Paul's message. It is not a zero-sum proposition where adding to the other means deducting from the one. That's his vision, and I think it is valid and important for us as another way of thinking about religious coexistence. Of course, people who speak like me are accused of, "So anything goes, eh?" No. Paul certainly knows he is right. "I know that I am right but I am not thereby justified, it is God who judges" (1 Cor. 4:4). So he is not backing down from his conviction. But since religion has to do with God, any doctrinal insight expressed by the human mind and grasped by a human will cannot claim ultimacy. Anything goes? No. Let's argue.

In a brilliant review essay of David Novak's *Jewish-Christian Dialogue: A Jewish Justification*,[2] Jon D. Levenson says that if anyone in dialogue has to presuppose that you are not allowed to witness to your conviction, then it is better just to go with Solivetszek's position that we should discuss only matters of common interest and not theology. Now Levenson doesn't quite say that it has to be so, but he is sort of teasing Novak for making it too easy to say that somehow you bracket your convictions when you enter into dialogue. That's a caricature of dialogue. For dialogue slowly creates a climate in which you can both speak and listen and find out what the real issue is. And ultimately perhaps we reach what I love to speak about, but will not speak about here — the Holy Envy: when we recognize something in another tradition that is beautiful but is not in ours, nor should we grab it or claim it. We Americans in our imperialism think that if we like something we just incorporate it and we think that we honor others by doing so. But that is not the way. Holy envy rejoices in the beauty of others.

To me "the Corinthian model" is the solution. Another point I have borrowed from Levenson is that if one wants to move toward dialogue, one has to give reasons for breaking with the tradition. For it is obvious that the Christian tradition, generally, in relation to other religions has not been dialogical. Sometimes it has been more dialogical on the mission stations than we have been given to believe, as Kenneth Cracknell of Wesley House in Cambridge has always pointed out. If you read the diaries of the missionaries, you see how much there is of "presence" and "dialogues," but when they wrote home often the jargon of the home office won out. Levenson says that No-vak has not demonstrated that dialogue is so essential that it justifies changes of that magnitude; namely, bracketing both, the witness and the critiques of one another.

Two Models

I happen to think that dialogue is essential in a world where reli-gion is often part of the problem rather than part of the solution in the relations between people. It is of much importance that we make our hermeneutical moves honestly and openly. I have lifted up Paul's warning in Romans 11 and Paul's idea in 1 Corinthians of a coex-istence that is not a zero-sum order that is to him totally secular. Actually, in both cases he is referring to something that is different because it has to do with God and not with philosophy, not with de-fined thinking systems, for any thinking system that claims ultimacy is a form of idolatry. "I think I am right but I am not thereby justified" is Paul's wonderful safeguard.

The first model deals with Jewish-Christian relations and the sec-ond model deals with intra-Christian relations, based on the fact that Christ is the foundation on which the house is being built. I would like to suggest a modern typology in which one says that these spiri-tual models of attitudes, these awarenesses of the fact that under God we are not locked in a zero-sum society, can be extended, and that we have valid reasons to extend both the Jewish-Christian and the intra-Christian model of Paul's toward interreligious attitudes in general. We are thereby making a deliberate move. We are not smuggling it in; we should know what we are doing. But I want to do it openly and give the reason for it as a valid way of utilizing the model.

The book by David Novak that Levenson critiques strikes me as unattractive in one way because it really sees the task of Jewish-Christian dialogue as one of banding together in an alliance against all the others, and I don't think that we are much helped in this world, in which we are all minorities from God's perspective, by alliances among sub-groups. This doesn't seem to be what the situation calls for. But as has often happened in Christian history, coming back to my beloved image of the laboratory, I would say that somehow when we Christians have found a model that works for us, it might be ready for export, to try these things out.

Now my final point is this. It is a well-known one, and I don't know why it has dawned on me so slowly. I have referred to texts. These are *our* texts. Each minority has its texts, what its history has recorded, what God has recorded in the hearts of the people. Their writing is shaped by their experiences.

These are *our* texts. Out of our perspectives we interpret them. When a child is born — I guess women can talk better about this — but I would guess that the child's, the baby's, world does not consist of much more than itself and the mother's breast. That's the whole world, and one of the things that happens as we grow up is that it dawns upon us that other children have sucked other breasts. The process of sorting out such facts is called maturation. That's what maturation is. Now one of the most intriguing texts on the universal and the particular that I know of in my beloved Bible is the passage in 1 Corinthians 15. (This is just an attempt to help those who love the Bible to think about these things, although others are allowed to listen in!) Let me tell it in the form of a Jewish-style Midrash.

It is the day of consummation and the whole world is gathered and there we are, we Christians. Now as we look up there is God and Christ on God's right hand exactly as we have been told. So we turn around and see that there are also all the others. We see a sort of pan-religious and ecumenical representation, and we turn around with a Christian smile that says: "You see, it is just as we said and isn't it wonderful that our God is so generous that you can all be here!" When we turn back toward God there is no Christ to be seen on God's right side because Christ will never be there to feed into the smugness of his believers; or, as the text says: "And so when the end comes, Christ will lay it all down before the Father and God will become *panta en pasin*, all in all." That is another way of witnessing to the mystery — lest I be conceited.

Notes

1. E. E. Urbach, "Self-Isolation or Self-Affirmation in Judaism in the First Three Centuries: Theory and Practice," in *Jewish and Christian Self-Definition,* ed. E. P. Sanders et al. (Philadelphia: Fortress, 1981), 2:298.

2. Jon D. Levenson, "Must We Accept the Other's Self-Understanding?" *Journal of Religion* 71 (1991): 558–67, review essay on David Novak, *Jewish-Christian Dialogue: A Jewish Justification.*

Chapter 4

Anti-Judaism and Anti-Semitism
A Complicated Convergence

Mary C. Boys

Many involved in Jewish-Christian dialogue differentiate between theologically motivated attitudes toward Jews and Judaism — *anti-Judaism* — and the racist ideology of modern *anti-Semitism*. *Anti-Judaism* refers to Christianity's negative theological judgment of Judaism because of its rejection of Jesus as Lord and Christ. *Anti-Semitism* denotes hatred of and hostility toward Jews, and may be based on little or no theological animus. While the term itself, coined in 1879 by Wilhelm Marr, is modern in origin, anti-Semitism has roots in antiquity — Robert Wistrich has called it "the longest hatred."[1] Yet nineteenth-century racist theories added a deadly dimension to anti-Semitism, which became the official policy of Germany with the ascension of National Socialism in 1933.

Although there is not a clear consensus on the precise meanings of the terms, William Farmer offers a typical definition in differentiating anti-Semitism and anti-Judaism. The latter he identifies as "a specifically Christian, theologically driven attitude toward Jews, including concepts of divine rejection and punishment of Jews as well as Christian supersessionism and triumphalism."[2] The 1998 Vatican document *We Remember: A Reflection on the Shoah* also distinguishes the terms, yet refers to both as "spoiled seeds" that "must never again be allowed to take root in any human heart." It speaks of anti-Judaism as "longstanding attitudes of mistrust and hostility of which Christians have also been guilty." The anti-Semitism of the Nazis, however, "had its roots outside of Christianity."[3]

The distinction is a useful one for Christians because it focuses on the theological legacy that the churches must confront, the "teaching of contempt" that has so poisoned relations with the Jewish people.[4] Nevertheless, despite the usefulness and relative clarity these distinctions offer, the relationship of anti-Judaism and anti-Semitism is more complex and troubling than the differentiation suggests. Thus, understanding the relationship of the two terms is more than a matter of mere semantics.

What is most compelling is the haunting question: In what ways is Christianity implicated in this "longest hatred"? It is a "well-proven fact," as the Catholic bishops of France said in 1997, that the "anti-Jewish tradition stamped its mark" on Christian teaching, theology, preaching, and liturgy. Moreover, they continue: "It was on such ground that the venomous plant of hatred for the Jews was able to flourish."[5] Stated baldly, the question might be posed: Are Christians anti-Semites? Or, to ask the question in a more nuanced manner: In what ways has the longstanding legacy of anti-Judaism shaped Christian attitudes and behavior toward Jews? To what extent has Christianity's theological legacy supported, fostered, or even engendered anti-Semitism?

Another question arises with urgency: Given the commitment in many churches "never again" to allow the "spoiled seeds" of anti-Judaism and anti-Semitism "to take root in any human heart," how will they respond to the replanting of these spoiled seeds in many quarters of the Arab and Muslim world today?

Anti-Judaism, not Anti-Semitism

Most Christians understand their relation to Judaism on the basis of the New Testament — on the texts themselves, as well as the way the churches preach and teach those texts. Without question, the texts suggest varied perspectives. On the one hand, they show Judaism in a positive light, especially through presenting Jesus of Nazareth as a faithful Jew. The Gospels report him citing scripture, going to the Temple, speaking in the synagogue, and debating knowledgeably about the Law. On the other, significant texts portray Jews negatively. For example, their depiction of the Pharisees as legalists and hypocrites provides an effective foil for representing Jesus as compassionate and upright. Their account of the passion and death of Jesus emphasizes Jewish leadership, culminating in the frenzied crowd — "the Jews" — crying out to Pilate, "Away with him! Away with him! Crucify him!"(John 19:15). The Acts of the Apostles describes Paul and Barnabas as deciding to turn to Gentiles and away from preaching to Jews, since the latter rejected the word of God and thereby judged themselves unworthy of eternal life (13:46). Revelation (2:9) accuses those "who say they are Jews and are not" of being the "synagogue of Satan."

In short, many texts throughout the New Testament contribute to a negative appraisal of Judaism. Lacking any contextual knowledge to the contrary, its readers might reasonably infer that Judaism in the time of Jesus was hostile to the revelation of God in Jesus. Further, those readers might assume that Judaism, although the religious tradition from which Jesus came, remains opposed to the message of Jesus by following the Law rather than the Way of Jesus.

Such an inference, while lacking a fuller context and deeper understanding, is reasonable — though no longer defensible. It does not, however, make a person an anti-Semite, though it certainly predisposes one to view Judaism negatively. It does recapitulate some of the arguments of the early church.

Such a conclusion, however, is unfaithful to the spirit of the contemporary church, as well as to the burgeoning body of scholarship that sheds new perspectives on the world of antiquity. Christians must become better interpreters of their sacred texts.

A New Lens on an Ancient Text

Biblical scholars have bequeathed the Christian churches valuable new understandings for interpreting the New Testament. The knowledge base they provide enables Christians to situate the texts within the fuller milieu of Second Temple Judaism (Judaism in the approximately six-hundred-year period from the return from Babylonian Exile in the sixth century B.C.E. to the destruction of the Temple in 70 C.E.). In particular, this larger context opens up a more complex picture of the sibling relationship of Christianity and (rabbinic) Judaism as they emerged from biblical Israel.[6] It also affords a more nuanced and accurate insight into the varied factors involved in the eventual separation of the two traditions. Contemporary scholars also challenge Christians to confront the way their texts have functioned in history, such as the way the liturgical proclamation of the passion narratives on Good Friday "inspired" Christians to taunt and even beat Jews. They show as well how the dependence of early Christianity on Jewish patterns and practices of worship meant "the urge to differentiate led to denigration of the Jews."[7] After all, "anti-Judaism was never mere theorizing without significant practical implications. . . . [It was] part of preaching, pastoral care, and community formation."[8]

Such scholarship has played a major role in stimulating leaders in many churches to challenge their members to repent of attitudes that have had tragic consequences for Jews and have distorted Christian self-understanding. Among the most poignant examples is the prayer Pope John Paul II inserted in the cracked stones of the Western Wall in Jerusalem in March 2000 asking God's "forgiveness for Jewish suffering caused by Christians" — the same prayer offered just weeks before in St. Peter's Basilica on the First Sunday of Lent.[9] An understanding of the multidimensional character and tragic consequences of anti-Judaism will contribute to repentance — and thus, one hopes, to its eradication.

Anti-Judaism: Variations on a Theme

While "anti-Judaism" has become something of an umbrella term for a variety of views, it is necessary to fold up the umbrella and peer more closely at the various perspectives it has covered.

Anti-Judaism in the New Testament: A Largely Intra-Jewish Debate

Even within the New Testament we find significant variants. Jesus' mission to proclaim God's reign in word and deed put him at odds with his Jewish contemporaries on various matters. Yet debate over interpretation of Torah was typical of Judaism in the first-century; no single understanding was normative. Whatever disputes Jesus may have had with other Jews of his day, the differences lay *within* Judaism. Moreover, the prominence Judaism accorded prophecy meant that Israel had a strong tradition of self-criticism. Thus, his hearers would likely have understood Jesus' challenges within the context of prophetic speech.

Paul's differences with Judaism were more complicated. Writing in the 60s C.E., Paul was both an insider — Jews were "his kindred according to the flesh" (Rom. 9:3) — and an outsider — "*They* are Israelites . . ." (Rom. 9:4). Judaism in many respects lay in the past for him, as he redirected his energies to Gentile converts. His argument, however, was not directed against Jews as such, but against what he regarded as traditional Judaism — Judaism that follows the way of Torah rather than the way of Jesus Christ. Paul believed passionately that Christ had brought Gentiles into the covenant, and that faith in Christ transcended covenantal laws. To be sure, this was an argument with Judaism — but an argument indicates a difference with, not opposition to, the people as such.

Yet we do have one text where Paul's passion leads him to cross the line. In 1 Thessalonians 2:14–16, Paul levels the accusation that the Jews killed both Jesus and the prophets. Further, they hindered him and his disciples from preaching to the Gentiles. Thus, Paul writes, the Jews have displeased God and "God's wrath has overtaken them at last." This passage is indeed anti-Jewish. Likely shaped by Paul's apocalyptic outlook, this text does not represent how deeply he cared for the Jewish people, nor does it reflect his utter commitment to Israel's God and its scriptures. In Romans 9–11 — a dense thicket of Paul's thought — he speaks of his "kindred according to the flesh": "to them belong the adoption, the glory, the covenants, the giving of the law, the worship, and the promises" (10:5). Paul's complicated thought requires painstaking explication.[10]

In general, as the Gospels move toward the end of the first century, they reflect a greater degree of tension with Judaism, even though the evangelists' communities were still inextricably connected to it — "Christianity" had not yet parted ways with "Judaism." Hence, we find the scathing denunciation of the scribes and Pharisees (Matthew 23), and the scurrilous "You are from your father the devil" in John 8:44. Clearly, the argument had become heated. The rhetoric of defamation had become part of the proclamation of the gospel — though let the reader note that Jesus rebukes Peter as "Satan" in the Gospel of Mark (Mark 8:33), with a parallel in Matthew 16:23.

The New Testament writers were not alone in drawing upon such derogatory language. Vitriolic attacks on one's opponents, even one's co-religionists, were part of the Greco-Roman culture. Jewish writings of a roughly comparable period attest to this. The Dead Sea Scrolls provide vivid examples of one group — a dissident community gathered at Qumran along the Dead Sea — excoriating other Jews as "lying interpreters" and as "teachers of lies and seers of falsehood." Neither the Qumran community nor the writers of the *Psalms of Solomon* spared harsh language in denouncing the Jewish priesthood.[11]

The fact the New Testament's rhetoric of defamation has counterparts in Jewish sources explains but does not justify it. Situating the texts in their sociocultural world, however, permits us to understand the dynamics that gave rise to such language — and challenges us to become judicious interpreters.

Douglas Hare, a New Testament scholar, contributes to the interpretative process in his identification of three kinds of anti-Judaism in the texts: *prophetic anti-Judaism, Jewish-Christian anti-Judaism,* and *Gentilizing anti-Judaism.*[12]

- *Prophetic anti-Judaism.* From its inception, Jesus' movement was a conversionist sect within Judaism. Like others caught up in the eschatological expectations of his day, Jesus found support in the sacred writings for his particular interpretation. Even his controversies with the Pharisees mirrored a well-established prophetic tradition in which the prophets accused priests and teachers of Torah of special responsibility for Israel's apostasy.[13]

• *Jewish-Christian Anti-Judaism.* This postresurrectional form of anti-Judaism includes elements of prophetic anti-Judaism, but adds a new element: Israel manifests its apostasy not only by failing to repent and return to God in ways prescribed by the prophet Jesus, but also by refusing to acknowledge the critical importance for salvation history of the crucified and risen Jesus. Hare writes, "As a conversionist sect, it [Christianity] could grant validity to the religion of its opponents as little as today's Jehovah's Witnesses can acknowledge the authenticity of the established churches."[14] Jewish-Christian anti-Judaism, however, retained the basic assumption of prophetic anti-Judaism that repentance was possible because God had *not* rejected his people. Nevertheless, it fostered a breach with the larger Jewish community. Because they subordinated the primary symbols of Jewish identity — Torah, temple, circumcision, Sabbath, food laws — to the central Christian symbol of the crucified and risen Jesus, Christian Jews "challenged ethnic solidarity too severely to be tolerated.... Ordinary Jews correctly perceived that Christianity constituted a genuine threat to Jewish identity."[15]

• *Gentilizing Anti-Judaism.* This form sublated prophetic and Jewish-Christian forms of anti-Judaism, and added the conviction that Israel's apostasy was incurable and that God had finally and irrevocably rejected his people. It drew upon prophetic texts that seemed "to speak of Israel as incurably obdurate, and which can be taken as suggesting that God will create a new people for himself."[16]

Hare's typology allows readers to recognize the way in which anti-Judaism developed in the New Testament itself. It is particularly helpful in distinguishing intra-Jewish debate from the rhetoric of a largely Gentile church. This "Gentilizing anti-Judaism" assumed new force in early Christian writings.

Anti-Judaism in Early Church Writings: A Rivalry Intensifies

Christians might well have regarded the New Testament passages that disparage various Jewish beliefs and practices as a "period piece" if the rivalry with Judaism had not widened and deepened in Christianity's formative years. Early church writers added new layers to anti-Judaism in their assertions that Judaism had become obsolete.

Christianity was a minority religion without legal status in the Roman Empire until early in the fourth century. Thus, we must read the church writers in the second and third century as apologists for an insecure, fledgling group experiencing opposition on three fronts: pagan, Jewish, and Christian.

To many in the pagan world, Christians must have seemed a strange lot. They claimed continuity with Israel, even to be the *new* Israel. They retained Israel's scriptures and asserted they had inherited its covenant. Yet they had abandoned to one degree or another the very practices commanded in those scriptures: circumcision, dietary laws, festivals, and observance of the Sabbath. The philosopher Celsus wondered in the late second century if God had given "contradictory laws to this man from Nazareth," given the differences in the teaching of Jesus from that of Moses. "Who is wrong?" Celsus asked, "Moses or Jesus?" "Or when the Father sent Jesus had he forgotten what commands he gave to Moses? Or did he condemn his own laws and change his mind, and send his messenger for quite the opposite purposes?" (*True Doctrine* 7:18).[17]

The apologists had to justify Christianity vis-à-vis Judaism, which was well established and respected, and undergoing its own process of transformation as it adapted to the loss of the Temple and Jerusalem. In retrospect, it is clear that Christianity's inextricable connection to Judaism complicated its theological differences: The closeness of the traditions, perhaps best imaged as a sibling relationship, made the disagreements all the more powerful.[18] For example, over against the more authoritative Jewish tradition, Christians brashly asserted that *their* interpretation of the scriptures was the correct one — even as they used some of the same exegetical techniques.

Within Christianity itself, Marcion (d. 160) elicited a heated debate by declaring that the God of Abraham, Isaac, and Jacob was a cruel and capricious God of Law, utterly unlike the loving God of Jesus Christ. Therefore, he argued, the Christian Bible should not include either the Old Testament, or any texts that reflected Jewish influence. Marcion's Bible was thus a slender volume: ten letters of Paul and an edited version of the Gospel of Luke.

The challenge to articulate Christian identity in relationship to these three audiences demanded a finely tuned articulation of both continuity and newness — an arduous task for a small band belonging to an illicit religion in the Roman Empire.

In many respects, Marcion's radical proposal sharpened the terms of the debate. Those who refuted him, most notably Irenaeus, Origen, and Tertullian, maintained that the God of Israel was indeed the God of Jesus Christ. They explained: Salvation unfolded in history, first in the promises to the Jews and now fulfilled in Jesus Christ. Thus, Christians must retain the scriptures of the Jewish people as the "Old Testament" because those texts contain the story of the promise essential to the narrative of the fulfillment. Augustine's later formulation synthesized their perspective in a dictum that has exercised a great deal of influence on Christian interpretation of the Bible: "In the Old Testament the New Testament lies hid; in the New Testament the Old Testament becomes clear" (*Questions on the Heptateuch* 2.73).

While the apologists maintained the superiority of the Christian revelation, their emphasis on continuity with Israel countered the extreme anti-Judaism of Marcion, who was condemned as a heretic and excommunicated.

Nonetheless, even as they reacted to Marcion's antipathy to Judaism, early Christian writers added a new layer to the disagreement with the synagogue. They believed a new era had arrived, and that Judaism would, therefore, give way to Christianity. After all, the Jews no longer had a Temple since the Romans destroyed it in 70, and after 135 Jerusalem had become a Roman city, *Aelia Capitolina*. So history seemed to confirm what their theology suggested — Judaism had been unfaithful to the covenant, and now its time was over.[19]

Origen (ca. 185–254) is explicit: the Jews had committed "the most impious crime of all when they conspired against the Savior" of humankind in the "city where they performed to God the customary rites" that symbolized profound mysteries. "Therefore," he concluded, "that city where Jesus suffered these indignities had to be utterly destroyed. The Jewish nation had to be overthrown, and God's invitation to blessedness transferred to others, I mean the Christians, to whom came the teaching about the simple and pure worship of God" (*Against Celsus* 4.2.3).

In the late second century, the bishop of Sardis (in modern Turkey), Melito (d. ca. 190), preached an eloquent sermon articulating what became the leitmotif of anti-Judaism: in killing Jesus, the Jews had murdered God. This charge of "deicide" echoed in the church for nearly two thousand years, formally repudiated only in 1965 by the Second Vatican Council in its decree *Nostra Aetate.* Major Christian figures of the fourth and fifth centuries, Augustine of Hippo

(354–430) and John Chrysostom (347–407), intensified the separation. Augustine argued that because the Jews had rejected Jesus, they were cursed to wander in exile as reprobates. Yet they must not be killed so that the world will see the consequences of rejecting the Christ. Chrysostom authored some of the most vitriolic denunciations of Jews, who were "called to sonship, but . . . degenerated to the level of dogs" (*Homily One against the Judaizers*). (We understand something of the rhetorical style of this period when we see how Chrysostom re-cycled some of the same vitriol in attacking Arian Christians, whom he regarded as heretics.)

These texts vividly describe what the more abstract term "super-sessionism" means: to Christians belong the blessing and the cove-nant because of the infidelity of the Jews. Judaism is obsolete. The logic of the early church writers established a theological tra-jectory: antiquated Israel would give way to the new creation of Christianity.

But Judaism did not vanish. Meanwhile, Christianity had acquired political ascendancy in 379 as the official religion of the Roman em-pire. As a result, the church found itself without a theology adequate to explain itself in light of the enduring character of Judaism, but with the political power to advance its own growth while placing restrictions on Judaism. Regional councils in various areas from the late fifth through late seventh centuries reflected the church's inse-curity by decreeing the separation of Jews from Christians. They had two preoccupations: to keep Jews from proselytizing and to persuade them to convert.

The Middle Ages:
More Virulent Forms of Anti-Judaism

Over the centuries, the church allowed or even encouraged defama-tion of Jews, although various popes periodically issued statements denouncing violence against Jews and condemning forced baptisms. While Christians and Jews co-existed in various places, warily, if often peacefully, church leaders overall treated Jews harshly. In the High Middle Ages, anti-Judaism took a more vicious turn. Hostility against Jews captured the popular imagination, spawning outbreaks of violence. The call for a crusade against the Muslim "infidels" occupying the Holy Land in 1096 resulted in the massacre of Jews in the Rhineland.[20] If traditionally Jews had been perceived as the historic enemy, now they were regarded as a menace to Christian society.

Sociocultural dynamics help to probe the various layers of anti-Judaism. In late twelfth-century Rhineland, for example, Jews inspired popular antipathy for a variety of reasons, including their status as immigrants, business competitors, and allies of the political authorities. Moreover, they were religious dissidents in a dominantly Christian realm. Add the overlay of their role as historic enemies of Christianity, and we find a formula for a virulent new strain of anti-Judaism. Just as Jews had persecuted and killed Jesus, so now Christians perceive them as a threat to their society.[21]

Popular legends about Jews as ritual murderers became widespread. During the thirteenth century, Christians charged Jews with desecrating the host so as to reenact their original deicide. They accused them of blood libel — using the blood of Christians, preferably children, for their Passover rituals. Preachers spread tales based on such fabrications and vilified Jews in passionate sermons. The violence against Jews — both verbal and physical — suggests that anti-Judaism had come to resemble what the modern world calls anti-Semitism. It had, however, one major difference: Christianity provided no sanction for genocide.

Anti-Judaism in the Modern Period: The Virulence Spreads

For the modern Christian, these medieval accusations appear particularly irrational and outrageous — and they were.

They were also enduring, despite the attempts of many popes to refute the charges. The charges exacerbated popular hostility toward Jews, leading in many cases to persecutions and even death. Yet the blood libel was the fantasy of the masses rather than church leaders, at least until the nineteenth century, when the Vatican itself became identified with the charges. Articles in official and unofficial publications repeated the charges against the "miserable race of Judah," assuring their readers that the Talmud commanded Jews to murder Christians for their blood. Vatican officials intensified efforts to convert Jews; for example, they held them against their will, confined them in ghettoes, and compelled them to listen to sermons.[22]

The Vatican was not alone. Sixteenth-century reformer Martin Luther had issued a vicious tract, *On the Jews and Their Lies,* in 1543, which recommended that Jews be dealt with by "severe mercy," including setting fire to synagogues and forbidding rabbis to teach. The Lutheran tradition portrayed Jews as the living embodiment of legalistic religion — like Catholics, only worse.[23] This carried over into nineteenth- and twentieth-century German Protestant thought and exercised a particular effect on the development of modern biblical scholarship. Indeed, its leading lights — Ferdinand Weber, Julius Wellhausen, Wilhelm Bousset, Emil Schürer, and Rudolf Bultmann — presented Judaism as a desiccated, ritualistic religion of works-righteousness.

Anti-Judaism, Anti-Semitism, and the *Shoah*

This brief review of history suggests that anti-Judaism has absorbed new layers over time, becoming ever more deadly. What initially grew out of an argument over differences hardened into harsh treatment of Jews over the course of many centuries. The church consistently rationalized its actions by defaming Jews as a "deicide people" and "Christ-killers." At the heart of anti-Judaism is the charge echoed repeatedly that the Jews bear the burden of responsibility for the death of Jesus.

As shameful as this legacy is, it is not identical with the genocidal anti-Semitism of the Nazis, which sought to eliminate Jews entirely.

Moreover, secular culture shaped modern anti-Semitism to a considerable degree. The Enlightenment philosopher Voltaire, for example, represented Jews and their Christian descendants as impediments to the development of European culture. He considered Jews outsiders to European society by their nature. From Czarist Russia came the *Protocols of the Elders of Zion* — later proven to be a forgery — which alleged a Jewish secret government existing since the time of Christ was conspiring to overthrow Christendom and inaugurate the reign of the devil.[24] Race theories provided a "scientific" basis for maintaining the outsider status of Jews. Jews were "Semites," a separate race. Social engineering through eugenics provided a way of fashioning a homogeneous society without "inferior" peoples, such as Gypsies, homosexuals, the mentally ill, and the physically disabled. Above all, for Adolf Hitler, the "Jewish race" had to be obliterated. The Third Reich, with its tools of an efficient bureaucracy and scientific method, had the means of carrying out Hitler's fixation. The *Shoah* (Holocaust) was state-sanctioned genocide, a product of the modernization process in which government officials authorized violence and routinized the means to exercise it over a people whom it had demonized and dehumanized.[25]

The *Shoah* may defy explanation, but it demands examination. For the sake of the integrity of the gospel as well as for establishing a just relationship with the Jews, Christians must confront their lethal legacy: Although distinguishable, anti-Judaism and anti-Semitism intersect. The consequences of this meeting have been unspeakable.

Anti-Judaism and Anti-Semitism: "Never Again"

When contemporary Christians hear New Testament passages proclaimed in a liturgical context, they typically know nothing of the layers of anti-Judaism that developed over nearly two thousand years. Thus, they seem in most cases not to take in the harshness of passages such as John's narrative of the passion (read on Good Friday in many churches) in which "the Jews" as a whole clamor for Jesus' crucifixion.[26] While most today would be horrified to hear Jews characterized as "Christ-killers," let alone as ritual murderers, Christians generally have no idea of the "journey" such passages have traveled since the evangelists penned them. Yet knowledge of this journey is requisite if we are to do justice to those texts in context — and to Christianity itself.

We must factor in demographics as well: Christians in vast areas of the world will have little chance to meet Jews face-to-face. Thus, the New Testament provides their sole point of reference for Christianity's relationship to Judaism. It is, then, all the more important that teachers and preachers help Christians enter both into the world from which these texts came and the "worlds" that used those texts.

A bitter irony has arisen. Even as the contemporary church is facing its responsibility for anti-Judaism, anti-Semitism is enjoying resurgence. Just as the churches have made a commitment to healing their relationships to Jews, growing numbers of those outside Christianity (and some within it) are drawing upon its tragic legacy of anti-Judaism to fuel anti-Semitism. Many, particularly in Arab and Muslim nations, seem to regard the conflict in the Middle East as a justification to recycle the worst of medieval accusations. For example, when Pope John Paul II visited Syria on May 8–9, 2001, Syrian president Bashar al-Assad gave a welcome speech that included an attack on Jews as those "who try to kill the principles of all religions with the same mentality with which they betrayed Jesus Christ." The Syrian minister of religious affairs, Muhammad Ziyadah, added: "We must be fully aware of what the enemies of God and malicious Zionism conspire to commit against Christianity and Islam."[27] The charge of blood libel is back — circulated now around the globe via the Internet. So, too, is the *Protocol of the Elders of Zion,* widely available in the Middle East and the subject of an Egyptian thirty-part series by Arab Radio and Television in December 2002. Medieval images of demonic Jews have reappeared in contemporary cartoons. Once again, a swarthy, bearded man with a long nose and repulsive visage lurks menacingly. Jews are presented as diabolical liars, hiding now behind the "Auschwitz lie."

Modern technology plays a major role in this. It may be, as Thomas Friedman muses, that the Internet, fiber optics, and satellites collectively form a "high-tech Tower of Babel. It's as though God suddenly gave us all the tools to communicate and none of the tools to understand."[28] As images have become international, fellow journalist George Packer observes, people's lives have remained parochial.[29]

The same technology can, however, be a force for change, as the resources for Jewish-Christian relations available through the Internet are substantial and impressive, whether for study of biblical texts or for tracing the progress of the churches in the arduous work of reconciliation. For those willing to explore and reflect, a world of thought is available in ways our ancestors could not imagine.

For example, I belong to an ecumenical group of Christian scholars who published a ten-point statement in September 2002, *A Sacred Obligation: Rethinking Christian Faith in Relation to Judaism and the Jewish People.* One paragraph of the introduction reads:

> We believe that revising Christian teaching about Judaism and the Jewish people is a central and indispensable obligation of theology in our time. It is essential that Christianity both understand and represent Judaism accurately, not only as a matter of justice for the Jewish people, but also for the integrity of Christian faith, which we cannot proclaim without reference to Judaism. Moreover, since there is a unique bond between Christianity and Judaism, revitalizing our appreciation of Jewish religious life will deepen our Christian faith. We base these convictions on ongoing scholarly research and the official statements of many Christian denominations over the past fifty years.[30]

Our principal interest in promulgating the statement is to stimulate thoughtful conversation in the churches. Yet we are a group of twenty-two persons of modest means — most of us academics — who would have little chance of disseminating our thinking so widely were it not for the Internet. As theologians for whom rebuilding the broken bridges between Jews and Christians is a sacred obligation, we hope that wider access to the rethinking in the churches will become a well-traveled road.

Without question, the anti-Judaism of Christianity has contributed to anti-Semitism. The challenge to the churches is to repent of this legacy and replace it with one that does justice to Judaism and the Jewish people. May all Christians come to see this as their sacred obligation.

Notes

1. Robert S. Wistrich, *The Longest Hatred* (London: Thames Methuen, 1991).

2. Cited in Amy-Jill Levine, "Anti-Judaism and the Gospel of Matthew," in *Anti-Judaism and the Gospels,* ed. William R. Farmer (Harrisburg, Pa.: Trinity Press International, 1999), 13, n. 10. Supersessionism (from the Latin, *supersedere,* to preside over, to sit upon) is the theological claim that Christians have replaced or superseded Jews as God's people.

3. Secretariat for Ecumenical and Interreligious Affairs of the National Conference of Catholic Bishops, *Catholics Remember the Holocaust* (Washington, D.C.: United States Catholic Conference, 1998). This monograph also contains statements from various episcopal conferences, most notably that of the bishops of France (see n. 4). Virtually all documents from the various churches on Jewish-Christian relations are available in various languages at *www.jcrelations.net.*

4. The term "teaching of contempt" originates with the French Jewish historian Jules Isaac; see his *The Teaching of Contempt,* trans. H. Holt (New York: Holt, Rinehart, and Winston, 1964). For an account of his meeting with Pope John XXIII and the effect that meeting ultimately had in placing the Catholic Church's relationship with Judaism on the agenda of the Second Vatican Council, see Michael Phayer, *The Catholic Church and the Holocaust, 1930–1965* (Bloomington: Indiana University Press, 2000), 204–8.

5. "Declaration of Repentance," in *Catholics Remember the Holocaust,* 31–37.

6. See Christopher M. Leighton and Daniel Lehmann, "Jewish-Christian Relations in Historical Perspective," in *Irreconcilable Differences: A Learning Resource for Jews and Christians,* ed. D. F. Sandmel, R. M. Catalano, and C. M. Leighton (Boulder, Colo.: Westview Press, 2001), 18–19. Judaism as we know it today was shaped significantly by rabbinic thought and practice. Thus modern Judaism is "rabbinic" more than "biblical."

7. Stephen G. Wilson, *Related Strangers: Jews and Christians 70–170 CE* (Minneapolis: Fortress, 1995), 257.

8. Clark Williamson, *A Guest in the House of Israel: Post-Holocaust Church Theology* (Louisville: Westminster/John Knox, 1993), 5–7.

9. For a summary of church statements in the Protestant and Catholic traditions, see Mary C. Boys, *Has God Only One Blessing? Judaism as a Source of Christian Self-Understanding* (New York: Paulist, 2000), 247–66.

10. For an especially helpful exposition, see Williamson, *A Guest in the House of Israel,* 77–106.

11. See Luke Timothy Johnson, "The New Testament's Anti-Jewish Slander and the Conventions of Ancient Polemic," *Journal of Biblical Literature* 108, no. 3 (1989): 419–41.

12. Douglas R. A. Hare, "The Rejection of the Jews in the Synoptic Gospels and Acts," in *Anti-Semitism and the Foundations of Christianity*, ed. Alan Davies (New York: Paulist, 1979), 27–47. George Smiga, *Pain and Polemic: Anti-Judaism in the Gospels* (New York: Paulist, 1992) renames Hare's categories: prophetic polemic, subordinating polemic, and abrogating anti-Judaism, respectively.

13. See John Gager, *The Origins of Anti-Semitism: Attitudes toward Judaism in Pagan and Christian Antiquity* (New York: Oxford University Press, 1985). Gager claims this term is misleading in "that it implies a negative attitude toward Judaism as such, although it is actually meant to describe an internal debate in which, though the meaning and control of the central symbols — Temple, Torah, ritual commandments — are in dispute, the symbols themselves are not. Therefore I shall substitute the phrase 'intra-Jewish polemic.' "

14. Hare, "The Rejection of the Jews in the Synoptic Gospels and Acts," 31.

15. Ibid., 32.

16. Ibid.

17. See Robert L. Wilken, *The Christians as the Romans Saw Them* (New Haven: Yale University Press, 1984), 94–125.

18. Gager provides an important interpretation of this proximity: "In short, *if* we are dealing with a religious community whose view of its own legitimacy is fundamentally dependent on a set of symbols, viz., the Hebrew scriptures, which are simultaneously claimed by another religious community; *if*, in addition, this other religious community is able to present arguments which appear at least initially to establish the priority of its claims (continuity of ritual observance, use of scriptures in the original language, and so forth); and *if* this other community not only continues to flourish but exercises an appeal among the faithful of the new religion, then, under these circumstances, the task of conceptual nihilation will appear all the more urgent and continuous." Or, as the psychoanalyst Rudolph Loewenstein puts it in *Christians and Jews: A Psychoanalytic Study,* the negative images of Jews and Judaism within the Christian tradition are indicative of "the Christian reaction to their moral debt to the Jews. All reflect also Christianity's incomplete victory over Israel" (cited in Gager, *The Origins of Anti-Semitism,* 22–23). For a development of the axiom that the closer the relation, the more intense the conflict, see Georg Simmel, *Conflict and the Web of Group Affiliations,* trans. K. Wolff and R. Bendix (New York: Free Press, 1964).

19. See Robert L. Wilken, *Judaism and the Early Christian Mind* (New Haven: Yale University Press, 1971), 1–38; 222–30.

20. See Robert Chazan, *In the Year 1096: The First Crusade and the Jews* (Philadelphia: Jewish Publication Society, 1996); also his *Medieval Stereotypes and Modern Anti-Semitism* (Berkeley: University of California Press, 1997).

21. See R. I. Moore, *The Formation of a Persecuting Society: Power and Deviance in Western Europe, 950–1250* (Oxford: Basil Blackwell, 1987).

22. See David I. Kertzer, *The Popes against the Jews: The Vatican's Role in the Rise of Modern Anti-Semitism* (New York: Alfred A. Knopf, 2001).

23. See Heiko A. Oberman, *The Roots of Anti-Semitism in the Age of the Renaissance and Reformation* (Philadelphia: Fortress, 1984).

24. See Goran Larsson, *Fact or Fraud? The Protocol of the Elders of Zion* (Jerusalem: AMI–Jerusalem Center for Biblical Studies and Research, 1994).

25. See Donald J. Dietrich, *God and Humanity in Auschwitz: Jewish-Christian Relations and Sanctioned Murder* (New Brunswick, N.J.: Transaction Publishers, 1995).

26. See Adele Reinhartz, *Befriending the Beloved Disciple: A Jewish Reading of the Gospel of John* (New York: Continuum, 2001), for an insightful wrestling with the rhetoric of the Fourth Gospel.

27. See Thomas L. Friedman, "Foreign Affairs: Empty Deeds, Ugly Words," *New York Times,* May 11, 2001; Susan Sachs, "Anti-Semitism Is Deepening among Muslims," *New York Times,* April 27, 2002.

28. Thomas L. Friedman, *Longitudes and Attitudes: Exploring the World after September 11* (New York: Farrar, Straus, and Giroux, 2002), 373. Friedman observes about the Internet: "It is not only the greatest tool we have for making people smarter quicker. It's also the greatest tool we have for making people dumber faster. Rumors published on the Internet now have a way of immediately becoming facts" (374).

29. Cited in ibid., 375.

30. The statement is available in full online at: www.bc.edu/research/cjl/meta-elements/partners/CSG/Sacred_Obligation.htm as well as in various languages at www.jcrelations.net.

Chapter 5

What Alexander the Great Did to Us All

James A. Sanders

Since September 11, 2001, the Western world has become starkly aware of the deep-seated cultural differences between the Muslim and Western worlds, between the cultures of the Eastern and Western hemispheres of Planet Earth, and between individual rights and national security. I shall attempt to draw some lines between East and West in antiquity but also show how they became interfused and interrelated in Early Judaism and in the Bible itself.

The Bible, both Jewish and Christian, is basically Semitic in culture and outlook, not European or Western. This is the case not only of the Hebrew Bible, or First Christian Testament; it is also true of the Second Christian Testament. It was not until Alexander's Greece conquered the pre-Christian world of the late fourth century B.C.E. that European cultural values and Semitic cultural values came into critical contact, conflict, and a fusion called Hellenism, thus creating the cultural crucible in which both Christianity and rabbinic Judaism were born.

Alexander's Conquests

In order to appreciate what Jesus was doing in his time, to understand what the figure of Christ meant in early Christianity, and to understand how and why rabbinic Judaism arose, we need to comprehend the vast importance of what Alexander the Great did to the Eastern Mediterranean and Near Eastern worlds, and eventually to the Western world. The Bible as a whole is based on an understanding of humanity that was centered in the patriarchal family and clan.[1] Individuals had their worth but only in the context of family, clan, and people. This was a corporate view of human worth and responsibility. When Alexander, however, fought the non-Semitic but nonetheless

Asian Persian Empire, and brought it to its knees in the late fourth century B.C.E., he radically challenged the social system of most of the world. There has rarely been a force more powerful unleashed on the world than this son of Philip of Macedonia, dedicated student of the great Athenian philosopher, Aristotle.

The Greek geographer Strabo relates anecdotes about Alexander that help understand how his early admirers understood him.[2] Alexander conquered Egypt when he was only twenty years old, Persia when he was twenty-five, and the world (at least to the Indus Valley in current Afghanistan) when he was thirty. Strabo relates an incident that showed who the young man in childhood was in the eyes of his followers (cf. Luke 2:40–52). When Alexander was a child twelve years old he watched his father's best horsemen fail at taming a wild horse. The lad asked his father, King Philip of Macedonia, if he, Alexander, could try. He gave his son permission and Alexander proceeded to tame the horse and make it his own! His father, according to Strabo, told Alexander he would have to create a larger kingdom of his own because Macedonia would soon prove too small for him.

But Alexander's lasting power was not in horsemanship and military prowess; it was in his dedication to Greek culture and philosophy, which challenged abuses in patriarchal systems throughout the known world. Alexander was an evangelist for Greek ways of thinking. Everywhere he went he established Greek-type cities, the *polis,* and in those cities, which he usually named Alexandria, he established schools to propagate what he himself had learned in Athens. I imagine he established a "peace corps" in Athens to staff the schools and to teach the world what Aristotle had taught him. And at the heart and core of what they taught was individual worth and responsibility. Greece was indeed the birthplace of democracy and individual human rights, though it often violated those rights.

Socrates was sentenced to die in 399 B.C.E., not because he had "corrupted the youth of Athens," as was officially charged, but because he had defended the Athenian constitution's guarantee of an individual's right to a fair trial. After the ignominious defeat of the glorious Athenian navy by the Spartan, in the Battle of the White Isles in 406 B.C.E., many citizens wanted to have the six admirals tried in one mass trial, because they had competed with each other for personal gain in the battle instead of fighting the Spartans. In order to do so, the constitution would have to be suspended by a unanimous vote of the Senate, but Socrates defended the constitution against popular demand, and alone voted against suspension. This was not forgotten.

Against the popular demand for "justice," Socrates defended each individual's right to a fair trial.

Hellenization and the Bible

A few examples will have to suffice to explain how Alexander's Hellenization of the known world affected Early Judaism. The Hellenization process was the historic interaction between the Hellenic culture that Alexander espoused and the local Semitic and other cultures of the eastern Mediterranean world.

The Bible is basically a community literature. Most of it is anonymous. We have no idea who wrote most of either testament, with the exception that the Apostle Paul wrote some letters to some churches he had founded. Even modern scholarship, which itself is very influenced by Hellenism's focus on individual worth and responsibility, has attributed signs to ancient hypothetical sources of biblical literature — such as J, E, D, P, Q, Mk, L, etc., in order to account for the contradictions, anomalies, and different points of view in the Pentateuch and Gospels. We have no idea who wrote the great stories and histories of the Bible, or the books of Psalms, Proverbs, Ecclesiastes, the four Gospels, or some of the New Testament epistles.

In the Semitic world anonymity of inspired literature put the focus on God as the author(ity) of what would become sacred literature, instead of on human authors. This is generally true in Oriental cultures, where traditional art and literature are anonymous. But when the Greeks came calling, they inevitably would ask who wrote this great literature. The Jew would have responded, "Why, the Torah is our Book, it tells us who we are and what we should do." "Yeah," the Greek would say, "but who wrote it? We know who wrote the *Iliad* and the *Odyssey*, so who wrote the Torah?" That information was far more important to Greeks than it was to Jews, until they too became Hellenized. Then they could answer, Moses wrote the Torah, David wrote all the Psalms, Solomon authored the Book of Proverbs, etc. This despite the fact that it is clear they did not, and the fact that such claims were superimposed later. Attribution of a biblical book to a well-known name from the community's past is called pseudepigraphy, which happened, because of the Greek cultural focus on individual responsibility, when a Semitic community was forced to assign original authors to its common literature.

So-called conservatives today are so Hellenized that they are offended when this is pointed out. They think it is an attack on the Bible to say the truth about its anonymous or community origins.

But we have no idea who wrote the Gospels. Superscriptions, such as "According to Luke," were not affixed to manuscripts of the Gospels until well into the second century C.E. It has been convincingly shown that whoever wrote Luke did not use any of the Greek medical terms of the time, but the tradition of Luke being the same person as the beloved physician who was companion to Paul in Colossians 4:14 is so imbedded in popular thinking it is difficult to surrender it. The truth is that the Bible is so Semitic in basic outlook that it is essentially a community literature, formed and shaped in the ancient communities that found value in its stories and wisdom, with later communities adapting them, glossing them, and adding to them, to speak more directly to their later situations, until the canonical process came to a close. Western insistence on locating an "original" author is deeply Hellenistic.

The prophetic books in the Hebrew Bible, which bear in their superscriptions the names of ancient figures, have many additions appended by later communities which found value enough in them to adapt them to their later situations and thus add to them to make them relevant to their own community needs — until the canonical process ceased, and took another turn.[3] The individual prophets' names in those books are presented in them as those through whom God worked; the focus in the prophetic corpus is always on God's word working through such persons and their followers, not on the prophet as a great individual through whom God worked. Books in the Hebrew Bible do not have titles or "by-lines," as the ancient Greek translations of the Hebrew Bible gave them, and New Testament books in Greek have, but are referred to by the first words, or the salient word of the first verse of the book.

So-called conservatives in the neo-Puritan tradition today confuse personal morals with social ethics. They think that if an individual leader is personally upright his policies will be good for the nation as a whole, but this is clearly not true, as some "evangelicals" admit.[4] A leader may indeed be faithful to his wife and family but still practice greed, selfishness, and subtle forms of bigotry, and sponsor policies that encourage greed and corporate irresponsibility. The Bible Belt has as high a rate of divorce and unmarried couples as any other. Focus on individual salvation and personal morals does not necessarily issue in worthy social behavior. There is an ancient saying from early Christianity, "God's grace works through human sinfulness" (*errore hominum providentia divina*). Paul stressed the very point in his Epistle to the Romans. Then he asked, "Shall we therefore sin the more that grace may the more abound?" And his answer, of course, was, "By no means" (Rom. 6:1–2). On reading any biblical passage one must always ask what God was doing, and only thereafter focus on what humans should do in the light of God's grace, whether personally or collectively. Celebration of God's works should precede deciding human works. Saying one is committed to "the whole law" is impossible. One generation stresses "laws" important to them (tribalism, patriarchalism, slavery, genocide, segregation, misogyny, homophobia), while the next sets those aside and stresses those that suit them.

The upshot of Alexander's revolution for the biblical world was to bring focus as never before to individual worth and responsibility within the community. Both Jeremiah (31:29) and Ezekiel (chap. 18) had earlier introduced the idea of generational (not yet individual) responsibility in the context of the devastating defeat of Judah in the Babylonian conquest of the early sixth century B.C.E. It was designed to help the destitute survivors, the remnant in Babylon, to understand that their generation would not have to continue to pay for "the sins of the fathers," or of earlier generations, as the Torah, on the contrary, insists they would (Exod. 20:5; 34:6–7). This patent contradiction was the major reason some rabbis later doubted whether the Ezekiel book "soiled the hands," or was "canonical."

The corporate or family dimension of the Bible and subsequent Judaism never ceased, but it became infused with the idea of individual worth and responsibility. The book of Chronicles is a revisionist history of Israel with focus on individual responsibility. For example, in the earlier book of Kings Manasseh is depicted as a scapegoat and the symbol of all that had gone wrong with the monarchy, while in Chronicles Manasseh repents and his repentance is accepted by God. The "Prayer of Manasseh," which is in some Eastern Orthodox canons, is a model for how in Early Judaism the individual could repent and be restored. In the classical Tiberian Masoretic manuscripts of the Hebrew Bible, Chronicles is placed first in the Writings, or third section of the Jewish Bible, followed immediately by the Book of Psalms, the first of which focuses on individual responsibility: "Blessed is the person who walks not in the council of the ungodly. . . . "

The concept of resurrection was originally a collective concept, as in Ezekiel 37, God's resurrecting the new Israel, Early Judaism, out of the ashes of old Israel and Judah in the Babylonian Exile. The focus was on the act of God who willed the restoration of his people. But later, after the gradual Hellenization of Judaism, resurrection began to be seen as an individual affair, as in Isaiah 24 and

Daniel 12, Pharisaic Judaism, and Christian Judaism. The extended Torah story, or epic poem, in Sirach 44–50 that begins, "Come, now, let us praise famous men . . . " (meaning the patriarchs, prophets, scribes, and priests) would have been anathema to traditional Judaism, which had always praised God and God only in retelling the biblical story. The focus was on God's working through those humans. But in Sirach the story of God's promises to and work with the patriarchs and prophets was in the Greek form of the encomium, or praise of the humans through whom God worked.[5]

Hellenization and the Renaissance

We can see the effects of Hellenization in many ways in our own lives. The Protestant Reformation was a child of the Renaissance, and the Renaissance was the "rebirth" of the Hellenization process after the Christian Dark Ages in Europe. One of the most interesting ironies of history, looking back from the present, is that it was the rise of Muslim civilization and culture, which flourished from the eighth to the fourteenth centuries C.E. across the Near East and North Africa into Europe, that was the cradle of the great Golden Age of Jewish culture of the time, and became the catalyst for the Renaissance in Christian Europe. In the wake of its sweep westward across the Mediterranean world, Islamic scholars translated Plato and Aristotle and the other great Greek philosophers and poets into Arabic. When Cordoba in Spain was the cultural jewel of the world of the time, Baghdad's only rival in that regard, Paris, was a backwater.

Medieval Jewish culture flourished under Islam and produced some of the greatest Jewish thinkers of all time: Maimonides, Yefet ben Ely, Abulwalid, Saadya Gaon, Ibn Ezra, and others. But when Christians came into power in Spain, under King Ferdinand and Queen Isabella, the same royal couple who financed Christopher Columbus's adventures west across the Atlantic, they expelled the Jews from Spain. The date that Americans celebrate as "the discovery of America," 1492, Jews lament as the date of the Expulsion of Jews from Spain. The great achievements of the Muslim culture of the time, algebra, calculus, engineering, medicine, anatomy, optics, and the inclusivist tendencies of a vigorous belief in One God, were the major stimulants that brought about the Renaissance in Europe and its child, the Protestant Reformation.

After the fall of the Roman empire the Christian West went into a gradual but serious decline during the European Dark Ages. And out of those Dark Ages in Europe came the medieval Christian crusades against Islam and Judaism. Islam then went into serious decline because of attacks also from northeast Asia. But it was because of Islam's achievements, largely stimulated by the ancient Hellenic and Hellenistic civilizations from which Islam had learned so much, that the Renaissance could take place in Europe. Alexander's influence continued to be felt fifteen centuries after he had conquered the Mediterranean and Near Eastern worlds.

Hellenization and the Reformation

When Martin Luther read the Bible for himself in the sixteenth century, and then translated it into German so others could as well, he could do so largely because Muslim culture had invented paper for use in the newly invented printing press, to replace parchment. Luther severed the Bible from Roman Catholic accumulated doctrine, called the Magisterium, to which for centuries it had been tethered. Luther thus invited individuals to interpret the Bible for themselves. Luther's doctrine of *sola scriptura* was a direct result of the Renaissance emphasis on individuals' worth and ability to read the Bible and think for themselves about it without the church's interpretation. Finally, in 1943, the Catholic Church, in the encyclical *Divino Afflante Spiritu,* allowed Catholic scholars to study scripture historically, apart from the Magisterium. In the secular world one need but think of Rodin's famous statue *Le Penseur.* And what was the sculpted serf or slave thinking as he pondered his condition? I suggest that he was asking himself whether God really intended him to be a serf or slave all his life, as his masters had taught him. In Martin Scorsese's film version of *The Last Temptation of Christ,*[6] Pilate remarked to Jesus after his arrest, "You do not want simply to change the way people live and act: you want to change the way they think. And Rome does not want that!" I suggest that it was Jesus' teaching of a new way for humans to think that Paul intended when he spoke of having "this mind in you, which was in Christ Jesus, that, being in the form of God he did not count equality with God a thing to be grasped, but humbled himself" and took on human form (Phil. 2:5–11). If one thinks radical "class-inversion" thoughts like that about the heavenly realm, one might be tempted to ask radical questions about class structures in human society.

The Reformation did not stop with Luther, of course. It eventually developed the left-wing Reformation of those who almost obliterated the corporate or community dimension from their forms of Christianity. Thus arose the Anabaptists and their heirs the Baptists, such as Roger Williams who founded Rhode Island and who insisted that each individual should read the Bible for him/herself, and that each reading was valid for that individual. Protestantism generally is a trip into the world of individualism. Some Protestant churches, however, (such as the Episcopal, Lutheran, Presbyterian, and Methodist) continue to practice infant baptism and reading scripture from a common lectionary, marks of corporate worth and responsibility. Others practice only "adult baptism," meaning that the individual must make the decision to be Christian, not the individual's family. They usually support the freedom of individual pastors to select whatever passage they want to preach from — permitting them to leave the congregation ignorant of vast portions of scripture (except to engage in trivial pursuit of superficial data?). Protestants speak of the number of members in their congregations while Jews, Catholics, and the Orthodox speak of the number of families in their congregations. Many Protestant groups developed their own "magisteria," particularly in the seventeenth century, through which so-called conservatives insisted that the Bible must be read.[7] This developed into heresy trials of individual scholars, who insisted on reading scripture historically apart from the post-Reformation magisteria, during the so-called modernist-fundamentalist controversies of the nineteenth century.

Reformation or Enlightenment came comparatively late to Judaism. The Reform Jewish movement evolved out of the rise of the Jüdische Wissenschaft (Jewish Science, or Enlightenment) movement in Germany in the mid-nineteenth century.[8] When it then moved to America, it flourished under the direction of the brothers Isaac Mayer Wise in Cincinnati and Stephen Wise in New York City, and it continues to grow. At the heart of the movement was belief in God's purpose for Jewry in dispersion and the adaptation of Torah and tradition to Enlightenment thinking. The "mission of Israel" was to bear witness to a contemporary understanding of Torah and to be a catalyst for ethical standards in the larger community wherever Jews settled. The Reform movement in Germany, and its heirs in the new world, is seen as Judaism's re-entry into the general cultural history from which nascent rabbinic Judaism had departed into ghettoes in the second century C.E., after the Bar Kochba Revolt, to resist further influence from the Greco-Roman world.[9] According to David Hartman, of the Shalom Hartman Institute in Israel today, a major result of the Enlightenment in Judaism was the establishment in the mid-twentieth century of the State of Israel, a Jewish, Western-style, democratic state, in the Middle East. While this is well supported in the West, it has not been well accepted in much of current Islam, which is still basically "family" oriented and suspicious of the trappings of democracy.

Hellenization and Early Christianity

Alexander's cultural conquest had a profound effect on enough pre-rabbinic Jews that some were able to hear a message in the first century, emanating from the Galilee, that God in their time had been incarnate in one person, or one Jew, for the sake of all persons of whatever tribe or family anywhere. "Emanuel=God with us" had always meant God's being with the Jewish people ("with us"). Early Christians, however, resignified it and applied it to their belief in God's being incarnate in one Jew, the Christ, whom God sent to be with the whole world. Hellenistic individualism permitted them to hear the message that God had resurrected that one person for the sake of every individual in the world. When those Hellenized Christian-Jews emerged into the Greco-Roman world outside Palestine the message was rapidly embraced by many. It is astounding to the historian how rapidly Christianity, with its almost uncanny combination of Semitic emphasis on corporate worth and Greek emphasis on individual worth, spread through the world Alexander had Hellenized. There were many Jews, like those at Qumran and the Pharisees, suppressed and oppressed as they were by the Greeks and the Romans, who resisted such individualization in the Christian message. For Jews who bravely resisted Hellenization, the idea of God's incarnation in one person was pagan and should be rigorously opposed. But it spread with amazing speed out in the Greco-Roman world. Later Maimonides would speak of God's incarnation in "the people" (ha-'am).

Others would develop the idea of God's incarnation in scripture,[10] but never before in one person. Messiahs would be anointed and appointed by God, but would not appear by incarnation.

Alexander had paved the way, and so had the Hellenization of a good portion of Early, pre-Christian Judaism. It was the combination of the two worlds, the Hellenic and the Semitic Jewish, that gave Christianity its basic character. When Paul and John tried to develop an ecclesiology, a biblical view of the nature of the church, they drew upon the corporate idea of the church being En Christo, "in Christ." This eventually led to the doctrine of "the church as the corporate body of Christ resurrected." The left-wing churches in the continuing Reformation developed the further idea that salvation was not in the church, but came about when individuals accepted "the Lord Jesus Christ as their personal savior." The left-wing Reformation went its own way in embracing individualism to the point of understanding the church as the sum of the individuals who make personal decisions "for Christ." They in effect set aside the earlier tradition of the church being the heir of Israel called forth by God in a pastoral call on Abraham and Sarah in Genesis 12 but expanded by Christ to the whole world. Such minority forms of highly Hellenized, so-called conservative Christianity today tend to be sectarian and exclusivist, admitting only those individuals who recite the same confession of personal faith and share similar emotions about a personal experience of salvation.[11]

The Catholic-Jewish statement of August 12, 2002, *Reflections on Covenant and Mission*,[12] that there should be no Christian effort to convert Jews because they are a people of an earlier covenant with God, exhibits a typically Catholic understanding of salvation in community, or in the church. Southern Baptists objected vigorously because they reject anything but the idea of a personal decision of the individual for their particular understanding of Christ.

The New Family in Christ

Viewed from the standpoint of the development of biblical thought from emphasis on the worth and responsibility of the family, tribe, clan, and community, to embracing the idea that anyone anywhere from any ethnic family or tribe could become a member of a new family in Christ, the phenomenon of the advent of Christ into the world was culturally revolutionary. But it was truly revolutionary only as long as a balance was kept between the community and the individual. In Christ a new family was formed in which, it was claimed, anyone on earth could join the mighty flowing stream that had begun when God made those promises to Abraham and Sarah in Genesis 12. Christianity did this by keeping the older testament in its double-testament Bible despite efforts to exclude it. The two things on which all early Christians agreed, whether Hellenizers or Judaizers, Pauline or Petrine, were (*a*) monotheism and (*b*) the belief that the church superseded Judaism as God's true Israel.

Jesus, the Galilean, who was himself considerably influenced by Hellenism, is reported as saying that unless one hates his mother and father, wife and children, sisters and brothers, even his own life, he could not join the new family in Christ being formed of folk from many families, clans, and tribes (Luke 14:26=Matt. 10:37; cf. Luke 8:21; 9:59–60). This notion is then explicitly developed in the Book of Acts. That was a serious challenge to those who revered the Fifth Commandment (Exod. 20:12 and Deut. 5:16), which was used to claim that one could not leave the God-given identity of the family or clan into which one was born from his mother's womb, still largely the case in the non-Western world today. Christian converts from Islam anywhere in the world are very few after centuries of missionary effort. Luke also reports Jesus saying, "My mother and my brothers are those who hear the word of God and do it" (8:21). And it is Luke also who reports that Jesus advised one, who excused himself from following Jesus because his father had died, that he should leave the dead to bury their own dead, and that he should instead go and proclaim that a new family, a new kingdom indeed was being formed (9:60). These are radical challenges to all earlier genetic views of the family. The new day of focus on individual worth and responsibility, throughout the Mediterranean world, was dawning in which the Jesus movement would rapidly spread out in the Greco-Roman world. This new family was not just another clan, in Christian belief, but "in Christ" a new multicultural family in which each individual was precious.

Because of the transcultural and multicultural nature of the Bible as a whole there has always been a mix of understanding of corporate worth and responsibility and individual worth and responsibility in the Bible, with focus often more on the one than the other, but moving generally from corporate to individual. Any viable society or culture has to find its own balance between the two. Individual responsibility recognizes human rights, including the right of the individual to migrate culturally and change community identity, as nearly every second-generation migrant family has done. Second-generation Americans are usually bilingual and bicultural. But their children, the third generation, become monolingual and monocultural English-speaking Americans. This country is, so to speak, at the far western end of the Hellenization process and at least theoretically sponsors human rights, that is, individual rights.[13]

If one wants to be true to the Bible, in all its dialogical strength and power, one should come to a true appreciation of the importance and power of the family to the human enterprise. The tension or dialogue between Israel's center in the patriarchal family and Jesus' radical openness to the worldwide human family as a whole can be resolved or understood as a biblical pilgrimage from the Bronze Age to the Greco-Roman, which indicates how we ourselves should continue by dynamic analogy on a similar but different route in our day. Understanding the Bible as a paradigm or model for how continually to bring the biblical past into the ongoing present in contemporary terms provides a map of God's will and desire for the progressive pilgrimage of constantly breaking through old patriarchal and tribal limits to new horizons about the worth and responsibility of all families and of all individuals in God's creation — the common good.

Israel as a Pilgrimage

Just as prominent as the metaphor of the family for the covenant relationship between God and Israel is the metaphor of Israel or the church being a pilgrim folk. Pilgrims cannot limit God's Word to a meaning from the past, either traditional or scholarly. Believers of all stripes regularly resignify the Bible in order to render it relevant to the present. Moses asked God one day on a desert mountain, "Is it not in your going with us, I and your people, that we are distinct from all other peoples on the face of the earth?" (Exod. 33:16). In David's consecration of the massive gifts offered so that Solomon could later build the temple, David prayed thus, "But who am I, and what is this people, that we should be able thus to offer gifts so abundantly? For all things come from you, O God, and of your own have we given you. We are strangers before you, O God, and sojourners, as all our ancestors were; our days on earth are like a shadow, and there is no abiding" (1 Chron. 29:14–15). And the psalmist sang, "Hear my prayer, O Lord, and give ear to my cry.... For I am your passing guest, an alien, like all my ancestors" (Ps. 39:12). Abraham Heschel called it a fatal illusion to assume that a human being is the same as being human. "Being human, he said, means being on the way, striving, waiting, hoping."

Israel, in this view, is a pilgrim folk constantly on the move from bondage to freedom. This should never be understood as a form of escapism — the "this world is not my home" syndrome — but as the essential character of any people who would claim to be Israel, to be on the move to address ever new challenges, to sing a new song to the glory of God, to break camp morning by morning to seek God's will to live by it, to change what can and should be changed, to accept what cannot be changed, with a prayer for wisdom to know the difference — constantly vigilant to oppose dehumanizing others on the way because they are different. This would truly be a move beyond tribal thinking.[14] Such vigilance is to witness to the power of Torah and tradition, or of scripture and Christ, as led by the Spirit.

Jesus was a clear embarrassment to the conservatives of his day. Luke reports that Jesus accepted invitations to many parties in the Galilee and on his fatal trip to Jerusalem. At one such party Jesus showed the depths of God's grace to a woman of ill-repute who bathed his feet in her tears and kissed them unashamedly in public, as the prime example of what *agape* (God's love) means (Luke 7:36–50). That story in the gospel ought to shock every Christian who ever claimed to read the Bible literally, and it ought to shame any who forget the radicality of Jesus' teaching in the context of first-century Judaism, and of God's divine love and grace that know no bounds.

The key is first to focus in biblical stories on what God was doing through the sinful humans in them, and to moralize later, that is, to celebrate God's creativity, love, and grace first, and thereafter to ask what humans should do in the light of that celebration. The day may yet come when Christians will develop a vigorous theocentric Christology, and thus move on in their pilgrimage from traditional Christocentric theologies. And if God is truly One, as we all claim we believe, the day may also come when Jews, Christians, and Muslims will have the humility to see the need to learn from each other, and be afraid neither that one is trying to convert the other, or that learning from others dishonors Torah, Qur'an, or Christ. On the contrary, it would honor them all.

Notes

1. Johannes Pedersen, *Israel: Its Life and Culture,* 2 vols. (Copenhagen: Povl Brawer, 1926); Leo G. Perdue, Joseph Blenkinsopp, John J. Collins, and Carol Meyers, *Families in Ancient Israel* (Louisville: Westminster/John Knox Press, 1997); Erhard S. Gerstenberger, *Theologies of the Old Testament* (Minneapolis: Fortress Press, 2002), 25–91; James A. Sanders, "The Family in the Bible," *Biblical Theology Bulletin* 32, no. 3 (2002): 117–28.

2. Strabo, *The Geography of Strabo,* vol. 7, Loeb Classical Library 241 (Cambridge, Mass.: Harvard University Press, 1967).

3. James A. Sanders, *The Issue of Closure in the Canonical Process: The Canon Debate,* ed. Lee McDonald and James A. Sanders (Peabody, Mass.: Hendrickson Publishers, 2002), 252–63.

4. George Barna, *Index of Leading Spiritual Indicators* (Dallas: Word Publishers, 1996).

5. Burton Mack, *Wisdom and the Hebrew Epic* (Chicago: University of Chicago Press, 1985).

6. Nikos Kazantzakis, *The Last Temptation of Christ*, trans. P. A. Bien (New York: Simon & Schuster, 1960), 373–76, Scorsese's film version.

7. James A. Sanders, *Scripture as Canon in the Church: L'interpretazione della Bibbia nella Chiesa* (Vatican City: Libreria Editrice Vaticana, 2001), 121–43.

8. Max Wiener, *Abraham Geiger and Liberal Judaism: The Challenge of the Nineteenth Century* (Philadelphia: Jewish Publication Society, 1962).

9. Lou Silberman, "From Apocalyptic Proclamation to Moral Prescript: Abot 2, 15–16," *Journal of Jewish Studies* 40, no. 1 (1989): 53–60.

10. Michael Fishbane, *The Garments of Torah* (Bloomington: Indiana University Press, 1994).

11. Sanders, *Scripture as Canon in the Church*.

12. *Reflections on Covenant and Mission*, Consultation of the National Council of Synagogues and the Bishops Committee for Ecumenical and Interreligious Affairs, August 12, 2002.

13. Michael Mandelbaum, *The Ideas That Conquered the World: Peace, Democracy and Free Markets in the Twenty-first Century* (Baltimore: Johns Hopkins University Press, 2002).

14. Gerstenberger, *Theologies of the Old Testament*.

Chapter 6

Catholic-Jewish Relations, 1995–2002

Eugene J. Fisher _____

1995–97

International Relations

January 27, 1995, marked the 50th anniversary of the liberation of Auschwitz. The differing tones of three major statements by the German, Polish, and American Bishops conferences, while not contradictory, illustrated the very different experiences of the three Catholic communities during World War II (texts in *Origins: A Documentary Service of the Catholic News Service* for February 9 and 16, 1995, vol. 24, pp. 563–64 and 585–88). The German Bishops appropriately stressed the guilt of the "unprecedented crime...put into action by the National Socialist rulers in Germany" and acknowledged with candor that "Christians did not offer due resistance to racial anti-Semitism. Many times there was failure and guilt among Catholics. Not a few of them got involved in the ideology of National Socialism and remained unmoved in the face of the crimes committed against...Jews," while others "paved the way to the crimes or even became criminals themselves."

The Polish and the German bishops' conferences had originally planned to make a joint statement on the commemoration, but could not agree on the proper wording. While the German bishops needed to make the articulation of the need for repentance first and central, the Polish bishops, representing a country that was conquered and occupied by the Nazi death machine against its will, needed first to articulate the Polish sense of victimhood: "We bow our heads before the infinite suffering which was often accepted in a deep Christian spirit." Only then could they begin to articulate the deeper suffering of the Jews during the war: "Extermination, called *Shoah*, has weighed painfully not only in relations between Germans and Jews, but also to a great extent in relations between Jews and Poles, who together, though not to the same degree, were victims of Nazi

ideology.... Seeing the Nazi extermination of Jews, many Poles reacted with heroic courage and sacrifice, risking their lives and that
of their families.... Unfortunately, there were also those who were
capable of actions unworthy of being called Christian.... There were
those who remained indifferent to that inconceivable tragedy, [those]
who in some way had contributed to the death of Jews. They will
forever remain a source of remorse." While affirming, as a matter of
historical fact, that the creators of Auschwitz were the Nazi Germans,
not Poles, and that many Poles shared "a dramatic community of fate"
with Jews, the bishops note, "however, it was the Jews who became
the victims of the Nazi plan of systematic and total liquidation.... It
is estimated that more than one million Jews died in Auschwitz-
Birkenau alone. Consequently, even though members of other nations
also perished at this camp, nevertheless, Jews consider this camp a
symbol of the total extermination of their nation."

Given the contentious atmosphere that surrounds Auschwitz-
Birkenau, and how its memory is to be preserved not only for Polish
Catholics and Jews but for all humanity, this very clear acknowledgment by the Polish bishops of the symbolic priority of the Jewish
memory is in many ways a remarkable and potentially very healing
statement on the part of the Polish episcopate.

The American Catholic statement, issued by Archbishop Oscar
Lipscomb of Mobile as chairman of the Bishops' Committee for Ecumenical and Interreligious Affairs (BCEIA), took up the themes from
a third perspective, recalling with "profound gratitude the tremendous sacrifices made by the generation of American Catholics which
defeated Hitler," but also recalling "with humility and a sense of regret the opportunities that were lost to save lives." Here, the BCEIA
listed the American failure "to bomb the railroad lines which led to
Auschwitz" (though flying daily bombing runs over them!) and the
"draconian immigration laws of the period, which kept this country from becoming an asylum for Jews, Catholics and others that it
should have been."

Archbishop Lipscomb carefully distinguishes between "personal
guilt," which is felt by few American Christians, who after all "fought
the war against Hitler," and a "sense of responsibility for what fellow
members of the community of the baptized did not do to save lives."
"Our spirit in remembering the 50th anniversary of the liberation of
Auschwitz," he concludes, "must be one of repentance and resolve to
build a world where never again will such evil be possible."

On February 6, 1995, the governing board of the American Jewish
Committee met with the pope, who told them that "the horrors of the

Shoah" must lead to a greater commitment by Christians and Jews to work together for justice in the world and "peace in the Holy Land, which is so dear to Jews, Christians and Muslims alike." The meeting noted the thirtieth anniversary of *Nostra Aetate* and both the pope and American Jewish Committee president Robert S. Rifkind spoke of the "profound changes" in Catholic-Jewish relations as a result of the Council. Rifkind also raised AJC's concern about "those who distort the history of the Holocaust" and asked that the Holy See open the archives of its Secretariat of State for responsible research by Jewish and Catholic scholars working together to preserve the historical record. A B'nai B'rith delegation headed by its president, Tommy Baer, raised the same issue in meeting with the pope on March 10, 1996.

In March of 1995, Cardinal Joseph Bernardin of Chicago (of blessed memory) traveled to Israel with a group of Jewish leaders. His lecture, "Antisemitism: The Historical Legacy and Continuing Challenge for Christians," which he gave at the Hebrew University of Jerusalem on March 23, 1995, has been included in a volume of his addresses on Jewish-Catholic dialogue entitled *A Blessing to Each Other* published in 1996 by Liturgy Training Publications of the Archdiocese of Chicago. It is also available in pamphlet form from the Center for Christian-Jewish Understanding of Sacred Heart University (5151 Park Avenue, Fairfield, CT 06432), which in 1995 also published a volume of essays edited by Anthony Cernera in honor of Cardinal John O'Connor (of blessed memory) of New York under the title *Toward Greater Understanding*. It contains essays by Cardinals Bernardin, Cassidy, Keeler, Law, and O'Connor, and by Chaim Herzog, Elie Wiesel, David Novak, and Rabbis Mordecai Waxman and Walter Wurzburger. It was the first publication of Sacred Heart University Press.

In September of 1995 in France, the publisher of the *Bible des communautés chrétiennes*, SOBICAI-Mediaspaul, announced that it was withdrawing the book from publication. This came after Bishop Thomas of Versailles in February revoked its imprimatur and after the Holy See and the French Bishops' Conference had declared the notes and commentaries attached to the translation (which had been done from an earlier Spanish text) to be inaccurate and anti-Semitic. While the Spanish version, which was published shortly after the Second Vatican Council, badly needs updating today, its notes do not reflect the blatant anti-Semitic elements that pervade the French text.

Similarly, in early 1997 a church history text containing anti-Semitic themes authored by a Catholic priest was published in Italy. Again the local ordinary with the public support of the Holy See's

Commission for Religious Relations with the Jews responded by denouncing the text, which was then taken out of circulation by the publisher. In Poland in this period as well an anti-Semitic sermon was given by a parish priest. The local bishop condemned the sermon and issued a public apology to the Jewish community. In Minneapolis–St. Paul in the United States, Archbishop Harry Flynn refused to meet with representatives of a pro-life group, Human Life International, when it came out that there was a chapter in a book written by its founder (and still distributed by the organization) in which anti-Semitic sentiments could be found, and which the author refused to modify. The archbishop, instead, met with Jewish leaders and issued a statement condemning the anti-Semitism, which he mandated to be read in the cathedral during the mass celebrated by the group.

Such events illustrate, on the one hand, that the Catholic community of some one billion people around the world is not yet entirely bereft of anti-Semites. On the other hand, they illustrate as well that the Catholic hierarchy will indeed act definitively to oppose their teachings.

In late September of 1995 a monument was unveiled near the Warsaw Ghetto monument to honor the Polish Catholic organization Zegota, which was formed to save Jews from the Nazis. One of the founders of Zegota, Poland's foreign minister Wladyslaw Bartoszewski, spoke along with local and foreign Jewish and Catholic leaders.

In November 1995, the Catholic Bishops of the Netherlands issued a statement on Catholic-Jewish relations entitled "Living from One and the Same Root," arguing that the relationship should not be one of "condemnation and vilification but of respect and modesty." In December of 1995, the pope addressed a celebration of the thirtieth anniversary of *Nostra Aetate* by the International Catholic-Jewish Liaison Committee, saying: "What you are celebrating is nothing other than the divine mercy which is guiding Christians and Jews to mutual awareness, respect, cooperation and solidarity. The universal openness of *Nostra Aetate* is anchored in and takes its orientation from a high sense of the absolute singularity of God's choice of a particular people. . . . The Jewish people, this community of faith and custodian of a tradition thousands of years old, is an intimate part of the mystery of revelation and of salvation."

In April of 1996, the chief rabbi of Rome, Elio Toaff, visited the pope at the Vatican to celebrate the tenth anniversary of the pope's visit to the Great Synagogue of Rome. They hailed a "new spirit of friendship" between Jews and Catholics.

On September 10–12, 1996, the Centre for the Study of Jewish/Non-Jewish Relations of the University of Southhampton, England, organized a symposium entitled "Tolerance and Intolerance: An International Conference to Mark the Centenary of James Parkes's Birth." Sessions discussed not only Parkes's seminal contributions to the dialogue but also theories and patterns of tolerance and intolerance in Jewish-Christian relations, and their practical implications for today.

The 450th anniversary of the death of Martin Luther elicited statements from the World Lutheran Federation and the Evangelical Lutheran Church in America disassociating the Lutheran Church today from the anti-Jewish writings that marred Luther's later years. The president of the Council of Protestant Churches in Germany, Klaus Engelhardt, in a Brotherhood Week statement in March 1996, warned strongly against any attempts to explain or justify Luther's anti-Judaism on theological grounds.

In June of 1996, during a visit to Germany, Pope John Paul II beatified two German Catholics who died as a result of their opposition to Nazism. Bernhard Lichtenberg used the pulpit of the Catholic cathedral of Berlin to denounce time and again the Nazi attacks on the Jews. He died on the way to Dachau.

On February 10–11, 1997, a symposium on Jewish-Catholic relations was held in Jerusalem co-sponsored by the Rabbi Marc H. Tanenbaum Foundation, the Foundation to Advance Interfaith Trust and Harmony (FAITH), the Interreligious Coordinating Council in Israel, and the Israel Jewish Council for Interreligious Relations. The papers presented by Cardinal Edward I. Cassidy, the president of the Holy See's Commission for Religious Relations with the Jews, and Rabbi Mark Winer, president of the National Council of Synagogues (USA) were published in *Origins* 26, no. 41, pp. 665–74. Other speakers included Judith Banki of the Tanenbaum Foundation, Bishop Alexander Brunett of Helena, Montana, chairman of the Bishops' Committee for Ecumenical and Interreligious Affairs (USA), and Dr. Ron Kronish and Daniel Rossing of Israel.

In August of 1997, Cardinal John O'Connor of New York visited Buenos Aires. In a major speech and in a homily delivered in Spanish in the Cathedral of the Most Holy Trinity he denounced anti-Semitism in the strongest terms and added his voice to the Jewish community's demand to the Argentinian government for a full investigation and justice in the wake of the bombings of Jewish community centers that killed more than a hundred people since 1994. The homily, Rabbi Leon Klenicki of the ADL noted, "was the talk of the city" and will have a very positive impact on Catholic-Jewish relations in Argentina.

Three major events were scheduled for September/October 1997 in Rome: (1) An international symposium on "Good and Evil after Auschwitz," sponsored by SIDIC, the Pontifical Gregorian University, and the University of Rome, (2) the meeting of the International Council of Christians and Jews, and (3) a scholars conference on the church and anti-Semitism, scheduled as part of the preparations for the Millennium by a commission of the Holy See. Selected papers from the SIDIC symposium were published in a special issue of its journal in 1998.

Relations in the United States

The 15th National Workshop on Christian-Jewish Relations was held in Stamford, Connecticut, on October 27–30, 1996, with over a thousand people attending from the United States, Canada, Europe, Israel, and, thanks to a large contingent of Sisters of Sion from around the world, from Australia as well. Under the theme "Seeking God: The Challenge of Being Religious in America," the program was once again rich and varied, providing opportunities for those involved in the field to update their experiences and understandings as well as offering an excellent program for "first timers," including many theology students and educators. Highlights included plenaries titled "The Search for Religious Identity" (Margaret O'Brien Steinfels, editor of *Commonweal*, and author Julius Lester of the University of Massachusetts), "Authenticity without Demonization" (Mary Boys, SNJM, of Union Theological Seminary, Neil Gillman of Jewish Theological Seminary, Anthony Saldarini of Boston College, and Paul van Buren, emeritus of Temple University), "The Impact of Religion on Society" (David Saperstein of the Union of American Hebrew Congregations and Cecil Murray of the African Methodist Episcopal Church), "Religion, Society and State" (Stephen L. Carter of Yale University), and "Educating with and about the Other" (Sr. Audrey Doetzel, NDS).

In addition, each day was begun with joint reflections of the biblical texts of Romans 9–11 and Leviticus 25, led by scholars such as Michael Cook of Hebrew Union College and Krister Stendahl, emeritus of Harvard University. As Sr. Marge Boyle, NDS, reported in her account of the Workshop in SIDIC (vol. 30, no. 1, 1997, published in English and French in Rome by the Sisters of Sion), there were over a hundred individual workshops dealing with education, theology, dialogue, social action, biblical studies, Israel, church-state relations, anti-Semitism, and even the Internet. The National Workshop has an Internet page linked to the Jewish-Christian Relations website, which I urge all to visit: www.jcrelations.com. The site contains documents, essays, and bibliographies in both English and German. It was developed by Fritz Voll of Calgary, Alberta, Canada, and is now maintained by the International Conference of Christians and Jews, posting documents and articles in several languages.

The Workshop honored several pioneers of the dialogue with special awards: Frank Brennan (of blessed memory), who founded and published *The National Dialogue Newsletter*; Sr. Katherine Hargrove, who has been active in the field since 1951 and has published *Seeds of Reconciliation* (1996); Rabbi Leon Klenicki of the Anti-Defamation League; Dr. Franklin Sherman of the Institute for Jewish-Christian Understanding at Muhlenberg College in Pennsylvania; and Rabbi Walter Wurzburger of the Union of Orthodox Jewish Congregations of America and the Rabbinical Council of America.

Also in the United States, the newly constituted National Council of Synagogues (representing Reform and Conservative Judaism in this country), the National Conference of Catholic Bishops, and the National Council of Churches of Christ in the USA issued a joint statement calling for a return to civility in public discourse on the eve of the presidential elections. On October 10, 1996, Niagara University sponsored a conference on Jewish-Christian history over the ages featuring Eugene Fisher as keynote speaker. Boston College sponsored a symposium titled "Jerusalem and the Holy Land in the American Consciousness," with Fisher and Michael Neiditch of the Jerusalem Foundation speaking. On November 21, the U.S. Holocaust Museum sponsored a discussion of Polish Catholic-Jewish Relations featuring Rev. John Pawlikowski, OSM, who also chairs the Museum's Church Relations Committee, which met at the Museum on December 11, 1996. The Fall 1996 issue of the *Journal of the Religious Education Association* contains a report, papers, and reflections on a unique Catholic-Jewish Colloquium of educators from both traditions sponsored by the Institute for Christian-Jewish Studies in Baltimore. Information on this and their other very useful programs and resources is available from Rev. Chris Leighton at the Institute (1316 Park Avenue, Baltimore, MD 21217). They also have a link on the jcrelations.com website to their own home page, which is well worth a virtual visit.

On April 14, 1997, Cardinal Achille Silvestrini, prefect of the Vatican Congregation for Eastern Rite Churches, in a ceremony in Pittsburgh presented to Rabbi A. James Rudin the first Joseph Award for his lifelong contributions to reconciliation between Christians and Jews. The papal medal struck for the occasion is believed to be the first ever to be inscribed with Hebrew letters. "The building of human bridges is one of the great success stories of this terrible, bloody century," Rudin said in accepting the honor (text in *Origins* 26, no. 45 [May 1, 1997]: 742–44).

On April 15, 1997, the twice-yearly consultation between the National Council of Synagogues (NCS) and the Bishops' Committee for Ecumenical and Interreligious Affairs (BCEIA), chaired respectively by Rabbi Mordecai Waxman and Cardinal William Keeler of Baltimore, met for the first time at the U.S. Holocaust Memorial Museum in Washington. After the meeting, the group participated in a ceremony sponsored by the museum to honor the Catholic rescuers of Jews during the Holocaust, many of whose names are memorialized in the museum. Cardinal Keeler addressed the group:

> The saving deeds and lives of Catholics that we remember here today represent crucially important moral lights in a period of darkness. Tragically, the world at large believed what it wanted to believe and did what it wanted to do, which was virtually nothing. Today we celebrate the memory of some non-Jews — specifically Catholics — who did do something at a time of utmost crisis when most European Catholics either could not, or would not help their neighbors in desperate need.... We Catholics who are teachers need such models if we are to be able to prepare the next generations of Christians properly for living moral lives in a world that can, as it did in the 1940s, descend into absolute moral chaos with dizzying rapidity. (Text in *Origins* 26, no. 45 [May 1, 1977]: 739–41)

The event concluded with a ceremony honoring Père Jacques Bunel of France, a Carmelite killed by the Nazis for attempting to rescue four Jewish children. The ceremony initiated a small temporary exhibit at the museum featuring the story.

On March 18, 1997, the NCS and the BCEIA co-sponsored a meeting of leading Catholic and Jewish educators in what would be the first of a series of such meetings probing how each presents the other in our respective classrooms and whether joint programming, such as is already being done in Los Angeles and Brooklyn, is possible on a wider scale.

Facing History and Ourselves is a national educational and teacher training organization begun in 1976, whose mission is to engage students of diverse backgrounds in an examination of racism, prejudice, and anti-Semitism. Over the years they have developed a variety of sound programming and materials for educators. Their address is 16 Hurd Road, Brookline, MA 02146. Their Web address is www.facing.org.

Merrimack College has established the Center for the Study of Jewish-Christian Relations. For information write to Prof. Martin S. Goldman, Merrimack College, 315 Turnpike Street, North Andover, MA 01845 USA.

On December 18, 1997, John Cardinal O'Connor hosted and co-chaired with Rabbi Fabian Schonfeld the BCEIA consultation with the Rabbinical Council of America/Orthodox Union. The meeting considered a joint statement on school vouchers and perhaps other forms of assistance to private education, which they strongly support.

Catholic-Jewish Relations, 1998–99

Participating in the BCEIA/Jewish Council for Public Affairs (JCPA) Interfaith Journey to Israel and Rome led by Cardinal Keeler and Rabbi Joel Zaiman of Baltimore on March 8–19, 1998, were Bishops John J. Nevins of Venice, Basil Losten of the Ukrainian Diocese of Stamford, Stephen E. Blaire of Los Angeles, John P. Boles of Boston, and John C. Nienstedt of Detroit, and Rabbis Allen Friehling of Los Angeles, Michael Menitoff of Boston, Dannel Schwartz of Detroit, and Mark Winer of London. The delegation was staffed by Rabbi A. James Rudin of the American Jewish Committee, Msgrs. Robert Stern and Dennis Madden of the Catholic Near East Welfare Association, Dr. Lawrence Rubin of JCPA, and Dr. Eugene Fisher of the BCEIA.

Highlights of what the participants came to consider a joint pilgrimage to Israel included a dialogue in the ancient synagogue of Capharnum, perhaps the first ever between successors of the Apostles and of the Pharisees since the generations immediately following Jesus' time; a celebration of Purim in the bomb shelter of a Moshav (kibbutz) in the Galilee; a memorial service at Yad Vashem; Shabbat dinner with residents of Jerusalem; and meetings with the president of Israel and the Latin patriarch of Jerusalem.

In Rome, the group, which by this time had grown quite close, was met at the airport by a Vatican representative and given copies of the statement of the Pontifical Commission for Religious Relations with the Jews, *We Remember: A Reflection on the Shoah,* which

had been issued while the group was in the air between Jerusalem and Rome. The meeting the next morning with His Eminence
Edward Idris Cardinal Cassidy, president of the commission, gave
him his first awareness of the likely response to the text by the
Jewish community. While much of the text was warmly welcomed
by the Jewish spokespersons for the group on this occasion, Rabbis
Waxman and Rudin, especially the sincerity of its call for Christian
repentance (*teshuvah*), certain of the phrasings describing historical
events appeared to them to be problematical. Cardinal Cassidy took
notes carefully, it must be said, during this discussion and during the
meeting the next week of the International Catholic-Jewish Liaison
Committee (ILC), which Cardinal Keeler and Dr. Fisher also participated in. In this way the Cardinal was quite well prepared to
clarify the perceived ambiguities when in May of 1998 he met with
the American Jewish Committee at its annual meeting in Washington. To help Catholics and others to understand the church's stance
on the *Shoah* in the context of all of the various statements issued
by local churches and by the Pontifical Commission from 1995 to
1998, the Bishops Committee for Ecumenical and Interreligious Affairs issued a collection of all of them, including the cardinal's crucial
clarification, in September 1998 under the title *Catholics Remember
the Holocaust* (USCCB publication no. 5-290). The communiqué for
the March 25–28, 1998, ILC meeting and the joint statement "Care
for the Environment: A Religious Act" were published in *Origins* 27,
no. 42 (April 9, 1998): 701–4, and subsequently in the Information
Service of the Pontifical Council for Christian Unity.

In 1998, the Christian Scholars' Study Group on Jews and Judaism,
formed in the late 1960s by leading Catholic and Protestant scholars
involved in the dialogue, suffered the loss of two of its founding
members, A. Roy Eckardt and Paul M. Van Buren. May they rest
in peace and be remembered for their great contributions to the
reformation of Christian theology on Jews and Judaism.

The issuance on March 16, 1998, of the Holy See's *We Remember:
A Reflection on the Shoah* added a substantive topic to the agenda of
the BCEIA/NCS meeting in Baltimore on May 4–5, 1998. Co-chaired
by Cardinal Keeler and Rabbi Mordecai Waxman, the consultation
also discussed and issued its joint statement, "Reflections on the
Millennium" (published in *Jubilee 2000* by the National Conference
of Catholic Bishops: www.usccb.org/jubilee). At the conclusion of
the meeting, Rabbi Mordecai Waxman was made a papal knight of
the Order of St. Gregory, the first rabbi ever to be so honored. Sirs

Sigmund Sternberg, Gilbert Levine, and Joseph Lichten, of blessed memory, have also been knighted by the Holy See.

On May 12, Dr. Fisher addressed the first meeting of the National Association of Boards of Rabbis on the topic of the Vatican *Shoah* document, which he also discussed with the New York Board of Rabbis on June 10, 1998.

On February 17–18, 1999, there took place a joint consultation of fifteen Catholic and fifteen Jewish educators and scholars at St. Mary's Seminary in Baltimore to begin a process of developing educational principles and guidelines for Holocaust education in Catholic schools in order to implement the mandate of the March 1998 statement of the Holy See's Commission for Religious Relations with the Jews, *We Remember: A Reflection on the Shoah.* The Jewish scholars' participation was sponsored by the American Jewish Committee. Cardinal William Keeler of the U.S. Bishops' Conference and Msgr. John Radano of the Holy See's Commission took part. Other conferences on the Holy See's *Shoah* document that took place in this period include March 11, 1999, at St. Charles Seminary in Philadelphia and March 15 at the Theological College of the Catholic University of America, and major joint consultations in Florida at St. Leo's College, also co-sponsored by the American Jewish Committee, and in Chicago at the Cardinal Bernardin Center, co-sponsored by the Tanenbaum Foundation of New York.

The March 23, 1999, meeting of the Catholic Bishops' consultation with the National Council of Synagogues, held at St. Mary's in Baltimore and co-chaired by Cardinal Keeler and Rabbi Joel Zaiman, continued the discussion of theological and social issues. The consultation's most recent statement was a joint reflection on the implications of the Millennium/Jubilee 2000 Year commemorations for Jewish-Christian relations. It and other relevant statements, such as those of Cardinal Keeler condemning the attacks on the three synagogues in Sacramento, can be found on the Bishops' Conference website (www.usccb.org) and on the website of the Center for Christian-Jewish Learning of Boston College (www.bc.edu/bc_org/research/cjl/documents.html).

On June 22, 1999, Cardinal Keeler issued in the name of the conference a sharp condemnation of the attacks on the three synagogues in Sacramento. On July 15, Bishop Fiorenza sent a check for $25,000 to Bishop Weigand to give to the rabbis of the synagogues to assist their rebuilding efforts. The latter had already donated $20,000 in the name of the diocese. These gestures of solidarity were deeply appreciated by the local and national Jewish communities. The American

Jewish Committee sent to Bishop Fiorenza a formal letter expressing the gratitude of American Jewry.

A continuing series of controversies continues to draw media attention away from the larger story of ongoing progress in Catholic-Jewish relations. These range from Edith Stein and Cardinal Stepinac to the Holy See's document, *We Remember: A Reflection on the Shoah,* and the cross (and crosses) at Auschwitz. While each is in itself relatively minor, all revolve around the Holocaust and the key question of how it will be remembered by future generations. Increasingly, the memory of the figure of Pope Pius XII is emerging as a sort of symbolic "lightning rod" for Jewish concerns about how Christians will remember and teach about the Holocaust. Dr. Eugene Fisher discussed the implications of the controversy in the John Courtney Murray Lecture at Fordham University in May. An excerpt from the paper was published in *America* (September 11, 1999).

The Millennial Year 2000

In March 2000, Pope John Paul II made a historic and, for him, long-awaited trip to the Holy Land. In late February, he visited Egypt and Mt. Sinai, praying at the ancient monastery there with the Greek Orthodox monks who keep penitential vigil at the foot of the mountain where God revealed the Ten Commandments to the Jewish people. The papal pilgrimage then took John Paul to Bethlehem and Jericho in the Palestinian Authority. Then he came as a pilgrim to Nazareth and Jerusalem, sites pregnant with sacred memories for Jews and Christians alike. As a pilgrim he prayed, not only at Christian sites but at Jewish ones — the Western Wall (the *Kotel*), the only remnant of the Temple of Jerusalem at which Jesus prayed and which he sought to cleanse, and Yad Vashem, Israel's profoundly moving memorial to the six million lives so brutally ended by Nazism in its short time of power. Despite the hoopla of the media and the various ongoing differences in viewpoint between Catholics and Jews, the pope's prayers were healing ones, offering reconciliation to both ancient communities. They were yet further steps taken by this most remarkable pontiff in building the bridge of trust between the church and the Jewish people.

These steps recalled earlier historic gestures by the pope. They recalled his surprising 1979 visit, shortly after he became pope, to Auschwitz, where he prayed in particular for its Jewish victims in a time when Communist orthodoxy wanted to "universalize" Nazi genocide as a general "crime against humanity," with no particular victims, just as they had done with regard to Babi Yar. They recalled the pope's geographically shortest yet historically longest trip across the Tiber from the Vatican to the Great Synagogue of Rome in 1986, where John Paul became the first bishop of Rome to visit and to pray in a Roman synagogue since St. Peter (who never stopped going to synagogue even after becoming a Christian). They recalled the historic 1987 meeting in Miami between the pope and over four hundred leaders of the world's largest Jewish community, where the pope took as his own the Jewish watchword after the Holocaust: "Never Again!" They recalled the pope's consistent and urgent appeals to the Catholic community to reform its teachings on Jews and Judaism and to incorporate Holocaust studies into Catholic education on all levels and in all places throughout the world.

In Jerusalem, the pope met with the two chief rabbis of Israel. Imagine: the successor of Peter, "chief" as it were of the apostles after the death and resurrection of Christ, meeting with respect, dignity, and due deference the heirs of the Pharisees. It was a meeting of dialogue not diatribe, a meeting of reconciliation after centuries of alienation. It was a meeting neither the pope's nor the chief rabbis parents' could have dreamed to be possible in their wildest imaginations. Truly, we live in a sacred time, a time blessed with the opportunity to change the course of human history. This pope from Poland, which had the largest number of Jews in the world when he was born and only a pitiful remnant by the time he was ordained a priest (three million Polish Jews were killed during the Nazi occupation), has seized the opportunity not just of a lifetime but of the millennium. The world will be forever better for it.

At Yad Vashem, the pope observed a moment of prayerful silence and then intoned:

In this place of memories, the mind and heart and soul feel an extreme need for silence.

Silence in which to remember.

Silence in which to try to make some sense of the memories which come flooding back.

Silence because there are no words strong enough to deplore the terrible tragedy of the Shoah.

My own personal memories are of all that happened when the Nazis occupied Poland during the war.

I remember my Jewish friends and neighbors, some of whom perished while others survived. . . .

We wish to remember. But we wish to remember for a purpose, namely to ensure that never again will evil prevail as it did for millions of innocent victims of Nazism. . . .

As Bishop of Rome and successor of the Apostle Peter, I assure the Jewish people that the Catholic Church, motivated by the gospel law of truth and love and by no other consideration, is deeply saddened by the hatred, acts of persecution and displays of anti-Semitism directed against Jews by Christians at any time and in any place. In this place of solemn remembrance, I fervently pray that our sorrow for the tragedy which the Jewish people suffered in the twentieth century will lead to a new relationship between Jews and Christians.

Let us build a new future in which there will be no more anti-Jewish feeling among Christians or anti-Christian feeling among Jews, but rather the mutual respect required of those who adore the one Creator and Lord, and look to Abraham as our common father in faith.

(Jerusalem, March 23, 2000)

Many Israelis in attendance, survivors and politicians, religious leaders and security officers, cried. They were healing tears, tears of hope and reconciliation. Prime Minister Ehud Barak, himself a former general not given to sentimentality, spoke equally from his heart and, I believe, from the heart of the land and people of Israel, the sons and daughters of Abraham:

When my grandparents, Elka and Shmuel Godin, mounted the death trains at Umschlagplatz near their home in Warsaw, headed toward their fate in Treblinka — the fate of three million Jews from your homeland — you were there, and you remembered.

You have done more than anyone else to bring about the historic change in the attitude of the church toward the Jewish people, initiated by the good Pope John XXIII, and to dress the gaping wounds that festered over many bitter centuries.

While the secular press, its own heart seemingly melted for the moment, called this exchange "soaring rhetoric," it was in fact much more than that. It was the simple, unadorned truth.

In late May and early June of 2000, two remarkable theological dialogues took place, the first in London, the second at our own Catholic

University of America in Washington, D.C. Both were international in scope, involving distinguished Catholic and Jewish thinkers from five continents around the world (North and South America, Europe, the Middle East, and Australia). One Orthodox rabbi, who came to the London conference from Israel, had been born in South Africa and had served for a time as the chief rabbi of Ireland.

The London conference in May was co-sponsored by the British Conference of Catholic Bishops, and the CUA conference (most graciously hosted by its Law School) was co-sponsored by the U.S. Catholic Bishops' Conference. Both conferences were initiated by the Jewish side of the dialogue, the World Union of Progressive Judaism, on the one hand, and by a new, international gathering of rabbis dedicated to dialogue with Christianity, the Rabbinical Association for Interreligious Dialogue. These remarkable Jewish initiatives came in response to a 1999 plea in Baltimore by Cardinal Edward Idris Cassidy of the Holy See's Commission for Religious Relations with the Jewish people for intensified dialogue.

The pope's historic pilgrimage to Israel likewise, I believe, opened the hearts of many in the Jewish community to move the relationship to a new plane. The very titles of the sessions of the London "Millennium Conference" reflected this optimistic vision of joint witness and action by God's people, Israel, and God's people, the church. The one assigned to me, for example, called for the church and the Jewish people to covenant together to form "a partnership for the Glory of God, the Good of Humanity, and the Future of Humanity."

Along the way in the often profound and always spirited discussions that followed such major presentations, there emerged from the Jewish side time and again the conviction that it was time that Judaism acknowledge the divine origins of Christianity as a response to God's revelation, just as the Catholic Church has acknowledged Judaism's divine origins and continuing place — on its own terms — as a living response to God's call to the Jews to be "a light to the nations." No formal resolutions were made at this initial gathering, of course, but opportunities and challenges were mutually explored. Differences of viewpoint were as often noted within the representatives of the two world religions as between them. The papers of the major presenters and the discussants were published in T. Bayfield, S. Brichto, and E. Fisher, editors, *He Kissed Them and They Wept: Towards a Theology of Jewish-Catholic Partnership* (London: SCM Press, 2001).

I coordinated the Catholic side of the June 2000 symposium at the Catholic University of America (CUA) at the request of the Holy

See. It was in many ways an unusual event. The rabbis present were brought together by two American institutes of Jewish-Christian studies, one freestanding, the other associated with a Catholic university, Sacred Heart University in Fairfield, Connecticut. Rabbi Joseph Ehrenkranz, who is Orthodox, directs the latter; Rabbi Jack Bemporad (Reform) directs the former. The two have had a long association with each other and with the Catholic Church on the national and international levels, counting many cardinals, among them the late, beloved John Cardinal O'Connor, as close friends.

Like Rabbi Mark Winer of the World Union of Progressive Judaism, who helped set up the London Millennium Conference in May 2000, Rabbis Ehrenkranz and Bemporad were responding to a plea for intensified religious dialogue between the church and the Jewish people. All who participated were intellectually stimulated and spiritually moved by the event. Truly, it was a graced moment in the history of an ancient relationship too often marred by mistrust and violence. Rabbis and Catholic theologians exchanged views and insights into scripture and what it means to respond to God's call to each of us as individuals and as members of God's people on earth.

The theme of the conference, the theology of repentance and forgiveness, was highlighted by Father James Loughran, SA, ecumenical officer of the Archdiocese of New York, and Rabbi Ehrenkranz, who presented the Catholic and Jewish understandings of divine and human forgiveness. The discussion after both presentations ranged from sophisticated theological enquiry into the precise meaning of the language used, to numerous "Oh, Wow!" expressions as the Catholic and Jewish thinkers realized that, underlying two very diverse traditions of biblical interpretation over the centuries, lies a very similar vision of what true repentance (*teshuvah* in Hebrew, *metanoia* in the Greek of the New Testament) actually entails for the penitent: not only sincere sorrow, but more deeply the firm resolve never to commit the sin again, and, in the case of sins against fellow human beings, the necessity of reaching out to the one sinned against in a spirit of repentance.

This perhaps became most clear when the group considered jointly the sacred liturgical texts of our two traditions, those of the Canon of the Mass and of Holy Week for Christians, and those of Yom Kippur for Jews. Both liturgical traditions, not surprisingly, rely on similar passages from Pentateuch and the prophets. Again, emphases and spiritual understandings diverge but do not contradict one another as once we thought. Reflection on both together, indeed, can bring both Jews and Christians to a deeper understanding of their own tradition.

In the Spring of 2000, also, a diverse group of fifteen Catholic, Protestant, and Jewish scholars was gathered by Carol Rittner and John Roth at King's College in Pennsylvania to discuss the then (as now) heavily emotional topic of Pope Pius XII and the Holocaust. The papers were published by the organizers of the symposium under that title by Leicester University Press and Continuum International in 2002.

Catholic-Jewish Relations 2001–2

The millennial year discussions, here vastly oversimplified of course, would not have been possible even a generation ago. The practice of medieval disputations forced upon Jews by Catholic rulers (with the setting always "stacked" in favor of the Christian disputants, so that if the rabbis argued too well they would face exile, if they were lucky) soured Jews for centuries from exposing themselves to Christians in discussion of serious religious matters. No more. The Catholic Church since the Second Vatican Council, and most significantly under the inspired leadership of John Paul II, has so visibly and so sincerely come to repent of its sins against Jews that many (albeit by no means all!) Jews have seen the beginning of the possibility for true, full reconciliation with the church. A follow-up to the Catholic University of America theological dialogue was held at Sacred Heart University in Fairfield, Connecticut, in December 2001. It featured a paper by Cardinal Walter Kasper, with response by Rabbi Norman Solomon of Great Britain.

In February 2001 the U.S. Conference of Catholic Bishops issued *Catholic Teaching on the Shoah: Implementing the Holy See's "We Remember."* The document, intended for all Catholic schools, universities, and seminaries, urges the incorporation of the Holocaust into their curricula, as appropriate, and offers guidelines, reflections, and resources for educators. It is available from the USCCB's Office of Publishing and Promotion Services, which can be reached through our website (www.usccb.org).

Further dialogue was invested in at the seventeenth meeting of the International Catholic-Jewish Liaison Committee, which occurred on May 1–3, 2001, in New York City. The ILC is co-sponsored by the Holy See and the International Jewish Committee for Interreligious Consultation (IJCIC). The main theme of the gathering, "Repentance and Reconciliation," was prompted by a desire to review the past eleven years, since Cardinal Edward I. Cassidy's remarkable statement made in Prague 1990, on *teshuvah.*

Introducing the main theme, "Repentance and Reconciliation," Rabbi Leon Klenicki argued that each of our communities needs to overcome its own form of triumphalism. "Christianity must overcome theological triumphalism: the conviction that it is the only way of salvation and has to be imposed on everyone. On our side, Judaism needs to overcome the triumphalism of pain and memories. We are obligated to respond to history with new affirmations of God's covenant and with new dimensions of faith in humanity despite human evil's potential." He pointed to the Jewish statement *Dabru Emet* (To Speak Truth), signed in 2000 by some two hundred American rabbis and scholars, as an example of this Jewish response to Christian outreach for reconciliation.

One of the difficult issues addressed by this seventeenth ILC meeting was the publication of *Dominus Iesus. Dominus Iesus,* Cardinal Kasper said,

> is an intra-Catholic document about interreligious dialogue addressed to Catholic theologians concerning problems with relativism, syncretism, universalism and indifferentism. It does not enter into the Jewish-Catholic dialogue. It must be noted first that the relationship between the church and the Jewish people is unique. Second, *Dominus Iesus* does not call into question the salvation of Jews. Third, the Jewish covenant has not been revoked and remains salvifically effective for Jews. Fourth, *Dominus Iesus* must be understood properly within the context of *Nostra Aetate,* papal encyclicals and other official documents of the church regarding Judaism. Fifth, there is no missionary activity on the part of the church directed toward converting the Jews. *Dominus Iesus* is not the end of our dialogue. It is a challenge for our dialogue.

In a sad turn of events, in June of 2001, the world of ecumenical, Christian-Jewish, and interreligious dialogue suffered a most severe setback with the untimely death of Father John Hotchkin, who for thirty-four years had been the director of the U.S. Bishops Secretariat for Ecumenical and Interreligious Relations. Starting with the conference just after the close of the Second Vatican Council, Father Hotchkin provided the intellectual and institutional framework for all that has been accomplished on the national level, and much of what has happened positively on the international level, between the church and the Jewish people since the Council. A man as humble as he was brilliant, Jack was my mentor and friend since he hired me for the Catholic-Jewish position in the summer of 1977. He shall be sorely missed.

Throughout this period the issue of the early release to scholars of the materials in the Vatican archives pertinent to the Holocaust became a matter of tension between Jewish groups and the Holy See. In December of 1999, at the suggestion of Cardinal Edward Idris Cassidy, the ILC established a working group of six Catholic and Jewish historians to examine what had already been released by the Holy See in the form of eleven volumes of *Actes et Documents du Sainte Siège Relatifs a la Seconde Guerre Mondial* (Vatican City: Libreria Editrice Vaticana, 1970–81), a massive collection of tens of thousands of documents edited by four Jesuit historians: Pierre Blet, Robert Graham, Angelo Martini, and Burkhardt Schneider. In the fall of 2000 the group reported back to the Holy See's Commission for Religious Relations with the Jews. They agreed that the selection of documents had been thoroughly and objectively done by the scholars, but that many questions were still not resolved and that in the intervening decades historical scholarship had raised new issues perhaps not anticipated by the original scholars. For this reason they requested some form of appropriate access to the unpublished documentation in order to proceed with their analysis. However, since the unreleased materials had not yet been catalogued by the Vatican archivists, this request simply could not be met at the time. The scholars suspended their work in July of 2001, an action attended by a great deal of unfortunate publicity. (In 2003 Cardinal Jorge Mejía, head of the Vatican Library, announced that the number of archivists working on cataloguing the materials from the pontificates of Pius XI and Pius XII had been increased from two to nine, so that the work would in fact be greatly accelerated. The first two large blocks of materials, those pertinent to the Holy See's relations with Germany under Pius XI and the work of the Holy See in responding to thousands of requests to find loved ones during the war and in its aftermath, have now been released.)

In the aftermath of this dissolution of the group, the ILC reaffirmed the need to move forward, and its resolve to do so. Though it did not achieve its goal, the historical team did show that Catholic and Jewish scholars, working together, could indeed make significant progress toward a common goal even faced with the most sensitive and complex of issues. The gratitude of Catholics and Jews everywhere should be theirs.

The spring 2002 meeting of the consultation with the National Council of Synagogues (Reform and Conservative Judaism), co-chaired by Cardinal Keeler, took place in New York on March 13, 2002. The draft of a joint statement on mission was considered, along with work on a series of six videos on Catholic-Jewish relations to be developed for use in parishes and synagogues. On March 18, a meeting of the ongoing consultation with Orthodox Judaism, co-chaired by Bishop Murphy, took place in Rockville Center, New York, centering on the possibility of a joint statement on school vouchers. On March 25, Cardinal Keeler met with Abraham Foxman, the national director of the Anti-Defamation League, and Rabbi Eugene Korn, interfaith director, in Baltimore, to discuss past difficulties and future promises.

On May 7, the Secretariat co-sponsored an international dialogue with the Rabbinical Council for Interreligious Dialogue on the statement of the Pontifical Biblical Commission, *The Jewish People and Their Sacred Scriptures in the Christian Bible* (Vatican City: Libreria Editrice Vaticana, 2002). The dialogue was hosted by the Law School of the Catholic University of America. The Catholic and Jewish scholars agreed on the significance of this text for religious education and as a basis for further dialogue in the future.

In August of 2002, delegates of the National Council of Synagogues and the BCEIA of the U.S. Conference of Catholic Bishops issued a joint statement entitled *Reflections on Covenant and Mission.* The preface to the document summarizes the two parts of the Jewish/Catholic reflections:

> The Roman Catholic reflections describe the growing respect for the Jewish tradition that has unfolded since the Second Vatican Council. A deepening Catholic appreciation of the eternal covenant between God and the Jewish people, together with a recognition of a divinely-given mission to Jews to witness to God's faithful love, lead to the conclusion that campaigns that target Jews for conversion to Christianity are no longer theologically acceptable in the Catholic Church.
>
> The Jewish reflections describe the mission of the Jews and the perfection of the world. This mission is seen to have three aspects. First there are the obligations that arise as a result of the loving election of the Jewish people into a covenant with God. Second, there is a mission of witness to God's redeeming power in the world. Third, the Jewish people have a mission that is addressed to all human beings. The Jewish community is

beginning to consider how Judaism's missions might be related to Catholicism's understanding of its mission for the world.

In welcoming the document, Cardinal Keeler said that it "represents the state of thought among the participants of a dialogue that has been going on for a number of years between the U.S. Catholic Church and the Jewish community in this country." Cardinal Keeler, the U.S. bishops' moderator for Catholic-Jewish relations, said that the document, entitled *Reflections on Covenant and Mission,* "does not represent a formal position taken by the United States Conference of Catholic Bishops (USCCB) or the Bishops' Committee for Ecumenical and Interreligious Affairs (BCEIA). The purpose of publicly issuing the considerations which it contains is to encourage serious reflection on these matters by Jews and Catholics in the United States. These considerations provide a basis for discussing both the similarities and the significant differences between the Christian and Jewish understandings of the call given by the one God to both peoples."

Cardinal Keeler said that, within the Catholic community, there has been a growing respect for the Jewish tradition and the lasting covenant that God made with the Jews. Judaism is "already a response to God's revelation in the Old Covenant" (*Catechism of the Catholic Church,* no. 839), a response to God's grace that requires religious freedom and respect for the faith relationship between God and the human person. This same respect for the freedom of faith requires us to be open at the same time to the action of God's grace to bring any person to accept what Catholic belief understands as the fullness of the means of salvation, which are found in the church.

Participants in the ongoing consultation are delegates of the BCEIA of the USCCB and the National Council of Synagogues (NCS), which represents the Central Conference of American Rabbis, the Rabbinical Assembly of Conservative Judaism, the Union of American Hebrew Congregations, and the United Synagogue of Conservative Judaism.

In September of 2002, the Christian Scholars Group on Christian-Jewish Relations, comprised of Protestant and Catholic scholars who have been meeting together regularly since 1969, issued a statement in response to *Dabru Emet,* which at the same time serves as an update or checklist of much of the best thinking in the dialogue on the Christian side. It contains eight sections affirming the irrevocable nature of God's covenant with the Jewish people and the relationship between the Jewish people and the land of Israel, eschewing supersessionism, anti-Semitism, and organized "missionary efforts directed at converting Jews," and calling on Jews and Christians to work together to heal the world. It can be found on the Boston College website: www.bc.edu/bc_org/research/cjl/documents.html.

Both of these statements have engendered considerable discussion within the Catholic and larger Christian communities. A visit of Cardinal Kasper to the Center for Jewish-Christian Learning in early November of 2002 provided him with the opportunity to comment on the entire discussion over *Reflections* within the larger context of the dialogue and from the vantage point of Rome and the Church Universal, while his predecessor, Cardinal Cassidy, now retired as president of the Pontifical Commission for Religious Relations with the Jews, similarly took the opportunity of an address he was asked to give in Wellington, New Zealand, to comment on the document as part of the ongoing dialogue between the church and the Jewish people. Like Cardinal Keeler, Cardinals Kasper and Cassidy welcomed *Reflections* as a step forward best understood as beginning a new phase of discussion, internally within the church no less than between the church and world Jewry. As the Irish would say, we certainly live in "interesting times."

Chapter 7

The Jews and Jesus in the Gospel Tradition
Common Features and Conflicts

Howard Clark Kee

The relation of Jesus to Jews — as evident in both the historical features of the social structures of Judaism and the understandings of the biblical traditions on which Judaism is based — is a pervasive and dynamic feature in the Gospels. In addition to references to (1) Jewish leaders, such as elders, priests, and scribes, and to (2) Jewish religious groups, such as the Pharisees and Sadducees, there are in the Gospels eighty occurrences of the term "the Jews." In the Acts of the Apostles — which is volume 2 of the Gospel of Luke — there are seventy-five occurrences of the term.

Analysis of these passages is essential for historical discernment of the role and intent of Jesus in redefining God's purpose for his people as it is portrayed in the diverse gospel traditions. It is also crucial for understanding historical relationships and issues between Judaism and Christianity.

These issues may be classified in three major categories — all of them representing central features in Judaism and, by extension, in early Christianity. They may be designated as follows: (1) messianic; (2) ritual, and (3) sociopolitical issues. The first two of these involve debate between Jewish leadership and the followers of Jesus as to the claim of the latter group for a redemptive role of Jesus and their defining the qualifications for sharing in the new community being called together in his name. Are ethical and ritual requirements of the Law of Moses as set forth by the priests and scribes to be essential qualifications for gaining and maintaining membership in God's covenant people?

The third feature — the sociopolitical — focuses on attitudes that the members of the Jesus movement had toward both the leadership of the Jewish community and the authority and policies of the Roman empire. The political issues concern the attitude God's people should adopt toward the ruling world power: Rome. Should the covenant people take part in the divine honors to the emperor fostered by the imperial authorities? Or should they engage in revolution in order to gain political freedom? Should they participate in the regional council (*synedrion*) fostered and controlled by the imperial authorities? Jesus was executed by the Romans on a charge that his message of the coming kingdom was promoting a political revolt. The inscription placed at the top of his cross to indicate the official charge against him was "King of the Jews," and the Roman soldiers who seized him mocked him as "the Messiah, King of Israel" (Mark 15:26, 32).

Both the Jews and the Christians in the first century had to decide to what extent, while identifying themselves as the people of God, they should collaborate with the Romans on political and cultural matters. Since Jesus was a Jew, how Jewish identity was defined had major implications for the response to him from the Roman rulers and agents, as well as for shaping the ways in that the early Christians perceived themselves as the properly defined people of God. Further, there were real differences in the ways which various groups — both Jewish and Christian — understood the bases for their participation in the people of God and developed the norms for that social grouping and the specifics of their hope for the ultimate divine triumph of God's purpose for his people and for the renewed creation. Each of the four canonical Gospels gives evidence of the diversity of identity, behavior, and expectations concerning the future fulfillment of God's purpose for his people that were operative in early Christianity, as well as the role that they perceived Jesus as fulfilling. These factors are evident in all of the canonical Gospels and in Acts, but each of these documents has a distinctive emphasis on the matter of the stance and attitude of members toward Jews.

The Jews and Jesus in the Gospel of Mark

In the earliest gospel, Mark, the term "Jew" appears only six times, all but one of which are in the account of Jesus' arrest, trial, and execution by the Roman ruler Pilate. In Mark 7:3 Jesus is told by Jewish leaders (Pharisees and scribes) that his followers do not obey the traditional laws for ritual purity, in that they do not wash their hands before eating. He dismisses this charge by quoting from Isaiah 29:11, where God is reported as saying, "The people draw near with their mouths and honor me with their lips, while their hearts are far from me, and their worship of me is a human commandment learned by rote." Thus Jesus is seen as dismissing certain Jewish ritual traditions, calling on the prophets of Israel to make the point that such rules are not divinely prescribed but humanly imposed by Jewish leaders.

The other references to Jews in Mark appear in the account of Jesus' trial before Pilate on the charge of his claiming to be king of the Jews. Pilate asks Jesus if he is king of the Jews (15:2) and then asks the Jewish leaders if they want Jesus to be released (15:4) or what shall be done with this man who is called King of the Jews (15:12). The Roman soldiers salute him with a mock acclaim, "Hail, king of the Jews," and then place an inscription on his cross, "The King of the Jews." The Jewish leaders join in the mockery by declaring, "Let the Christ, the king of Israel, come down from the cross" (15:32). Clearly, the reason the Romans are putting Jesus to death is political: he was perceived by his followers to be the divinely chosen and empowered agent to overcome the forces opposed to the purpose of God and to establish the rule of God over the world. This would result in the overthrow of the imperial power of Rome.

The Jews and Jesus in the Q Source

In the material in the Gospels from the hypothetical source Q, which scholars have reconstructed as having been drawn upon by Matthew and Luke, there is a theme that points to the inclusiveness of the new community founded by Jesus. While many features of Judaism are taken over into the new movement, there is an important theme that perceives the community as including in its membership persons who by genealogical, ritual, or social status did not conform to Jewish norms. Yet in the movement launched by Jesus they are to be identified as "children of Abraham" (Luke 3:8). Abraham was told by Yahweh that the relationship humans would gain by being descended from him, or in his tradition, would result in their sharing in a blessing that would, however, reach out to "all the families of the earth" (Gen. 12:3).

This outreach of divine grace and renewal across ethnic and social boundaries is attested in Q (Luke 7:1–10) when an officer in the Roman army — a centurion — asks some Jewish elders to go to Jesus with the request that he come and heal his slave who seems to be fatally ill. As Jesus approaches the centurion's residence the Roman official sends word that he has confidence in the authority of Jesus but considers himself to be unworthy to have Jesus come under his roof. Jesus declares that this statement by a Gentile of his confidence in Jesus' ability to heal is an indication of greater faith than he has found "even in Israel." When the bearers of his message return to the centurion's house, they find the slave fully recovered.

Thus, while the divinely chosen and empowered agent through whom God's renewal of his people is being launched is a Jew — Jesus — the healing and transforming power is available to all humans who seek it. Just as the message of the prophet Jonah reached out to the people of the pagan city of Nineveh (Jonah 3) and the wisdom imparted to Solomon was heard and heeded by the non-Israelite Queen of Sheba (1 Kings 10:1), so the message embodying the wisdom of Solomon and the prophecy of Jonah will be heard and heeded by non-Israelites in the present time (Luke 11:29–32). The door into the kingdom of God is narrow, and those who refuse to heed the message of Jesus will be thrust out, while those from all over the world who receive it will "sit at table in the kingdom of God." Invited to share in this community of faith are "the poor and the maimed and the blind and the lame" from "the highways and the hedges," while those preoccupied with ordinary domestic and commercial matters will not enter the kingdom of God (Luke 14:15–24). Ironically, those who remain faithful and obedient during the times of trial and difficulty that the new community will experience will not only "eat and drink at my table in [Christ's] kingdom," but will also "sit on thrones judging the twelve tribes of Israel," the traditional members of the people of God (Luke 22:28–30). Thus Jewish identity by ethnic or ritual criteria will not assure participation in the kingdom of God. The crucial factor is trust in God as called for and defined by Jesus.

The Jews and Jesus in the Gospel of Luke and the Acts of the Apostles

The Gospel of Luke

The Gospel of Luke is distinctive among the Gospels in several ways, including the following: (1) it emphasizes by direct claim and implicit point that what God is doing through Jesus for the renewal of his people and the establishment of the divine rule on the earth builds on both prophetic promises and biblical models from the Old Testament and is accomplishing their fulfillment. (2) Only Luke is followed by a writing — known as the Acts of the Apostles — which was the work of the same author as this Gospel, but, unlike the other Gospels, traces in detail the spread of the gospel from its origins in the land of Israel to major centers of Graeco-Roman culture, such as Athens and

Corinth, and its ultimate arrival in the capital of the pagan world: Rome. The initial divine steps toward the accomplishment of this goal are offered throughout the Gospel of Luke, including reports of conflict with Jewish authorities but with the major theme of the ongoing process of fulfillment of the divine purpose for the wider world, not the abandonment of Jewish hopes for cosmic renewal.

The term "Jew" is used only four times in this gospel. The first occurs in a more extended version of a story found in the Q source describing a Roman army officer (a centurion, commanding a hundred soldiers). He is able to engage some Jewish elders to go to Jesus and request that he heal the officer's ailing servant (Luke 7:1–10). As noted previously, Jesus commends his faith in the authority of Jesus — faith that resembles that of the centurion and that leads to the healing of the slave. In Luke 23:2–6 is a modified version of the Markan story of the trial of Jesus before Pilate, but it echoes the account of Pilate's question, "Are you king of the Jews?" to which Jesus responds with "You have said so." It is followed by Pilate's declaration to the Jewish authorities that he finds "no crime" in Jesus, and that the only significant charge against him is their accusation that Jesus' teaching has stirred people up from Galilee to Jerusalem. Only Luke reports here Jesus' address to the women of Jerusalem warning them of the divine disaster that will fall on their offspring (23:27–31).

Only in Luke's account of the crucifixion do the soldiers join in the mocking of Jesus as one who claims to be "King of the Jews" (23:36–37), and does one of the criminals crucified with Jesus join in this mocking as well. And only here does the other criminal ask Jesus to remember him when he comes into his kingdom — in which Jesus promises him participation (23:39–43). A Jew also has the major role in the burial of Jesus: Joseph, who is granted permission to bury the body of Jesus, is from Arimathea, a town of the Jews, and is accompanied by women who see to the proper preparation of the corpse of Jesus for burial just prior to the sabbath (23:50–56). It is these women who return to the tomb after the sabbath has passed. Finding it empty, they are greeted by two men "in dazzling apparel," who tell them Jesus has risen from the dead — which they report to the apostles, who initially do not believe this (24:1–11). A series of appearances of the risen Christ is recounted in Luke (24:12–53), culminating in his claim that what has occurred is in fulfillment of the scriptures and is to be preached in his name to all the nations — an undertaking that will be empowered by the Spirit that God is to send upon them from on high.

The Book of Acts

That promise is repeated in the opening lines of the Acts of the
Apostles (1:1–6) and is followed by Jesus' commissioning the apostles
for their world mission and the account of his departure from them
in his ascension (1:5–11). Then comes the report of the choice of an
apostle, Matthias, to succeed the traitorous Judas (1:11–26). A climax
comes in the story of the outpouring of the Holy Spirit on the apostles
(2:1–13), which results in their ability to speak in languages of people
from across the world, telling them of "the mighty works of God."
Peter addresses the throng, affirming that what is happening is in
fulfillment of the prophet Joel (3:1–5), who foretold the coming of the
Spirit upon all humanity [flesh], the marvels that would accompany
this, and the opportunity all will have to "call on the name of the Lord
[and] be saved" (1:26). God has confirmed this promise — uttered in
Psalm 13:8–11 — by raising from the dead the crucified Jesus (2:22–
36). This divine gift is available not only to Jews and proselytes (2:1)
and their children, but also to "all that are afar off, every one whom
the Lord calls to him" (2:39). The modes and messages by which this
promise of human renewal will be accomplished are set forth in the
account of the ministry and teaching of Jesus in the Gospel of Luke.
But their potential for reaching out to wider humanity across cultural, social, and ethnic lines is exemplified and demonstrated in the
narratives and messages that constitute the Book of Acts.

The central significance of this outreach in Acts is evident from the
response of Jesus to the question of the disciples when he appears to
them after his resurrection from the dead (1:6–8). They ask if the
time has come for him to "restore the kingdom to Israel," to which
he replies that they are not to know the time when God will fulfill his
purpose, but they are to be empowered by the Holy Spirit to begin
now their testimony concerning Jesus in Jerusalem — and then to extend it to "the end of the earth." The essence of the message to be
proclaimed worldwide and the strategies for the mission are demonstrated in detail in the Book of Acts as a whole. The empowerment for
this operation is seen as taking place — literally and symbolically —
with the outpouring of the Holy Spirit on the apostles on the Day of
Pentecost, whereby they are enabled to speak in a range of languages
and to be understood by those from many parts of the world then
gathered in Jerusalem. This happens when assembled there are "Jews
and devout men from every nation under heaven" who are enabled to
understand the apostles in their own language as the apostles recount
"the mighty works of God" through Jesus (Acts 2:5–11). Peter then

explains (2:14–21) that this is the fulfillment of the prophecy of Joel that God's Spirit will be poured out "on all flesh" — that is, on representatives of all humanity (Joel 3:1–5). Included among those who hear the message are not only Jews from across the known world, but also proselytes — persons identified by birth or by earlier cultural context with other religious traditions who have subsequently been moved to affirm beliefs and perform practices in the Jewish tradition. Thus the pattern of religious outreach beyond one's native ethnic traditions was already operative in Judaism, but now it becomes a central feature of the spread of Christianity.

Thus fulfillment of the divine promise to the Jews is now taking place among Gentiles as well. The divine origin of this program of comprehension and affirmation across ethnic, national, and cultural boundaries is seen to be confirmed by the healing of the lame man at the gate of the temple (3:1–10). The import of this manifestation of divine power and purpose is explained by Peter in his address to the throng in the Jerusalem temple (3:11–36). He declares that what is happening among them is the work of the God of Abraham, Isaac, and Jacob, who has now raised Jesus from the dead. The Jewish leaders deny his divine status and turn him over for execution to the Roman official Pilate, who is inclined to release him. They ask that instead a murderer be set free, and as a result the Author of Life is killed — but God raises him from the dead. Those who trust in Christ understand that his sacrificial death was essential to his role as Messiah: God has exalted him to heaven, from which he will return when God establishes his rule upon the earth. Then will be fulfilled the promise to Abraham that "in your posterity all the families of the earth shall be blessed" (3:25; Gen. 22:18; 26:4).

Peter declares that what is happening through the ecstatic speech of the apostles is not the result of their drunkenness. Rather, this is taking place in fulfillment of the prophetic promise in Joel 3:1–5 that God's Spirit will be poured out "on all flesh" — that is, on representatives of all humanity: "devout men from every nation under heaven" (2:5). As noted above, they include not only Jews but proselytes: non-Jews who converted to Judaism. That Gentiles would turn to trust in the God of Israel was foretold by Joel (3:2, 9, 11) but is now taking place. The divine promise to the Jews is now being fulfilled among Gentiles. Divine approval of the outreach across ethnic and traditional religious lines is evident in the healing of a lame man at the gate of the temple: there Peter declares, "In the name of Jesus Christ of Nazareth, walk!" — and he does (3:1–10)!

The import of these events is explained by Peter in his address to the throng gathered in the portico of Solomon in the temple complex (3:11–26), who are astounded at the healing that occurred. Peter identifies the source of this healing power as the "God of Abraham and of Isaac, and of Jacob," as the one who glorified his servant Jesus, in whose name the healing has occurred, though sadly the Jewish leadership denied him any link with God. This resulted in his execution by the Romans — though he is here declared to be "the Holy and Righteous One, and the Author of Life." This role is confirmed by God's having raised him from the dead, and faith in his name leads to life. That power of renewal is now demonstrated before them dramatically by the transformation of the lame man into one who walks, jumps, and praises God (3:7–10). The Jewish people and their leaders were not aware of the significance of their rejection of Jesus, but as the healing of this lame man makes clear, they must await the coming again in triumph of God's Messiah after God has made all things new as foreseen by the prophets of Israel. This is taking place in fulfillment of the promise to Abraham that through someone of his posterity "all the families of the earth shall be blessed" (3:15; Gen. 22:18).

The Jewish authorities are deeply disturbed by these claims, seize Peter and John, and take them for a hearing before the Jewish council — in Greek *synedrion*, which as noted was the agency of collaboration between the Jews and the Roman authorities. Later this term emerges in Jewish documents as "Sanhedrin," and is the designation for the central intra-Jewish authoritative body. Peter explains to this group that these events occurred through Jesus of Nazareth, whom he identifies as the "stone rejected by you builders who has now become the head of the corner" (4:11; Ps. 118:22). Then he adds the claim that human salvation is possible only through Jesus (4:12). The council forbids the apostles to speak in the name of Jesus, to which they reply that they can speak only concerning what they have seen and heard, which they view to be the work of God among them (4:17–20). Gathered in prayer, the new community perceives the opposition they are experiencing to be a part of what was foretold in scripture concerning the hostility of human leadership toward God and his Anointed One (Ps. 2:1–2). The coalition of Roman and Jewish leaders against this movement in the name of Jesus will not, however, be able to thwart God's purpose through the apostles. The convictions of the latter are confirmed by the Spirit that filled them, and therefore they "speak the word of God with boldness" (4:31).

The community is at one in its beliefs, its message to the world, and in its shared possessions and support of needy members (4:32–37). Divine judgment falls on members who violate the rule of fully shared possessions (5:1–11), but divine power and enablement are evident among the faithful in the increase in membership and the healing of the needy (5:12–16). Efforts by the Jewish leadership to halt the Jesus movement by imprisoning the apostles is thwarted by divine release of the members (5:17–26) and by their testimony to the council concerning God's exaltation of the crucified Jesus as "Leader and Savior" to give repentance and forgiveness of sins to Israel, even though their official council supported the Romans in their crucifixion of him. Trust in and obedience to him are confirmed by the Holy Spirit within them. One of the council members, Gamaliel, warns them to leave to God punishment of those in such a movement since they cannot be certain that it is not "of God." In spite of the council's forbidding them to speak in the name of Jesus, they continue to do so: "teaching and preaching Jesus as the Christ" (5:42).

Like Judaism as a whole in this time, the members of the new community include those of both traditional Jewish background and those whose origins and cultural orientation are based on inner religious experience or deeply influenced by the Graeco-Roman culture. One such leader, whose name and orientation derive from that culture, was Stephen. His perception, eloquence, and Hellenistic cultural features troubled the more traditionalist members of the Jewish council, who accused him of hostility toward the temple and the Law of Moses and arranged to have him tried before the council (6:8–14). His speech (7:1–53) traces the movement of the descendants of Abraham from Mesopotamia to what became the land of Israel, their stay in Egypt, the rise of Moses as their leader and the one through whom they receive the Law from God, their takeover of the land of Canaan, their establishment as a nation, and the building of the temple. Yet in spite of this extended history of divine favor to this people, they have persecuted the prophets, God's messengers to them, and now have shared in the death of Jesus, "the Righteous One." They continue to resist God's Holy Spirit and Jesus, nor do they obey the law that God gave them (7:1–53). The response of the people to Stephen is to assassinate him by stoning. In what becomes an irony, it is Saul/Paul who is identified as the leader of this fierce opposition to this new community (7:58–8:3). The persecution of the church in Jerusalem leads to the dispersion of its members throughout Judea and Samaria, which is the first stage in the spread of the gospel across the wider Graeco-Roman world. Significantly, the names of the church leaders shift from Semitic to Greek — as is evident in Paul, Stephen, and Philip.

One of the first places that the gospel takes root in Acts outside Jewish territory is in Samaria — a feature of the outreach of the good news which appears in the Gospel of Luke, as noted previously. Those converted and baptized in Samaria include Simon the magician, who was amazed by the signs and miracles performed by Philip, who represented the apostles. Peter and John went then from Jerusalem to Samaria to confirm what had been reported and what was seen to have happened to the new converts as taking place through the Holy Spirit (8:9–25). Philip had analogous experience of the movement reaching out across ethnic and traditional lines in meeting an Ethiopian eunuch who was an official returning from a visit to Jerusalem. He had been reading from the Jewish scriptures (Isaiah 53) and asked about the one mentioned there who was led as a sheep to the slaughter and whose life was snatched away. Philip explained that this prediction of a sacrificial death was the substance of the good news that was now fulfilled through Jesus. The Ethiopian believed the message and was baptized. Thus the new community was being extended to include those on the outer boundaries of Judaism.

Acts 9:1–18 describes how Saul, also known as Paul, who was from Tarsus in Asia Minor, had been on his way to Damascus under authorization from the high priest in Jerusalem to arrest and bring back to Jerusalem any individuals he might find, men or women, who had chosen to join "the Way." This was a designation for the new community of those who trusted in Jesus as the Messiah who had opened the way to God. As he approached Damascus he saw a flashing light from heaven and heard a voice calling him by name and asking him, "Why do you persecute me?" Saul asks who this is and learns that this is Jesus — as represented by his messengers, to whom he has been so cruel (Acts 9:6). Saul was blinded by this experience and had to be led into Damascus, where he was without sight for three days, and neither ate nor drank (9:9).

A disciple of Jesus named Ananias is told in a vision that he should go to the house where Saul was, lay hands on him, and thereby restore his sight. He learns further that Saul is to be God's messenger to carry the message about Jesus to Gentiles and kings, as well as to the children of Israel, and that he will suffer much for the sake of Jesus' name. Ananias goes and gives Paul the message, assuring him that he will regain his sight and be filled with the Holy Spirit (9:17). These promises take place, and Paul begins preaching in the synagogue about Jesus as the Christ. In spite of Jewish schemes to kill him, he is able to escape and returns to Jerusalem, where he is at first unable to join the disciples of Jesus, who fear he will harm them. Thus official Judaism is pictured in Acts as seeking to stamp out the new community and its leaders. Paul was escorted by members of the new community to the seaport, Caesarea, from which he sailed off toward his home in Tarsus (9:30).

From this point on, Acts narrates how various individuals in the wider Roman world seek to know God and how the apostles are empowered to inform them about Jesus — recounting his life of obedience, his death on the cross, his resurrection, and how he becomes manifest when, through preaching, his divine role as savior is proclaimed to non-Jews (10:34–43). It is through preaching and baptism that the new community expands and is empowered by the Holy Spirit, as reported by Peter to the church in Jerusalem (11:1–18). As persecution of the church intensifies, however, the apostles and their converts flee — proclaiming the good news as they go, across Syria and into Asia Minor. It is reported in 11:19–26 that it was in Antioch-in-Syria that the disciples were first called Christians. Hostility toward the movement from the Roman authorities resulted in imprisonment or martyrdom for its members and leaders (12:1–5), although divine action is said to have freed Peter from prison in Jerusalem. He believed that God had sent an angel to rescue him from harsh treatment by King Herod and "the Jewish people" (12:6–17). Herod was so angry at the escape of Peter from prison that he ordered the execution of the prison guards (12:18–19). When he was approached by a group from Tyre and Sidon asking for peace, he appeared to them on his throne in royal robes. When he was greeted by some of his subjects as divine, however, he was stricken by an angel and died (12:20–23). Yet this violent opposition did not hamper the spread of the word of God. Saul and Barnabas returned to Jerusalem.

After they had gone from Antioch the church there was told by the Holy Spirit to appoint Barnabas and Saul to launch a wider mission in the Mediterranean world, and they commissioned them to do so (13:1–3). Sent forth by the Holy Spirit, they sailed first to the island of Cyprus, where they were summoned by the proconsul to impart the word of God, but were threatened by a Jewish false prophet who was also a magician and who tried to divert the consul from the faith in Jesus. Paul confronted the magician and told him that the Lord was sending blindness upon him for a time. The proconsul thereupon became a believer and was astonished at the teaching about the Lord (13:4–12).

Paul and his associates sailed north to the mainland of Asia Minor and journeyed inland to Antioch-in-Pisidia, where they took part in worship at the synagogue (13:13–43). Invited to speak to the worshipers, Paul tells them that God has fulfilled the promise he made to David in bringing to Israel a savior, Jesus. The Jewish leaders in Jerusalem had failed to recognize him and unwittingly fulfilled the scriptures that spoke of his sacrificial death by asking Pilate to kill him (13:28), and through Jesus God grants forgiveness of sins, which is not made possible through the Law of Moses. On hearing this message, many Jews and devout converts to Judaism believed it and sought further instruction from the apostles. So great was the favorable response of the hearers to the apostles' preaching that the Jewish leaders were incensed and sought to discredit the apostles' message about Jesus (13:44–45). Paul and Barnabas responded by declaring that they would now turn to the Gentiles, which would fulfill the prophecy in Isaiah 49:6 about the salvation that will be brought to the ends of the earth. "The Jews" — which here refers to the Jewish leaders — "stirred up persecution against Paul and Barnabas, and drove them out of their district" (13:50).

A similarly mixed response came to the apostles' mission in the cities of Iconium and Lystra (14:1–7). In Iconium Paul and Barnabas went into the Jewish synagogue and spoke about Jesus, and a great number of both Jews and Greeks became believers. But the unbelieving Jews stirred up the Gentiles and poisoned the minds of some of them about these messengers. The residents of the city were divided — some siding with the Jews and some with the apostles. A plot was made by some Jews and Gentiles with the leaders to mistreat Paul and Barnabas and to stone them to death, but they learned of the plot and fled to the region of Lycaonia, where they preached the good news in both the cities and the countryside (14:8–20). After Paul healed a lifelong crippled man, the crowds were convinced that he and Barnabas were gods, and even after Paul spoke to them of the living God who does such things, they wanted to offer sacrifices to these two. Some Jewish leaders turned the crowds against them, and the crowds hit them with stones and dragged them out of the city, assuming that they were dead. But when the faithful gathered around them, they revived and went on to preach the gospel in the city of Derbe. From there they traveled back through the cities they had visited earlier and others on the way, encouraging the members of the new community that they must persevere in spite of difficulties and appointing elders to lead the new churches. They then reported to the faithful in Antioch on their successful mission (14:21–28).

Some people came to Antioch from the church in Jerusalem, telling the church members there that they must observe the Jewish law of circumcision. This policy is based on the report in Genesis 17:9–14, where Abraham is told that all male offspring of him and his ancestors, including their slaves, must be circumcised when they are eight days old. Paul and Barnabas go to Jerusalem to discuss this question with the apostles and church leaders there (Acts 15:1–2). On the way there, the two reported to churches in Phoenicia and Samaria the conversion of Gentiles, which brought a happy response, but in Jerusalem some members assert once more the rule of circumcision for all non-Jewish converts (15:3–5).

The apostles and elders who gathered to discuss this issue are told by Peter that it was through him that Gentiles first heard the gospel, and the Spirit confirmed that their hearts were cleansed by faith — not by obedience to the Law of Moses. Paul and Barnabas reported the wonders that had then occurred, confirming the transformation of these Gentile converts (15:12). James, who has become the leader of the apostles, declares that Gentiles should not be obligated by the Jewish law, except that they should "abstain from pollution of idols [eating food offered to pagan deities], from unchastity [sexual misdeeds], from what is strangled and from blood [expanding the prohibition of eating meat that was sacrificed to idols]." The Law of Moses has long been proclaimed "in every city," so these basic restrictions would be known among non-Jews, and should be observed by them as Christians. This kind of restriction on Gentile converts is not found in the letters of Paul, where the sole requirement placed on that group is that they should contribute to the support of the poor (Gal. 2:10). Acts reports, however, that the Gentile converts were well content with the requirements articulated by the apostles (15:30).

Paul and the other apostles chose their associates and accepted the assigned territory where their evangelism and community-building was to be continued (Acts 15:36–16:5). Paul, accompanied by Silas, is seen here as divinely guided to open a new area to the mission of the church. Passing through sections of Asia Minor, he is told in a vision to cross over to the mainland of Europe in the region of Macedonia (16:6–10) — which he did. There in the city of Philippi, at a "place of prayer" for Jews and God-seeking Gentiles, he met a gentile woman whose business was selling costly purple dye. She was persuaded by Paul's message, was baptized along with her entire household, and invited Paul to come and reside in her house (16:14–15). After Paul expelled a spirit from a slave girl, which had enabled her to foretell the future, her owners took him and Silas to court, charging them with "upsetting our city." They were beaten and imprisoned, chained deep within the jail. As they prayed after midnight, an earthquake shook the prison, and chains fell from all the prisoners. They did not flee, but urged the terrified jailer not to kill himself. He asked what he should do "to be saved" — evidently meaning to get out of his gross difficulty — and was told to "trust in the Lord Jesus." After telling all in the jailer's house about Jesus, they all believed and were baptized. In the morning he reported to Paul and Silas that they were to be set free. On learning that these two were Roman citizens, the local authorities apologized for their mistreatment and urged them to leave town. After reporting to Lydia and other believers what had happened, the two journeyed westward, stopping in Thessalonica (17:1).

There the claim made by Paul in the synagogue that Jesus was the Messiah was welcomed by some of the Jews, as well as by devout Greeks and leading women. But some Jews strongly opposed the movement and reported that the apostles were violating Roman law and promoting "another king, Jesus" (17:7). The supporters of Paul and Silas sent them off to Beroea, where the response was more positive, with daily scripture studies. But the Jews from Thessalonica stirred up strong opposition, and for safety, Paul was conducted to Athens. There — in the traditional intellectual center of the world — he also argued with philosophers, though some dismissed his message as nonsense (17:16–19). Summoned to give a public statement of his religion, he affirmed the one transcendent God of the universe who is at work sustaining the universe, who cannot be identified with an idol, but who calls on all humanity — his offspring — to be just and obedient. The divine model for judging the universe is one whom he has appointed and has honored by raising him from the dead (17:22–31). The response to this address was that some were persuaded, others scoffed, and others expressed interest in further information (17:32–34).

The message was then proclaimed in other major Greek cities — notably Corinth and Ephesus (18:1–19:41). Challenges came from Jewish leaders, but Paul returned to confirm and inform the members of the new communities. On leaving the church in Ephesus, Paul went to the port of Troas, had fellowship with the community there, and then set sail for Tyre on his way to Jerusalem. En route, at Miletus he sent for members of the church of Ephesus, whom he warned that they would experience not only attacks from outsiders but fierce disputes from members within (20:29–30). He was returning to Jerusalem, and knew that his colleagues and converts in Ephesus and the other Graeco-Roman cities would not see him again. On reaching the final port of Caesarea, he was warned about his being bound by Jews and turned over to the Gentiles when he reached Jerusalem. Nevertheless he continued the journey (21:1–14). After arriving in Jerusalem he greets James and the other leaders of the church there, who are elated to hear of the large numbers of Gentile converts, but who warn him that, since thousands of the members of the new community adhere to the requirements of the Law of Moses, Paul will be denounced by them for his law-free gospel. A minimum list of rules for Gentile converts has been drawn up, including some dietary laws and the avoidance of sexual intercourse in a mode prohibited by the Jewish law (21:15–26).

Paul is seized in the temple by the Jewish authorities and beaten, but is then taken and protected by the Roman military there (21:27–36). To the chief Roman officer he denies that he has been involved in Jewish insurrection. But initially his zeal for the Jewish law had led him to take initiative in trying to destroy the Christian movement — the Way — as it began among the Jews. He describes his conversion and the vision of Jesus he had in the temple, which led to his call to a mission among the Gentiles. The Jews now call for his execution, but he appeals to his status as a Roman citizen for protection (22:25–29). This is followed by a hearing before the Jewish council, where his affirmation of belief in the resurrection leads to a dispute within the council: the Pharisees believe in the resurrection and the Sadducees do not. The former declared that they did not find Paul guilty of anything, and the inner conflict of the council became violent, and he was removed to the military barracks by order of the Roman official (21:9–10). Other Jews joined in a conspiracy to kill Paul, which was reported to the Roman official, who moved the trial from Jerusalem to Caesarea on the seacoast (23:23–24:27).

Felix, the Roman governor there, on learning that Paul was a Roman citizen and that the charges against him by the Jewish leaders were based solely on violation of their law, allowed them to present their case against him. They charge him as an agitator of Jews throughout the world and as one who profaned the temple. Paul denies these charges and affirms his worship of the God "of our ancestors" and his belief in the Law of Moses. The charge against him as a violator of that law is based on intra-Jewish divergence about a religious belief: in the resurrection. Since Felix's wife is Jewish, Paul is invited to explain his faith to them, but Felix is perturbed by hearing Paul speak of justice, self-control, and the coming judgment (24:24–25). He is held in custody for two years, but when Felix is succeeded by Festus, Paul appeals his case to the emperor — which is his right as a Roman citizen (25:1–12) — and makes his case again before the puppet king Agrippa (25:13–26:31). Thereupon he is sent under Roman control to Rome (27:1–28:16). There, in spite of a fierce storm, he arrives three months later.

In Rome he is met by Jewish leaders (28:11–29), whom he seeks to persuade by evidence "from the Law of Moses and the prophets." Because many of the Jewish hearers of this message were those whose hearts had "grown dull and their ears heavy of hearing," as foretold by the prophet Isaiah (6:9–10), "this salvation of God has been sent to the Gentiles: they will listen!" (Acts 28:28). Paul is seen as fulfilling this divine assignment in Rome, where he lives in his own rented dwelling, "proclaiming the kingdom of God and teaching about the Lord Jesus Christ" (28:30–31).

The Jews and Jesus in the Gospel of John

One feature of the gospel tradition that has led to misunderstanding between Jews and Christians by implying an aggressive, hostile attitude on the part of Jews as a whole toward the Jesus movement is the phrase recurrent in the Gospel of John concerning the disciples' "fear of the Jews." The first occurrence of this phrase is in John 7, where it is reported that Jesus remained in Galilee rather than going to Jerusalem "because the Jews sought to kill him" (7:1). Much discussion about Jesus is assumed to have gone on within the new community, but it was not made public since "for fear of the Jews no one spoke openly of him" (7:13).

In 7:14–19 is reported another encounter of Jesus with the religious leaders in the temple. He asks them, "Why do you seek to kill me?" This rumor is said to have been confirmed by some people in Jerusalem who rightly think that Jesus is "the man whom they seek to kill" (7:25). In 9:1–22 is the account of the Jewish authorities' investigation of the reported healing by Jesus of a man born blind. The parents refuse to discuss this since "the Jews" had already agreed that if anyone should confess Jesus to be the Christ, he or she was to be put out of the synagogue. In 19:38 Joseph of Arimathea, who is said to be a disciple of Jesus — but "secretly for fear of the Jews" — after the crucifixion asks for and receives Pilate's permission to take away the body of Jesus for burial. After the appearance of the risen Christ to Mary Magdalene she reported this to the disciples, who met in secret in a closed place "for fear of the Jews" (20:19).

Jesus' involvement in and conflict with Judaism — including reports of both shared features and critical views of certain Jewish beliefs and practices — are depicted throughout the Gospel of John. The Jewish leaders send agents to ask John the Baptist about Jesus' identity (1:19). John does not identify himself with any of the roles that the inquirers ask about, but declares instead that he is the one foretold by the prophet Isaiah (40:3): the voice of one crying out in the wilderness, "Make straight the way of the Lord." He declares that there is one who is the Lord and is already among them, but they do not know him. So exalted is this one that John considers himself to be unworthy to perform such a menial task for this divine agent as to untie the thong of his sandal (1:27).

Conclusion

Thus it is evident in the traditions embodied in the Gospels and Acts that the early Christians were convinced that Jesus was the divinely chosen and empowered one through whom was revealed God's purpose in creating the world and disclosing to humans the means by which they might find justice and fulfillment. Both Jesus' role in this cosmic process and the guidelines for human participation in it were conceived in diverse ways, as is manifest in the range of perceptions of these features set forth in the early Christian writings examined above. This led to diverse modes of perception of the role of the traditional people of God — the Jews — in the fulfillment of the ultimate divine purpose for cosmic renewal and for the identity and responsibility of those people. This is by no means a repudiation of the Jewish traditions set forth in the scriptures. It is instead a radical appropriation of that tradition, with strong and repeated emphasis on the belief that the God now disclosed through Jesus is the God of Abraham, Isaac, and Jacob, of David and Solomon, and of the Hebrew prophets. The early Christian interpretation of these traditions offered new options for those drawn by and seeking to appropriate the traditions of Judaism.

Chapter 8

St. Luke's Message about the Christian Relationship toward Israel

Petr Pokorný

St. Luke, the author of the third gospel and the canonical Acts of the Apostles, is considered to be one of the anti-Jewish early Christian authors. In his writings Jews are the opponents of Jesus, organizers of all the riots dangerous for the empire, and unwilling to listen to the gospel. That is why the Good News has been sent to the Gentiles (Acts 28). This was the prevailing view until recent decades.

The fact that Luke is critical toward the Jews of his time cannot be denied; to some degree we can understand his position, since he wrote his two books when the division between the synagogue and the church had just been accomplished and the wounds were still fresh. However, his image as an anti-Jewish writer may be corrected by another set of important observations: According to St. Luke the Torah and the other parts of the Jewish scripture (Tanach) are indispensable not only for the synagogue, but also for the Christian church. A Norwegian scholar, Jacob Jervell, tried to rehabilitate Luke as a theologian with a clearly positive attitude toward Israel. Not all his arguments stood up to exegetical scrutiny, but some of his insights are — in my opinion — irrefutable. Most important is that Luke never blamed Israel as a whole. He never questioned the role of Israel in the history of salvation.

In this context I realize how interesting it is to discuss the impact of the famous parable of the Prodigal Son (Luke 15:11–23) on the Christian-Jewish relationship. In Luke's time the prodigal son was interpreted as representative of Christians of Gentile background, the sinners who used to live in a distant country, still "far off" (in Greek *makran* — Luke 15:13, 20), and yet children of God — "his offspring" (Acts 17:28). The older son, who becomes the main character in the second part of the parable, obviously represents the synagogue, the

Pharisees who try not to disobey the commands of God (Luke 15:29; cf. the Pharisees as hearers of the parable in vv. 2–3).

According to all the rules of telling tales, as they were described by Vladimir Propp, the roles should change at the end of the story: The younger son through his repentance should be the positive hero; his older brother should be considered the wicked one, because he was disobedient at the decisive moment, when the father invited him to join the feast celebrating the return of his prodigal brother.

Surprisingly, the father does not share such a conclusion. His attitude toward the older son does not change at all and in fact is the same as the attitude toward the younger one: "...all that is mine is yours" (v. 31). The parable has an open end as to the reaction of the older son. It reflects the rupture between the church and the synagogues in the time of Luke. The solemn proclamation about the full participation of Israel in God's eternal heritage is nevertheless valid without any additional condition. The older son is full heir of the eternal heritage of the heavenly father (see vv. 29 and 31), of the "kingdom of God," as Luke would say. In this respect Luke must have been — at least indirectly — acquainted with the Pauline view of Israel's future according to which Israel will be saved together with the fullness of the Gentiles, as it is expressed in Romans 11. Paul's stopping the mission of Israel, as Luke describes it in the last verses of Acts, is not identical with Israel's eternal damnation.

However, the impression could arise that Israel's future is dependent on its return into the paternal house and its reunion with Christians. This interpretation is readily available. However it is a false understanding. The parable was not intended as a missionary text concerning Jews. Its intention within the frame of Luke's work is to address the Christians. They should know that the older brother, the Jews, have the full rights of the firstborn, that they are the heirs of God's kingdom, even if they are not the addressees of the missionary preaching in the present age.

The legal problem of the parable, namely, that both the brothers are the heirs of all that is the paternal heritage, has to be solved by discovering the divine logic: in the Kingdom of God the fullness of the eternal heritage is shared by all (Luke 12:32; 22:29f.).

Together with the respectful confirmation of the Jewish scripture as a part of the Christian Bible, it is this exhortation to respect Israel — the older brother with his full rights in the sight of God — that changes the traditionally anti-Jewish image of Luke. The Christians should listen carefully to God's proclamation about Israel: "My son, you are always with me, and everything I have is yours...."

Chapter 9 _____

A Sharp Mercy for Jews

Barclay M. Newman _____

Anti-Judaism in the New Testament

Over the centuries, untold human suffering has resulted from the abuse of certain New Testament passages — especially those in the Gospels — that speak of "the Jews" in negative tones. Even the barbaric events of *Kristallnacht* (when Nazi mobs destroyed Jewish homes and synagogues in "celebration" of Martin Luther's birthday in 1938) have their roots in the reformer's words of 1543:

> ... those Jews should be treated with a sharp mercy, their synagogues to be set on fire with sulphur and pitch thrown in, their houses to be destroyed. They are to be herded together in stables like gypsies in order to realize that they are not masters in the land but prisoners in exile. Their prayer books, their Talmud, and their Bibles are to be taken from them in order that they should no longer have the power to curse God and Christ. Their rabbis are to be forbidden on pain of death to give instructions, to praise God in public, and to pray to him. This is to stop the blasphemy that they practice.... And strong young Jews and Jewesses are to be given flail, ax, spade, and staff and spindle in order that they might earn their bread in the sweat of their brows, although it would be in the interest of the public welfare that they be expelled.... ("On the Jews and their Lies").[1]

"The Jews" in the Gospels and Acts

Of the 192 times that "the Jews" appears in the entire New Testament, more than 150 of these are found in the Gospel of John and Acts, both of which date toward the end of the first century. However, before any of these passages are examined, it is worthwhile to note (1) the relatively few times that the Sadducees appear in the New

Jewish group for the month of June — *THE 16th* —

day of each month, once monthly

4 from our book of essays —

ism – A Complicated Convergence"

Testament (Matt. 3:7; 16:1, 6, 11, 12; 22:23, 34; Mark 12:18; Luke 20:27; Acts 4:1; 5:17; 23:6, 7, 8) and (2) their complete absence from the Gospel of John. In all probability this noticeable absence results directly from the destruction of the Jerusalem temple in 70 C.E. and the consequent disappearance of the Sadducees as a force to be reckoned with in Judaism. Moreover, their primary function in the New Testament is that of opposing the Pharisees (and Jesus!) over the doctrine of resurrection, while in Acts 5:17 they are described as a Jewish "sect" (as are the Pharisees: 15:5; 26:5). Elsewhere in Acts, the Jesus Jewish Community is itself spoken of as a "sect" — of the Nazarenes (24:5), of the Way (24:14), and without further qualification (28:22). In addition, at least three significantly different forms of this Jesus "sect" are reflected in the New Testament: the radical Jewish community of Paul, the reactionary Jewish community of Matthew and James, and the reflective Jewish community of John.

Such observations are of supreme importance, because they underscore (1) the diversity of Judaism, both during and after the lifetime of Jesus, and (2) some of the conflicts both between and within the various "Jesus Jewish communities," as well as between them and "other Jewish communities" toward the end of the century, when the Gospels were taking on their final form.

A few preliminary observations regarding the relation between the actual events and the recounting of those events in the Gospels should prove helpful in setting the stage. For example, even a passing remark such as "Let the reader understand!" (Matt. 24:15; Mark 13:14) — which finds its place among the oral instructions of Jesus to his disciples — confirms that the gospel writers were concerned primarily with the relevance of their message at the time of the recounting of the events. Moreover, teachings regarding such matters as forgiveness within the church (Matt. 18:15–17) become relevant only at a date considerably later than the ministry of Jesus. Finally, the unique theological framework of each gospel is a salient reminder that the "historical realities" at the time of composition have significant priority over any perceived realities on the part of the modern reader.

According to John 3:25, John the Baptist and his followers — themselves Jews — got into an argument about Jewish ceremonial washing with either another Jewish man or several Jewish men, depending upon the choice of Greek manuscripts. This, together with the observation that Jesus and his followers were also Jews, is enough to affirm unequivocally that in the Gospel of John "the Jews" should never be translated in such a way as to suggest that *all* Jews of that time were involved. (Christians believe X about the form of baptism! Christians believe X about the meaning of the Lord's Supper! Christians believe X about the inspiration of scripture!) Nowhere is this division among Jews more apparent than in John 20:19, which states, "The disciples were afraid of the Jews." At most, the phrase means no more than "the Jewish leaders/authorities," though when the emotional aspects of words are taken into consideration, it would be significantly better to translate "the Jews" as "the religious authorities" (leaving "Jewish" implicit), since that is the *contextual function* of the term, whether viewed from the temporal perspective of the event itself or from that of its final editing.

With the exceptions of Mark 7:5 (which distinguishes between Pharisees and other Jewish groups) and Matthew 28:15 ("this story is still told among the Judeans"), all references to "the Jews" in the synoptic Gospels occur in the phrase: "king of the Jews" (Matt. 2:2; 27:11, 29, 37; Mark 15:9, 12, 18, 26; Luke 23:3, 37, 38). In this regard, it is important to notice that with the single exception of the angel's promise (Matt. 2:2), each occurrence reflects either the official political charge of insurrection brought against Jesus by the Roman governor Pilate (Matt. 27:11; Mark 15:2, 26; Luke 23:3, 38) or indirectly by others in the course of the trial and crucifixion of Jesus (Mark 15:12, 26; Luke 23:37). Unlike the execution of Stephen by stoning (Acts 7:57–58) — which was an official Jewish method of execution — Jesus was crucified, which was a Roman form of the death penalty reserved for criminals judged to be the most dangerous to the government.

In those passages where "king of the Jews" is used in the passion narratives, a note such as the following would be advisable: "*King of the Jews:* The official charge brought against Jesus by Pilate, the Roman governor, was that of being a revolutionary against Roman rule, for which the penalty was death by crucifixion. Death by stoning was the Jewish method of executing fellow Jews for crimes against their religion (Acts 7:57–58)."

On the other hand, Matthew 28:15 may legitimately be translated as "the people of Judea still tell each other this story," because "the Jews" of the Greek text is equivalent to "people in the region of Judea" (see Mark 1:5; John 3:22). In fact, since Judea (epitomized by "Jerusalem") — as opposed to Galilee (where "Jews" also lived) — is the center of hostility against Jesus in all four Gospels, it would be more "historically correct" to translate "the Jews" as "the people of Judea," except in those contexts where the phrase is obviously limited to smaller (authoritative) groups of Jews within that region.

Moreover, an overriding translation principle is operative here: *Sensitivity* has priority over insensitivity in contexts where a literal translation might well incite prejudice and potential violence against any racial group, as has resulted from a well-intentioned, but misleading, literal translation of "the Jews." The remainder of this section will involve looking at several passages from the Gospel of John and Acts, where such sensitivity should — and indeed must — be given high priority, lest the Bible become its own worst enemy.

John 1:19 ("the Jews sent priests and Levites from Jerusalem"): From the mention of "priests and Levites from Jerusalem," it is clearly implicit that those who sent them would have been Jews, and so "the Jews" may be translated "the religious authorities."

John 2:18, 20 ("the Jews then said ... the Jews then said"): The context is the Jerusalem temple during "the Passover of the Jews" (2:13), and since the Jews who verbally attack Jesus are obviously "representative" of a larger group, which the reader will easily identify as Jews, the two occurrences of the phrase may be translated "some of the religious authorities ... the authorities replied."

John 5:1, 10, 15, 16, 18 ("[1]a festival of the Jews, and Jesus went up to Jerusalem ... [10]the Jews said to the man ... [15]The man ... told the Jews ... [16]the Jews started persecuting Jesus ... [18]the Jews were seeking all the more to kill him"): Once again, the setting for the controversy is Jerusalem during a Jewish festival, where all the participants, unless otherwise indicated, are clearly Jews, which means that the passage can be both accurately and sensitively translated without explicit mention of them except in verse 1 ([1]Jewish festival ... [10]the religious authorities ... [15]told the authorities ... [16]they started making a lot of trouble for Jesus ... [18]now the authorities wanted to kill Jesus).

John 6:4, 41, 52 ("[4]the Passover, the festival of the Jews ... [41]the Jews began to complain about him ... [52]the Jews began to dispute"). Interesting is the observation that in this episode, which centers around the Passover theme, the participants — other than Jesus and his disciples — are identified as "a large crowd" (2, 5), "the people" (14), "the crowd that had stayed on the other side" (22), "the crowd" (24), and otherwise as either "they" or "them." This ambiguity is probably intentional, since this scene takes place in Galilee. It is not until the controversy develops between Jesus and some of the crowd that "the Jews" (a term usually reserved in John for Jesus' opponents at Jerusalem) appear in the narrative (41, 52). Unfortunately, a literal translation might well suggest that before the Jews arrived, a non-Jewish crowd had initially received Jesus without hesitation.

Sense and sensitivity would demand that these two verses should be translated: "the people started grumbling... they started arguing."

John 7:1, 11, 13, 15, 35 ("[1]the Jews were looking for an opportunity to kill him... [11]the Jews were looking for him at the festival... [13]for fear of the Jews... [15]the Jews were astonished... [35]the Jews said to each other"): Of itself, verse 1 is a valuable commentary on "the Jews" in the Gospel of John: "After this, Jesus went about in Galilee. He did not wish to go about in Judea because the Jews were looking for an opportunity to kill him." Here "the Jews" are explicitly linked to Judea in contrast with Galilee, making plausible the following translation: "[1]the religious authorities (in Jerusalem) wanted to kill him... [11]the authorities looked for Jesus... [13]the people were afraid of the authorities... [15]the authorities were surprised... [35]the people asked each other."

John 8:22, 31, 48, 52, 57 ("[22]the Jews said... [31]Jesus said to the Jews who had believed in him... [48]the Jews answered... [52]the Jews said... [57]the Jews said"): The setting is that of Jerusalem, and since "the Jews" seem more confused than hostile, each of these occurrences may be rendered "the people."

John 9:18, 22 ("the Jews did not believe... they were afraid of the Jews; for the Jews had already agreed"): Here "the Jews" are contrasted with the rest of the people, and so the passage may be translated: "the religious authorities would not believe... they were afraid of the authorities. The authorities had already agreed."

John 10:19, 24, 31, 33 ("[19]the Jews were divided... [24]the Jews gathered around him... [31]the Jews took up stones... [33]the Jews answered"): In verse 19 "the Jews" are suddenly mentioned, without any specific point of reference, though the Pharisees are mentioned in 9:40, followed by an ambiguous "them" in 10:6. Since this verse speaks of a division among the Jews, the best solution would be to assume that all four occurrences in this chapter relate to a larger group, which may be designated "the people."

John 11:8, 19, 31, 33, 36, 45, 54, 55 ("[8]the Jews were... trying to stone you... [19]many of the Jews had come to Martha... [31]the Jews who were with her... [33]the Jews who came with her... [36]the Jews said... [45]the Jews, therefore, who had come with Mary... [54]openly among the Jews... [55]the Passover of the Jews... many went up... to Jerusalem"): This passage is intriguing, because in verse 8, the disciples — who are themselves Jews — inform Jesus that "the Jews" are trying to stone him. Then in verses 19–45 the Jews apparently are friends of Martha and Mary, while the use of "the Jews" in verse 54 is clearly inclusive of local Jews generally. Accordingly, the following proposals are appropriate: In light of verse 7 ("Now we will go back to Judea"), verse 8 may be translated "the authorities there want to stone you," while "the people" is valid for all that follows, except verse 55, which should be made explicit: "Many of the Jewish people who lived out in the country had come to Jerusalem." A note may also be helpful at verse 8: "*Stone you:* Stoning was the Jewish method of executing fellow Jews for crimes against their religion (Acts 7:57–58)."

John 12:9, 11 ("the great crowd of the Jews . . . the Jews were deserting"): A generic rendering is best: "A lot of people came when they heard that Jesus was there . . . many of the people were turning from them" ("them" = the "chief priests" of verse 10).

John 13:33 ("as I said to the Jews, so I now say to you"): Here Jesus addresses his disciples, all of whom were Jews, and indicates that he is telling them exactly what he told "the Jews." Translate: "I tell you just as I told the people."

John 18:14, 20, 31, 36, 38 ("[14]Caiaphas . . . who had advised the Jews . . . [20]where all the Jews come together . . . [31]the Jews replied . . . [36]keep me from being handed over to the Jews . . . [38]he [Pilate] went out to the Jews"): Most readers won't realize that Caiaphas, the Jewish high priest, was appointed to his position by Pilate, the Roman (Italian!) governor. Since the text explicitly mentions that Jesus was taken to the high priest (verse 13), even the uninitiated reader will quickly realize that the Jewish high priest is intended. So verse 14 may be translated: "This was the same Caiaphas who had told the religious authorities, 'It is better if one person dies for the people.'" In the remainder of the verses, except 36, "the Jews" are the Jewish people in general — as the context makes abundantly clear — and so may be translated: "[20]where all of our people come together . . . [31]the crowd replied . . . [36]keep me from being handed over to the authorities . . . [38]Pilate went back out and said" (contextually sufficient for "back out to the Jews").

John 19:7, 12, 14, 20, 21, 31, 38, 40; 20:19 ("[7]the Jews answered . . . [12]the Jews cried out . . . [14]he said to the Jews . . . [20]the Jews read this inscription . . . [21]the chief priest of the Jews said . . . [31]the Jews did not want the bodies left on the cross . . . [38]because of the fear of the Jews . . . [40]the burial custom of the Jews . . . [20:19]for fear of the Jews"): In verses 7–14, "the Jews" make up the crowd gathered outside Pilate's judicial hall and in each instance may be translated "the crowd," because Pilate's words in 18:39 more than imply a Jewish audience: "I usually set a prisoner free for you at Passover." Although the translation of "the Jews" in verse 20 as "the people" finds less support than in the other verses under consideration, it is always better to err in the direction of inclusion than otherwise. And "the chief priests" is certainly contextually sufficient for "the chief priests of the Jews" (19:21). Since 19:31, 40 merely describe Jewish customs, no harm can be done by translating literally as "the Jews." Chapter 19:38 is similar to 20:19, which has already been discussed, and so may be accurately translated "because they feared the religious authorities."

Acts 9:22–23 ("the Jews who lived in Damascus...the Jews plotted to kill him"): Since "the Jews" of verse 23 refer back to those of verse 22, the two verses may be translated: "the Jewish people in Damascus...some of them made plans to kill Paul."

Acts 14:19 ("Jews came from Antioch and Iconium"): It is obvious that not all of the Jews would have come, and so the phrase may be translated "some Jewish leaders from Antioch and Iconium came."

Acts 17:5, 13 ("the Jews became jealous...the Jews of Thessalonica"): Here again, not all of the Jews would have been involved, and so translate: "the Jewish leaders became jealous...the Jewish leaders in Thessalonica."

Acts 18:12, 14 ("the Jews made a united attack on Paul...Gallio said to the Jews"): As so often in the New Testament, "the Jews" is used in the same fashion as expressions involving "all" in both the Old and New Testaments (for example, "*all* the city went out"). Translate: "some of the Jewish leaders got together and grabbed Paul...Gallio said [to them]."

Acts 19:33; 20:3, 19; 21:11 ("[33]whom the Jews had pushed forward ...[20:3]a plot was made against him by the Jews...[19]the plots of the Jews...[21:11]the Jews in Jerusalem"): The same rule applies as in 18:12. Translate "the Jews" as "several of the Jewish leaders" (19:33); "several of the Jewish leaders" (20:3); "some of the Jewish leaders" (19); "the religious authorities in Jerusalem" (21:11).

Acts 21:20, 21 ("[20]thousands of believers there among the Jews... [21]all the Jews living among the Gentiles"): Paul is in Jerusalem to address the Jesus Jewish community, and verse 19 states, "Paul greeted them and told them how God had used him to help the Gentiles." So the context allows for the following: "[20]many tens of thousands of our people have become followers...[21]those who live among the Gentiles." Not only is this contextually accurate, it is much more appropriate English style for the apostle to use a first-person form ("our") when speaking of his own people.

Acts 21:27; 22:30 ("[27]the Jews from Asia...[22:30]wanted to find out what Paul was being accused of by the Jews"): Once again it is abundantly obvious that not all Jews are included. Translate "[27]some of the

Jewish people from Asia ... [28]wanted to know the real reason why the Jewish leaders had brought charges against Paul."

Acts 23:12–13, 20 ("[12]the Jews joined in a conspiracy ... [13]there were more than forty ... [20]the Jews have agreed to ask you"): In verse 13 "the Jews" are qualified by "more than forty of them"; so it is advisable to combine verses 12 and 13 and translate: "more than forty Jewish men got together." When the young man informs the Roman commander of the plot (23:20), the reader already knows that the conspirators are Jews, and so all that is necessary contextually is "some men are planning to ask you."

Acts 23:27 ("this man was seized by the Jews"): In the commander's letter to Felix, he would certainly not state that *all* Jews had attacked Paul. Translate "some Jews grabbed this man."

Acts 24:5, 27 ("all the Jews throughout the world ... he wanted to grant the Jews a favor"): Tertullus, the Jewish lawyer, is bringing charges against Paul in the court of Felix, and in so doing mentions "all the Jews throughout the world," which is more fittingly translated "our people all over the world." Moreover, the only persons whom Felix really desired to placate at the moment were the Jewish leaders, who had brought charges against Paul.

Acts 25:7 ("the Jews who had gone down from Jerusalem"): Since the reference is to "those in authority" (25:5), the text could be translated as either "the leaders" or "the authorities from Jerusalem."

Acts 26:2, 3, 7, 21 ("[2]all the accusations of the Jews ... [3]all the customs and controversies of the Jews ... [7]our twelve tribes ... accused by Jews ... [21]the Jews seized me"): In Paul's defense, he shifts from a third-person reference ("the Jews") to a first-person reference ("our tribes"), which would be unnatural in English. Paul's statement is more forceful when translated: "all the charges that my own people have brought against me" (2); "our religious customs and the beliefs that divide us" (3); "our twelve tribes ... some of their leaders have brought charges" (7). Since the temple in Jerusalem is the point of reference, verse 21 may be faithfully translated "some men grabbed me in the temple."

Acts 28:19 ("the Jews objected"): In light of verse 17, which reads literally "the first of the Jews," it is logical to translate here as "the Jewish leaders disagreed."

"The Jews" in the Letters of Paul

There are only a few places in the letters of Paul where "the Jews" may be misleading to someone who does not realize Paul's deep pride in his Jewish heritage (2 Cor. 11:21–25; Phil. 3:4–6) and his profound love for his own people: "Dear friends, my greatest wish and my prayer to God is for the people of Israel to be saved" (Rom. 10:1). However, from a few scattered verses (2 Cor. 11:24; Gal. 2:13–15; 1 Thess. 2:14), a reader might gather that "the Jews" as a race were Paul's most dreaded enemies. It is true that Paul faced hostility from certain segments of the Jewish community, including the apostle Peter, whose Christology was apparently not radical enough to suit Paul (Gal. 2:11–18). Add to this the fact that Paul's "door" to the Gentiles was most often through the synagogue, it is surprising that even greater conflicts with the Jews are not reflected in his writings.

Unfortunately, when the Gospels, Acts, and a few of Paul's letters are placed side-by-side in a Bible, the whole becomes much more than the sum total of the individual parts, and the unknowing reader assumes that a vicious giant-sized vermin collectively called "the Jews" is standing at every corner to prevent the spread of the gospel. Little do these readers grasp that quite often "the Jews" belonged to the Jesus Jewish community, which itself was experiencing a time of self-definition, as it still is today, both between and within denominations! Without apology, the conscientious Bible translator should exercise every legitimate technique in order to destroy the false notion that "the Jews" are "Christ killers." For the most part, all this requires is leaving "the Jews" implicit, rather than explicit in the text.

2 Corinthians 11:24 ("from the Jews forty lashes minus one"): Actually, Paul's words convey deeper pathos if translated: "Five times my own people gave me thirty-nine lashes with a whip."

Galatians 2:12, 13 ("certain people came from James...of the circumcision faction...the other Jews joined him in this hypocrisy"): Does the average reader gather that those who came from James were *Jewish* believers, as were *the other Jews,* and that the real bone of contention was how to properly define the relationship between Jewish believers and Gentile believers as regards the demands of the Law of Moses? Some of this will become clear, if the relevant portions of these two verses are translated: "He [Peter] used to eat with Gentile followers of the Lord, until James sent some Jewish followers. Peter was afraid of the Jews and stopped eating with Gentiles. He and the others hid their true feelings."

1 Thessalonians 2:14 ("as they did from the Jews"): Whereas the Jews of Galatians were insiders, these are outsiders, and Paul is comparing the suffering brought on the Thessalonian believers by nonbelieving Gentiles with that earlier brought on Jewish believers by nonbelieving Jews. As with 2 Corinthians 11:4, a shift to an inclusive form is significantly more effective in English: "My friends, you did just like God's churches in Judea and like the other followers of Christ Jesus there. And so, you were mistreated by your own people, in the same way they were mistreated by their people."

"The Jews" in Revelation

Revelation 2:9; 3:9 ("who say that they are Jews . . . who say that they are Jews"): The real thrust of these two verses is not so much a claim on the part of these people to be *Jewish,* as their claim to be the *people of God* because of their Jewishness. Each of these clauses may then be translated: "those who claim to be God's people." It is possible to accompany the translation with a note: "*God's people:* Literally 'Jews.' These people claimed to be God's people because they were Jews."

Epilogue

In my most recent read-through of the Gospels, I have concluded that "the Jews" may well be a less than accurate translation of the Greek phrase *'oi ioudaioi.* Instead it means "those Jews" or better still, "those *other* Jews," referring to those who were not followers of Jesus. In my judgment, such a translation best accords with the linguistic, literary, and historical context of these documents.

Postscript

The Center of Christian-Jewish Reference (CCJR) held its first annual meeting on October 27–28, 2002, at the Center for Continuing Formation at St. Mary's Seminary and University of Baltimore. The CCJR is currently hosted by the Center for Christian-Jewish Learning at Boston College and may be contacted by e-mail at cjlearning@bc.edu. The Council of Centers on Jewish-Christian Relations is an association of twenty centers and institutes devoted to enhancing mutual understanding between Jews and Christians. Most of these centers or institutes are located in the United States, and affiliated with Catholic universities, but there are also affiliated members from other countries. This institutionalization on the national level of so many fine and productive local-level efforts will provide exciting new possibilities for the dialogue, not only within the United States, but internationally as well.

Notes

1. John Stendahl, "With Luther, Against Luther," in *Removing the Anti-Judaism from the New Testament*, ed. Howard Clark Kee and Irvin J. Borowsky (Philadelphia: American Interfaith Institute/World Alliance, 1998), 167–68.

Chapter 10

Judaism and the Gospel of John

D. Moody Smith

Introduction

The Gospel of John seems on the face of it a poor basis for Jewish-Christian dialogue. The Protestant New Testament scholar Eldon Jay Epp in 1975 advanced the thesis that

> the attitude toward the Jews that finds expression in...the Gospel of John coacted with the extraordinary popularity of that gospel so as to encourage and to buttress anti-Semitic sentiments among Christians from the second century C.E. until the present time. This leads to the conclusion that the Fourth Gospel, more than any other book in the canonical body of Christian writings, is responsible for the frequent anti-Semitic expressions by Christians during the past eighteen or nineteen centuries, and particularly for the unfortunate and still existent characterizations of the Jewish people by some Christians as "Christ-killers."[1]

Similarly, the Roman Catholic theologian Rosemary Ruether characterized John as the gospel in which the Jews "are the very incarnation of the false, apostate principles of the fallen world, alienated from its true being in God." Moreover, "because they belong essentially to the world and its hostile, alienated principle of existence, their instinctive reaction to the revelation of the spiritual Son of God is murderousness" (John 8:40, 44).[2] If modern exegesis deemphasizes "the Jews" so as to understand the term to mean the unbelieving — as contrasted with the believing — mode of existence, rather than having a concrete historical referent or significance, well and good. "This indeed is...the only authentic way to read the antithesis between the 'believer' and 'the world' (qua 'the Jews') in John."[3] Theologically speaking, it is a proper reading. Nevertheless, Christians, historically, have not read John in this way, says Ruether, because the gospel does not, in fact, demythologize the Jews. Rather, it mythologizes the distinction between two modes of existence, the believing and authentic over against the unbelieving and unauthentic, by identifying them with two historically and empirically distinct communities, the Christian and the Jewish.

Whatever may be said about John on this score, modern exegetes agree that it does not represent the views of Jesus or his original disciples. "Jesus was a Jew, and so were his first disciples. In fact, the earliest Christians did not think of themselves as members of a new religion separate from Judaism. Yet from the beginning Jesus and his disciples represented something new."[4] That "something new," however, was not conceived of as the end of Judaism and the beginning of something called Christianity. As to the Law, Jesus did not reject it, but set about interpreting it anew for a new day. The famous statement in Matthew ("Do not think that I have come to destroy the law and the prophets; I have come not to destroy but to fulfill.") may not actually have originated with Jesus. It can reasonably be argued that on Jesus' lips such a statement would have been superfluous. He and his followers, as well as his hearers, would have assumed as much. However that may be, Jesus certainly reckoned most seriously with the Jewish belief that God had spoken, that his will was concretized in Law, and that the Hebrew scriptures were a faithful account of his speaking.

The new thing that Jesus proclaimed was the realization of the Rule of God, certainly no novel concept. But Jesus believed that its time had come and that his mission was to proclaim that the ancient faith in God as king was becoming reality in his own mission and message. Such an expectation and faith did not, of course, negate the Law and the prophets; rather, it was understood as their proper fulfillment. The Rule of God, expressed already in his Law, was to find effectual and final fulfillment. The question of exactly how Jesus conceived this fulfillment is one that has motivated and stimulated much New Testament scholarship, but probably admits of no final conclusion. In the synoptic Gospels and tradition the kingdom impinges upon the present and is enormously relevant to decisions people make here and now. Yet at the same time it is not an inner spiritual experience or dimension, but the reality that everyone will have to reckon with ultimately, for it will impose itself upon us.

The revival of scholarly historical interest in Jesus of Nazareth has for good reason centered upon his Jewishness, that is, upon his rootedness in the traditions of Israel. Apart from that rootedness he cannot be understood. There is, of course, a sense in which "Jewish" is an anachronistic term, and one imposed from without. It is a term that does not appear on the lips of Jesus in the synoptic Gospels. Ancient Jews did not ordinarily understand or refer to themselves as such, except when assuming an outsiders' perspective. (For example, the ancient lintel inscription from Corinth reads "Synagogue of the Hebrews.") Although the term "Jew" and the conceptualization of Judaism and Jewishness were certainly antecedent to the rise of Christianity, they have taken on a new and somewhat different significance as the two religions have separated from and interacted with one another. Nevertheless, it is not incorrect or misleading to speak of the Jewishness of Jesus as a way of indicating where he belongs historically and theologically. In one important sense, Bultmann was correct to see Jesus as a "presupposition" of New Testament theology and to place him within Judaism.[5] Insofar as Jesus may become the subject matter of New Testament theology, however, scholars must take seriously that theology's Jewishness. (Possibly because of Bultmann's own modern, existentialist, and Lutheran presuppositions, he was unable to accomplish this adequately.)

The Meaning of "the Jews" in the Gospel of John

The Jewishness of Jesus shines through the synoptic Gospels, even though they are all distinctly Christian documents, because it is enshrined in the traditions on which they draw. Those traditions, however much they may reflect — in their selection, arrangement, and editing or formulation — the interests of the early church, nevertheless enshrine the attitudes and emphases of Jesus. This fact becomes particularly clear in light of certain data of vocabulary and terminology, and especially when those data are compared with evidence from the *Gospel of John*.

In the synoptic Gospels, there are only sixteen occurrences of the term *Ioudaios* (pl. *Ioudaioi*), "Jew(s)." They are found mostly in the passion narratives, where the Roman authorities are interested in the question of whether Jesus is the king of the Jews. Otherwise, the term rarely appears, and where it does it also, as in the passion narratives, betrays an extra-Jewish (whether Christian or Gentile) perspective (e.g., Matt. 2:2; Mark 7:3). In the synoptic Gospels' narrative of Jesus' ministry, the term "Jews" is superfluous because everyone is a Jew, unless otherwise designated, and the perspective of the narrator lies within the Judaism of first-century Palestine, or so it seems. Although modern redaction criticism has rightly emphasized the underlying, and sometimes explicit, Christian perspective of the authors, a critically innocent or naïve reading of the texts sees in them a narrative of events transpiring within the world of Judaism and of the historical Jesus, as problematic as direct historical inferences from the narrative may be. It has often been observed that parties to discussion with Jesus are not called Jews, but are Pharisees, Sadducees, Herodians, scribes, disciples of John the Baptist, and chief priests. Jesus may even have had a Zealot among his disciples (Luke 6:15; Acts 1:13). Of these the Sadducees, Herodians, scribes, and Zealots do not appear at all in John.

On turning to John, we notice immediately that in contrast to synoptic usage, the Jews are spoken of quite frequently. There are seventy-one occurrences of the term in John, surpassed only by the eighty-odd occurrences in the Acts of the Apostles. (In the remainder of the New Testament, "the Jews" appears fewer than thirty times.) The preponderance of the term in John and Acts is interesting and significant. In both, disciples of Jesus (i.e., Christians) are clearly differentiated from Jews. This is not the case in the synoptic Gospels, and not for the most part in the letters of Paul, who contrasts Jews and Greeks, not Jews and Christians. The situation in John and Acts seems almost prescient of later usages and determines the traditional Christian reading of the New Testament and understanding of the apostolic generation in ways that are not always historically felicitous.

It is fair to say that in John the Jews stand over against Jesus and his disciples, who are distinguished from them. Yet the Evangelist obviously knows that Jesus is a Jew (4:9) from Nazareth, the son of Joseph (1:45). His disciples, some of whom were followers of John the Baptist (1:35), were Jews as well (see 18:15). Despite his knowledge of the historical facts, John insists on characterizing the Jews as somehow clearly different and distinguishable from the band of Jesus and his disciples. Understandably, when Jesus tells the Samaritan woman that "salvation is of the Jews" (4:22), modern exegetes ask whether the Evangelist could have written such a thing and suggest it may be a later editorial insertion. (Just what purpose it might have served, however, is not immediately clear.) By and large, "the Jews" in John are the opponents of Jesus.

As such, they are quite often identified with the Pharisees (e.g., John 9), who appear frequently in the synoptic narratives as well. In the synoptics the Pharisees are, of course, a group within Judaism, whereas in John they sometimes seem to be identical with Judaism, or at least with its essence. We shall later consider the possible historical reasons for this significant difference. For the moment it is sufficient to note it and to observe that it may be significant in coming to terms with the nature and identity of "the Jews" in the Gospel of John. In John the Pharisees seem to be taking over Judaism. It is quite interesting and typical that the familiar synoptic linkage of the Pharisees to the scribes is entirely missing from John, where scribes are not found. Instead, more than once the Pharisees are in league with the chief priests (7:45; 11:47). Probably they were unlikely political or religious bedfellows in the time of Jesus. Such a linkage occurs also in Matthew (21:45; 27:62), where a historical setting similar to John's, but different from Jesus' own, may be in view. It is not found in Mark and Luke, and when Pharisees and chief priests (or Sadducees) appear together in Acts, they are more often than not at odds with each other (Acts 5:34; 23:6–9).

In view of the prominence of the Pharisees, and their apparent identification with "the Jews," in John's Gospel it is all the more striking that they do not appear prominently in the passion narrative. True, only in John do the Pharisees appear in the party that goes out to arrest Jesus just before his trial and crucifixion (18:3). Yet thereafter they disappear completely (although there are Jews aplenty in the trial narratives). In this respect John agrees with the other Gospels: despite the prominence of the Pharisees as Jesus' opponents throughout his public ministry, they actually recede in the events leading up to his execution. This striking fact is more likely a reflection of history and tradition than of the author's mentality, however, for he tends to identify the Pharisees with the Jews, who are already presented as the mortal enemies of Jesus. (Christians have long felt that "Pharisaic legalism" opposed Jesus and essentially did him in. This questionable view is encouraged by the presentation of them in John, but even there at the crucial point the Pharisees disappear from the scene. Jesus falls victim to Temple or priestly authorities.)

Who are these Jews? We address this question first of all from the standpoint of the phenomenology of the text. They are clearly Jewish people, but they are not all Jewish people. To begin with, Jesus and his disciples are not among "the Jews," although they are plainly Jewish. Moreover, no Galilean or Samaritan is called a Jew, except in chapter 6. That "the Jews" are residents of Judea is probably the case in most instances, but simply to translate *Ioudaioi* as "Judeans" will not do. They are both more and less than "Judeans." In John 6 they appear as Jesus' opponents in Galilee. From John 9:22 one may infer that they are religious leaders exercising authority in the synagogues to which at least some followers of Jesus belonged. From John 12:42 the same inference may be made, except in this case the most authoritative figures are called "Pharisees." They are powerful or influential enough to exercise authority over other Jews, who are called "rulers" or "officials" of these synagogues. Particularly in view of the fact that both John 9:22 and 12:42 deal with expulsion from the synagogues, it is likely that the "Jews" in the one case and the "Pharisees" in the other are the same authorities. It is important to notice that they are authorities who exercise significant power over other Jewish people. At least in these contexts, "Jews" may be "Pharisees," but they are not to be identified or confused with the totality of the Jewish people.

Thus Jesus, his followers, Galileans, and perhaps Samaritans are Jewish, but they are not "the Jews." There are also people explicitly called "Jews" who are not enemies of Jesus. Prominent among them is Nicodemus, a ruler of the Jews (3:1), who keeps coming back to Jesus, speaks for him (7:50), and helps bury him (19:39). We never read that he believed in Jesus, though some Jews (or Pharisees) do (9:16; cf., 8:31). The people who mourn Lazarus with Mary and Martha are said to be Jews, although they are also not hostile to Jesus. Moreover, throughout John's Gospel "Israel" and "Israelite" are used in a positive sense. Thus Nathanael can be called "truly an Israelite in whom there is no guile" (1:47) and Jesus is hailed as "king of Israel" (1:49), a title whose entirely positive connotations contrast with "king of the Jews," which as a negative and sarcastic ring on the lips of the Romans (e.g., 19:3).

"The Jews" is, then, a term used of a group of *Jewish leaders* who exercise great authority among their compatriots and are especially hostile to Jesus and his disciples. A recent study of the Gospels' use of *Ioudaioi* confirms the view that when it is used in a peculiarly Johannine sense, that is, not with reference to Judeans or to Jewish customs, feasts, and so forth, it refers to certain authorities rather than to the people as a whole.[6] It is these authorities, not Jewish people generally, who are portrayed as hostile to Jesus throughout John and make that gospel appear anti-Jewish. This being the case, it is reasonable — and probably correct — to contend that the anti-Jewish aura of the Fourth Gospel is a misreading of the text and, presumably, of the intention of its author(s). Nevertheless, it is a misreading that has all too easily and understandably arisen in the history of Christian exegesis, and it may be well nigh impossible to put it to rest in all the circles in which the gospel is read and treasured.

Before dealing with this larger issue, however, it will be useful to inquire further into the historical setting and putative purpose of the portrayal of "the Jews" in the Gospel of John. We proceed on the assumption that only a setting different from the immediate historical setting and purpose of Jesus himself will explain the statements and perspective of the Fourth Gospel. Jesus of Nazareth did not distinguish himself from the Jews in the way the Johannine Jesus does. Nor did he dwell upon his messianic role. If he ever acknowledged the claim that he was the messiah (see Mark 8:27–30), he did not give it the emphasis it receives in the Fourth Gospel.

Expulsion from the Synagogue

The absence of Zealots, Sadducees, and Herodians in the Gospel of John and the tendency for Jews to be equated with Pharisees suggests that John appeared after the Roman War, that is, after 70 C.E. Following the war, the so-called Council of Jamnia began the process of retrenching and redefining Jewish life and collecting and codifying traditions that would eventuate in the emergence of rabbinic Judaism as the heir of Pharisaism. The language of John's Gospel apparently reflects this state of affairs when the Pharisees are equated with the Jewish authorities, precisely the authorities who are able to say who belongs within the synagogue and who must be excluded. They are in the Fourth Gospel, as in broader Jewish history, defining what Judaism shall be. In putting Johannine Christianity beyond the pale, the Pharisees of the Fourth Gospel affirmed a religion of law and absolute monotheism. They rejected a sectarianism based on charismatic inspiration and seemingly limitless transferal of divine prerogatives and attributes to a crucified messianic claimant whose followers believed had risen from the dead. Almost certainly John's Gospel reflects this post-70 situation in Judaism, as well as in what we might call Jewish-Christian relations.

Can the setting and purpose of the Fourth Gospel be defined more precisely? Nearly two decades ago, J. Louis Martyn made an ingenious proposal based primarily on the three instances in the Fourth Gospel in which the threat of expulsion from the synagogue is reflected or predicted (9:22; 12:42; 16:2).[7] If such a threat was not made and was scarcely even conceivable in Jesus' own day, Martyn asks when and under what circumstances it may have been found. His underlying assumption is that the statements in John mirror an actual historical situation and set of circumstances. In this respect the Gospel of John affords primary testimony for the circumstances under which it was written (a principle argued by many, esp. Bultmann, Wellhausen). These in turn have been retrojected into the time of

Jesus and his disciples. (It is thus only secondarily testimony for the times and events it purports to narrate.) This process took place without deliberate design and forethought over a period of years.

Martyn thought it likely that a primitive narrative gospel consisting of a collection of miracle stories and probably also a rudimentary passion narrative was used by Jewish followers of Jesus to attract adherents to their movement within the synagogue. Such a gospel had been analyzed from the canonical text by Martyn's student Robert T. Fortna on other, chiefly unrelated, grounds.[8] It was a missionary gospel, and its original conclusion (now found in John 20:30–31) reflects this fact. As Christian missioners, using such narratives or such a primitive gospel, attained success in persuading their fellow Jews that their Jesus was, in fact, the Messiah of Israel, a backlash or reaction among the majority who were not convinced set in. In this connection the Twelfth Benediction of the *Shemoneh Esreh* was reformulated, in such a way as to condemn sectarians (*minim*) and Nazarenes (*notzrim*).[9] Presumably its purpose was to smoke out Christ-confessors within the synagogue, who could not pronounce this benediction, or malediction, against themselves. This reformulation of the Twelfth Benediction took place in the rabbinic Academy at Jamnia. According to tradition, it was done by a sage called Samuel the Small under the auspices of Rabbi Gamaliel II, and it has been dated in the ninth decade of the first century. The status of the synagogue ban as a general edict or decree of Jamnia is inferred from the statement of John 9:22, that "the Jews had already agreed. . . . "

There is actually no direct evidence that the Twelfth Benediction was reformulated or originally used for the purpose of identifying Christ-confessors specifically and expelling them from the synagogue. If a dating in the 80s is correct, it would antedate the publication of the Fourth Gospel by about a decade (just the right amount of time) if that gospel were composed — as is usually thought — between 90 and 110. Before Martyn's book appeared, W. D. Davies had already proposed such a date and use of the Twelfth Benediction in his work on Matthew.[10] Davies also cited the several places in Justin Martyr's *Dialogue with Trypho* that can be construed as allusions to the use of the Twelfth Benediction to drive Christians out of the synagogues. The evidence is indirect and circumstantial, but impressive, particularly when it is correlated with the fears and predictions of expulsion from the synagogue found in the Gospel of John. As we have noted, this state of affairs scarcely corresponds to a setting in the ministry of Jesus, and one is impelled by its prominence in the Fourth Gospel, together with other evidence bearing on Jewish-Christian conflict, to seek a plausible setting for it. Martyn's proposal is then a logical — as well as a brilliant — intuition of the historical imagination.

Nevertheless, it is a proposal and not a demonstration, as subsequent discussion has revealed, and, indeed, as Martyn had recognized from the beginning. Between the initial publication of Martyn's work and the appearance of the second, revised edition a decade later, he had entertained, in conversation and correspondence, the objections and reservations of Wayne A. Meeks and Morton Smith.[11] Meeks and Smith were unwilling to assign the reformulation of the Twelfth Benediction as early a date as Martyn had proposed. Hence they raise questions about a direct connection between the Benediction and passages such as John 9:22 that Martyn had made. (Nevertheless, Meeks and Smith agree with Martyn that the Twelfth Benediction and the Johannine *aposynagogoi* are manifestations of the same or related historical developments.) Subsequently, others have more sharply questioned the early dating of the reformulated Twelfth Benediction that Martyn had accepted, its relation to the Fourth Gospel, and its possible reflection in patristic texts such as Justin's *Dialogue with Trypho*.[12] The authority of Jamnia to promulgate what in effect was a decree against Jewish Christians has also been challenged. Later rabbinic sources afford precious little evidence of its use in this way. On the contrary, the evidence of the fourth-century bishop John Chrysostom indicates that Christians were then welcome in synagogues and, in Chrysostom's view, had to be warned away from them. Moreover, even the question of when Samuel the Small altered *the text* of the Twelfth Benediction may presuppose a textual stability that did not exist at the time.[13] It can reasonably be argued that at most the evidence suggests local rather than universal measures against Christ-confessors in the synagogue and that these were, moreover, a passing phase. One sadly notes that Christian-Jewish conflict has apparently left bolder evidence than Christian-Jewish harmony or tolerance, which may have been as common in the pre-Constantinian era.

Martyn and others involved in the scholarly discussion are working on a problem of ancient historiography, and their honesty and integrity as historians can only be honored and admired. The possible bearing of this attempted historical reconstruction and objections to it upon modern Jewish-Christian dialogue is, however, interesting. The implication of Martyn's thesis is that the Gospel of John is not, as might first appear, a generally and vehemently anti-Semitic (more accurately, anti-Jewish) document, but a response to a specific crisis in Jewish-Christian relations that had been initiated, or at least exacerbated, by the promulgation of the revised Twelfth Benediction. (Of course, according to Martyn's thesis, the controversy began within the synagogue, among Jews, and that intramural status still pertained at the point of the reformulation of the Benediction.)

Ironically, the objections by Jewish scholars such as Kimelman and Katz, which are substantial, in distancing the Fourth Gospel from the Twelfth Benediction and its postulated function, tend to push it back in the direction of a generally anti-Semitic or anti-Jewish writing. Obviously, a scholarly historical issue cannot be decided on the basis of the needs of contemporary Jewish-Christian dialogue. Nor is it helpful, and it is probably not accurate, to say that the truth lies somewhere in between. It would perhaps be more accurate to say that the sources available to us do not permit us to say exactly what transpired to produce the tension between Johannine Christianity and Judaism that is evident in the Fourth Gospel. If the problem with the Martyn thesis is the lack of positive and explicit, as opposed to suggestive, evidence in the rabbinic sources particularly, the problem with simply dismissing it is the evidence — in John, and elsewhere in the New Testament and early Christian sources — of strong tension between Jews and Christians, and occasional persecution.

However that may be, it is unnecessary and hazardous hurriedly to draw parallels or relations between this ancient situation and the present, or between it and instances of Jewish-Christian tension and persecution in intervening centuries. If, in fact, Johannine Christians were persecuted by some Jews or Jewish authorities, as Saul at first persecuted the Christian sectarians, this is obviously no justification for Christians' persecuting Jews subsequently. Such persecution, or threat thereof, makes historically understandable certain statements in the Gospel of John that otherwise appear to be the product of a gratuitous anti-Judaism. If John is properly read only in the latter way, the consequences for Jewish-Christian dialogue are unfortunate, particularly in view of the virtual certainty that Christians will continue to accord John a high, canonical authority in their own religion and theology. But the seemingly anti-Jewish statements in the Gospel of John are disastrous theologically only on the basis of a rather narrow and literalistic conception of the authority of the New Testament scriptures.

"The Jews"
in Other Johannine Writings

The prominence of "the Jews" in the Fourth Gospel bespeaks a real, historical situation and confrontation, wherever and whenever it may have occurred. The Gospel of John, however, is only one of five "Johannine" writings in the New Testament. In none of the others do Jews or Judaism figure in the same way; in fact, even in a long section of the gospel (chaps. 13–17) this confrontation fades completely into the background. The Revelation of John stands at the periphery of the Johannine circle, and, in the judgment of some, wholly outside it. As I have suggested elsewhere, however, there are a sufficient number of points of contact and similarity to warrant the assumption of a significant relationship or consanguinity.[14]

Revelation, interestingly enough, reflects less hostility toward Jews than does John's Gospel. The term *Ioudaioi* appears only twice in Revelation (2:9; 3:9), in both cases in an indirectly positive sense. That is, members of the "synagogue of Satan" are said to claim to be Jews although in reality they are not. The presumption is that it is good to be a Jew. "Jews" is still used in a positive sense, even as it is in Paul's Letter to the Romans (2:17, 28, 29; cf., 3:1). This remains the case even if the "synagogues of Satan" means Jews in Smyrna, or Philadelphia, or even contemporary Jews generally. In that case, they have defected from proper Judaism, from what it should mean to be a Jew. It is not certain, however, that by the "synagogue of Satan" John means all Jews or Judaism generally, as many Christian exegetes have assumed.[15] He may mean only Jews in the aforementioned localities who have persecuted or driven out the followers of Jesus who are being addressed. In that case we may be very near the milieu of the Gospel of John.[16] It is not necessary to assume that John regards all Jews as necessarily members of the Synagogue of Satan, as the author of the Fourth Gospel would, at least if the evidence of passages such as John 8:44 is determinative. In other words, the Fourth Gospel may represent the expansion or tendency to generalize attitudes only nascent in Revelation. Revelation 2:9 and 3:9 may not be derived from, or inferred from, the broader condemnation of Jews and Judaism rather common in the Fourth Gospel. In Revelation, "Jew" is still a good word; in the Fourth Gospel, it is not, having been displaced by "Israelite." Revelation, if basically earlier than this gospel (as, for example, Barrett argues), may represent a period prior to the Gospel of John. Possibly Revelation 3:9 still contemplates the conversion of such Jews.

On the other side of the Fourth Gospel, then, one would locate the Johannine epistles. *Ioudaios/oi* appears not once in any of them, a remarkable fact in view of its frequency in John, which is in many respects so closely related theologically to them. There is an obvious reason for this. The opponents, who come frequently into view in the letters, are not Jews but other Christians, whose lifestyle, ethics, and theology do not meet with the author's approval. To hear him tell it, they are loveless heretics who falsely claim to be without sin and perhaps for that reason are especially incorrigible. If, as on other grounds appears likely, the Johannine epistles are later than the Johannine gospel and presuppose it, a significant change in fronts has occurred. The struggle with Jews seems to be a thing of the past. Perhaps significantly, the vehemence of the opposition is still by no means diminished for that reason. If the Christian opponents are not "children of Satan," they are children of the world, "anti-Christs" (1 John 4:3, 5; 2 John 7). This is not significantly better.

The farewell discourses of John are in some respects closer to the Johannine epistles than to the rest of that gospel, in which such open opposition to Jews is manifest. In chapter 13 through 17 *Ioudaioi* occurs only in 13:33, where Jesus tells his disciples what he says to them he has already told the Jews. The reference to being put out of the synagogues and being killed (16:2) would seem to have Jewish opposition in view, and Jesus' discussion of the world's hatred (15:18–16:4) doubtless includes Jewish opposition. But otherwise, the farewell discourses are concerned with distinctly Christian theological and related issues, not with external opposition. For good reason it has been argued that the farewell discourses are in some respects, or in some part, closer to the epistles than to the rest of the gospel.[17] The farewell discourses, then, represent a Johannine Christianity that has weathered the synagogue controversy and moved on to other concerns.

One cannot fail to note an anomaly present in both this gospel and these epistles. In no other New Testament opus is there stronger emphasis on God's love, as expressed in Jesus his Son (3:16; 1 John 4:10, 14, 16) or on the command to love as the expression of true discipleship. Only those who truly love one another can claim to be recipients of God's love or, for that matter, can claim to love God (1 John 4:20). Yet love is expressed only within the circle of believers: "Love one another" (John 13:34–35; 15:12–13; 1 John 3:23; 2 John 5). Commandments and exhortations to love the neighbor (Mark 12:31) — and even the enemy (Matt. 5:44) — are absent from the Fourth Gospel and

the Johannine epistles. Outsiders, whether because they have not believed or because they have believed wrongly, are not necessarily to
be loved. While the Gospel of John does *not* teach that Christians
should *hate* their enemies (cf. Matt. 5:43), 1 John comes close: "the
world" — those outside the faith (or the church) — is not to be loved
(1 John 2:15); "the world" will hate believers (John 15:18, 19). Believers are not told to love the emissaries of the world as if they too are
children of God. In fact, the only true children of God are believers
(1:12). The Johannine Jesus gives no instructions to disciples about
how they should behave toward those who hate them. Perhaps a position of relative powerlessness is assumed. They are simply warned
so that they will be prepared for the world's hatred and be able to
overcome it. Even the command to love is subsumed within John's
dualism, and does not overcome it. Only God does that: the world
may hate God (John 15:23), but God nevertheless loves the world —
in spite of, perhaps because of, its sinfulness. However that may be,
believers are not — at least not explicitly — urged to emulate God in
this respect.

Here we see a collision between the quasi-metaphysical dualism of
the Fourth Gospel and its basic theological-ethical affirmation. That
is, the dualistic conceptual framework seems to impede, if not prevent, the universal extension of the love of God and humanity which
is the fundamental axiom of John. This impediment obviously has to
do with role of belief (i.e., reception of that love). When revelation
meets unbelief all bets are off, and love's expression is thwarted, at
least among human beings. Nevertheless, in John's view, the love of
God is not defeated. Whether human love ought to stop at the boundary of belief and unbelief is a question that merits reflection. In the
view of the synoptic Jesus, who in this respect is also more likely
the historical Jesus, it should not. The fact that in John human love
does stop at this boundary is, as we have seen, related to the author's
and the community's dualism. How it is related is a good question.
Does that dualism set limits conceptually so as to override John's
intent? Is the love of which the author of John speaks effective only
within the limits set out by a fideistic, if not ontological, dualism?
Or is that dualism itself a product of the social situation of John, in
that the rejection of the community's claims, of its evangelical effort,
results in an ossification of boundaries? In that case, one might ask
whether John's response is the only, or the best, one in the face of
the rejection of missionary witness. John seems to know, however,
that the expression of love, even within the community, is the most
effective form of witness to those outside (3:16; 15:12; cf. 17:20–23). If

love within the community is a powerful witness, how much more might the expression of loves toward those outside the community witness to them?

Implications of the Issue for Contemporary Jewish-Christian Dialogue

A generation ago, scholarship tended to gloss over the Jews in the Gospel of John. For Bultmann the Jews were a surrogate for the world, their presence apparently accounted for by the historical setting of Jesus' ministry within Judaism.[18] John had no great interest in polemicizing against historical, empirical Jews in his own life-setting, although Bultmann notes that insofar as "the situation of the Church is reflected in the Gospel of John, its problem is the conflict with Judaism, and its theme is faith in Jesus as the Son of God."[19] Bultmann's interest was definitely the theological theme rather than the setting. His English contemporary and counterpart, C. H. Dodd, much more than Bultmann, took into account the Jewish and Old Testament conceptual background of John. Yet Dodd found in the Hermetic literature — of fundamentally pagan origin — the closest affinities with the Fourth Gospel.[20] Dodd saw John as a book addressed not primarily to Christians, much less to Jews or Jewish Christians, but to a non-Christian public, to "devout and thoughtful persons . . . in the varied and cosmopolitan society of a great Hellenistic city such as Ephesus under the Roman Empire."[21] For Dodd, even less than for Bultmann, a rather vociferous internecine conflict among Jews, or between Jews and Christians, was not the substratum of Johannine thought; and the exegete did not need to take it into account in order to understand John.

Developments of the past two decades, epitomized by Martyn's thesis, have wrought a significant change in Johannine exegesis and interpretation. In different ways, Raymond Brown, Wayne A. Meeks, Marinus de Jonge, Klaus Wengst, Oscar Cullmann, Georg Richter, and others have underscored and demonstrated the significance of the Jewish or Jewish-Christian milieu and affinities of the Fourth Gospel. The second edition of Barrett's justly famous commentary is an accurate barometer of this change.[22] Scholars seeking to understand and interpret the Gospel of John may no longer bypass or downplay this dimension of its historical setting or horizon, as had Bultmann and Dodd. Rather, the Jewishness of the Fourth Gospel has been established in such a way as to press upon us the importance of

Jewish-Christian relations — *and* Jewish-Christian disagreements — as ingredients of any historically responsible exegesis.

By the same token, the Jewish dimension of the origin and purpose of the Fourth Gospel can scarcely be acknowledged as something that, while real, belongs essentially to the past. In vital respects the issues upon which the Fourth Gospel focuses with such unremitting starkness and clarity remain before us. That is, Christians in the contemporary world, like the Christians of the Johannine community, live in the presence of Jews who do not accept the theologically daring — even extreme — propositions about Jesus that the author of John sets forth. They could not do so and remain Jews in the now generally accepted sense of the term. Thus the Fourth Gospel seems to offer little hope or basis for dialogue between Christians and Jews. At the same time, the fact that John belongs to the Christian canon of scripture — to the New Testament — make such dialogue all the more necessary.

As we have noted, the harshness of the alternatives as posed by the Jesus of the Fourth Gospel — and equally by "the Jews" mentioned in it — is somewhat mitigated by an appreciation of the dire historical circumstances of those ancient Jews and Christians. Both lived under conditions of great stress and duress. The stress under which those Jews lived is not always recorded in as direct or obvious a fashion as is that which beset the Johannine Christians (although, of course, in John theirs is also recorded indirectly, as if it applied to Jesus rather than his disciples). The portrait of late first-century Judaism is buried in the difficult, laconic, and often obscure statements of rabbinic sources. It comes to light in the imagery of the post-70 Apocalypses of Ezra and Baruch. And it is fleshed out in the long historical narrations of Josephus, which attempt both to justify the dominance of Rome in Jewish eyes and to define and defend the essential character of Judaism as a monotheistic religion and a sane and sober ethical philosophy rather than a dangerous and subversive movement. The Judaism of the late first century was badly, although not mortally, wounded after the bloody and disastrous war of 66–70 C.E. It was to suffer further trauma within another half-century in the wake of the suppression of the Bar Kokhba rebellion. The sober sages who were conducting the retrenchment of Judaism, preserving the ancient traditions along Pharisaic lines, truly had no need of the spiritual enthusiasm, messianism, sectarianism, and apparent challenge to the Law and to traditional monotheism that the Johannine community represented.

The Johannine Christians, on the other hand, had the uncompromising zeal of new converts. They were not so much converts from Judaism to Christianity as converts to Jesus, filled with his spirit, born from above, filled with power and glory. (But their conversion to Jesus took them sharply away from the direction in which contemporary Judaism was heading; hence the continuing controversy with "the Pharisees.") They believed that they had received — and would continued to receive — God's ultimate revelation of himself in the crucified Jesus, whom they believed to be the divine Son of God. If "the world," and particularly their Jewish confreres, insisted upon rejecting God's revelation, the only satisfying explanation was the darkness of their origin and their destiny of sin and death. On the other hand, God not only assured believers of eternal fellowship with himself, but granted them life and joy in this world. Thus the lines were fully and finally drawn; or so it seemed.

Historical circumstances have changed, and continue to change. The setting of modern Judaism is in many respects both more diverse and more hopeful than that of its late first-century counterpart. Yet the continued threat to the existence of modern Israel is almost universally viewed by Jews as a threat to Jewish survival. The Holocaust, of recent and bitter memory, represented a more dire threat to Judaism than the Roman war. After all, the Romans only wanted the Jews to be reasonable — by Roman standards, of course; they did not want to destroy the Jewish people or their religion. The Nazis wanted to destroy both.

There is something to the Johannine blacklisting of the Jews, the consigning of them to this world and to Satan, that in Jewish eyes foreshadows the Holocaust or the annihilation of Judaism. Such a dire, negative view of Jews and of the whole world is undeniably present in John. But, paradoxically, it is precisely John's Gospel that presents the motivation, meaning, and effect of God's revelation in Jesus as love. Furthermore, the love of God finds its true response in reciprocal human love that will lead to the unity of the community of love. It is a concept of revelation and response that is in principle universal. In the course of the vagaries and vicissitudes of history, the universal goal was jeopardized, and the dualistic division between truth and falsehood, light and darkness, seemed to be the last word.

Johannine Christianity and Pharisaic Judaism represent opposite poles and possibilities arising out of a common religious tradition. In its need to retrench and conserve the heritage the past had bequeathed to it, this Judaism appears in the Gospel of John as remarkably conservative, which in a sense it certainly was. If Johannine

Christianity would scarcely qualify as "liberal," it nevertheless enshrines and places a high premium upon elements of spontaneity, novelty, and uniqueness, which are, however, indigenous to — and derived from — the same parent tradition. Within that tradition it is in the nature of the new to take a critical stance toward the old, and of the old to look askance at the new. The potential polarities arising out of a common tradition could not be better illustrated. They stand over against each other as making mutually exclusive claims for allegiance and loyalty (e.g., John 9:28; 14:6). The resolution of those claims seems impossible apart from the dissolution of one side or the other. It belongs to the honesty and the integrity of the discussion to honor the reality of the opposing claims. It belongs to the necessity of our mutuality and coexistence, however, not to terminate the conversation but, despite the Pharisees and the Johannine Christians, to continue that dialogue for the sake of the revelation and tradition out of which we both live.

One final observation: it would be wrong to conclude from the tension between Pharisaic Judaism and Johannine Christianity that the one simply represents a conservative and defensive posture toward the inherited tradition while the other represents spontaneity and the claim to new revelations and insights. Within the former, the impetus to preserve the tradition precisely by correlating it with, making it applicable to, new and emerging problems and situations is a mark of Pharisaism's distinctiveness and originality. Moreover, within Johannine Christianity the need to hold on to what through revelation or experience has established itself soon became urgent, as Raymond Brown has shown.[23] The Johannine epistles are "Johannine Pastorals" (Conzelmann); that is, their goal is to assert and defend the revelation already given. Thus they lay heavy stress on what was "from the beginning" (of the tradition); they speak of the love command as the "old commandment" (1 John 2:7) rather than the new (John 13:34). This point is important to bear in mind, for it shows that the tensions between Pharisaic Judaism and Johannine Christianity are, phenomenologically speaking, not tensions between Judaism and Christianity as separate religions, but tensions that arise almost inevitably *within* a religion, particularly within religions such as Christianity and Judaism, whose essence consists both of the claim that God has spoken and of the claim, however refined or attenuated by qualification or concepts of inference or mediation, that God continues to speak in ways that are — or should be — determinative of human existence.[24]

Postscript 2003

Having now reread this essay, fifteen years after it was written, I am pleased with it, for I was able to say why and how historical investigations can illuminate and ameliorate doctrinal or religious controversies. "The Jews" of the Gospel of John are not all the Jews, although it is also possible to understand how that blanket interpretation arose. Would that John the Evangelist had chosen different terms, but I do not believe he was prescient, or even if he had been that he would have written differently. Yet since I am not a fundamentalist Christian, I do not feel bound by what may well be his limitations or mistakes. One can understand John without agreeing with him, as one can explain John without apologizing for the difficulties his language has created.

The bibliography on the subject of the Gospel of John and Judaism has grown considerably since this article was published. There is, for example, a valuable and representative collection of essays emanating from a Leuven (Louvain) University meeting, *Anti-Judaism and the Fourth Gospel,* edited by R. Bieringer et al. (Louisville: Westminster John Knox, 2001). I should also mention a couple of pieces that I have done. In an article entitled "John" in the volume *Early Christian Thought in Its Jewish Context,* edited by John Barclay and John Sweet (Cambridge: Cambridge University Press, 1996), I argued that the tension between the Johannine Jesus and "the Jews" is so great because their central bases for argument are held in common. They inhabit the same theological world, even though they disagree sharply on crucial issues. In 2003 Westminster John Knox published yet another edition of J. Louis Martyn's classic book, *History and Theology in the Fourth Gospel,* cited frequently above, for which I was asked to supply an introductory essay. In it my basic point is simply that Martyn's work, despite its controversial points, has led most exegetes to see John as a Jewish book, that is, a work quite unthinkable apart from Judaism, despite its tension with the form of Judaism the author knew. Yet their relation is not a friendly one, as Adele Reinhartz discovers in her challenging book *Befriending the Beloved Disciple: A Jewish Reading of the Gospel of John* (New York: Continuum, 2001). To review her book (*Theology Today* 59 [2002]: 323–26) was, I hope, to open a new phase of a discussion that began two millennia ago, with the prospect of more productive and positive results.

Since I wrote this essay more than fifteen years ago, one of my daughters married a Jewish man, and they have two daughters. So I can now say that not only are some of my best friends and colleagues

Jewish, but also members of my extended family. My daughter, as well as my son-in-law, are still touched by a fear of another Holocaust. Another Hitler might consider their children Jewish, although they are baptized Presbyterians. Nazi anti-Semitism was based on racial pseudo-science. In the Jewish tradition, only if the mother is Jewish are the children considered so, but if Jewishness were a racial distinction (which it is not), either parent's Jewishness might make the child Jewish.

John's description of "the Jews" as enemies of Jesus, who played a central role in causing his death, has undoubtedly stoked fires of anti-Judaism, if not anti-Semitism, among Christians. (Yet this did not happen in the church in South Carolina in which I grew up.) This hostility played a significant role in the atrocities of the twentieth century culminating in the Holocaust. Yet before the horrifying extent of Hitler's final solution of the Jewish problem was known, Confessing Christians in Germany recognized the profound opposition between National Socialism, and the popular Christianity it supported, and Christianity understood as obedience to Jesus and the good news of God's rule. To grasp the sharpness of this opposition requires a measure of historical, as well as theological, understanding and discernment. To begin with, John could not have conceived of post-Constantinian, not to mention early twentieth century, Christendom, or how his gospel might have been read in circumstances so far removed from his own. This is by way of saying that the cause of anti-Semitism is not the Gospel of John alone — it never was — but the gospel read through the eyes of a literalism or fundamentalism lacking any appreciation of the ancient evangelist's situation and purpose, but at the same time predisposed to opposition to Judaism. (That the Gospel of John played a role in developing such a predisposition is quite likely, but it was scarcely the only precipitating factor.) Such a reading also lacked the theological discernment to identify properly the center or burden of the Christian message. John's fundamental message is that God loves the world, not that God hates the Jews, or that his followers should. The latter is never said.

Although John does not espouse hatred of the Jews, hatred by the Jews is anticipated or reflected (John 9:22; 16:2; 15:18). Love and hatred rest uneasily close together in the Johannine literature, in a system of thought largely defined by an ethical dualism that verges on the ontological. (But in 1 and 2 John the enemy is no longer "the Jews," but other Christians, who are considered heretical.) The question is whether that system will rigidify, or whether the love of Jesus will break through the dualistic system and will overcome the danger of hatred — not only being hated, but hatred in response to hatred.

Notes

1. E. J. Epp, "Anti-Semitism and the Popularity of the Fourth Gospel in Christianity," *Journal of the Central Conference of American Rabbis* 22 (1975): 35. "Anti-Semitism," which has distinctly racial overtones, is inappropriate to describe the attitude of the Fourth Gospel, where the roots of conflict were theological and in all probability lay within the synagogue, between Jews who believed in Jesus and the majority, who did not. Nevertheless, the *reading of John* has contributed to the growth of anti-Semitism among Christians and others. See the excellent discussion of this matter and the entire question in R. A. Culpepper, "The Gospel of John and the Jews," *Review and Expositor* 84 (1987): 273–88, esp. 282–85. Culpepper's citation of the literature is a useful bibliographical aid. Note particularly the important article by J. Ashton, "The Identity and Function of the *Ioudaioi* in the Fourth Gospel," *Novum Testamentum* 27 (1985): 40–75.

2. R. R. Ruether, *Faith and Fratricide: The Theological Roots of Anti-Semitism* (New York: Seabury Press, 1974), 113.

3. Ibid., 116.

4. R. A. Spivey and D. M. Smith, *Anatomy of the New Testament*, 3rd ed. (New York: Macmillan, 1982), 13.

5. R. Bultmann, *Theology of the New Testament*, vol. 1, trans. K. Grobel (New York: Scribner, 1951), 1: "The message of Jesus is a presupposition for the theology of the New Testament rather than a part of that theology itself."

6. U. C. von Wahlde, "The Johannine Jews: A Critical Survey," *New Testament Studies* 28 (1982): 33–60.

7. J. L. Martyn, *History and Theology in the Fourth Gospel*, 3rd rev. ed. (Louisville: Westminster John Knox, 2003). The book was first published in 1968. See R. E. Brown, *The Gospel of John,* Anchor Bible 29 (Garden City, N.Y.: Doubleday, 1966), 1:lxx–lxxv, lxxxv, who also linked the origin of the Fourth Gospel to a similarly conceived synagogue controversy. Although their proposals were made independently, Martyn and Brown have subsequently carried on a mutually fructifying discussion. Brown's own position is set out most fully in *The Community of the Beloved Disciple* (New York: Paulist Press, 1979).

8. See R. T. Fortna, *The Gospel of Signs: A Reconstruction of the Narrative Source Underlying the Fourth Gospel,* SNTSMS 11 (Cambridge: Cambridge University Press, 1970), originally a dissertation with Martyn at Union Theological Seminary.

9. The form of the benediction, as reformulated, accepted by Martyn (*History,* pp. 62–63) is as follows:

For the apostate let there be no hope
And let the arrogant government be speedily uprooted in our days.
Let the Nazarenes [*notzrim* = Christians] and the *Minim* [heretics] be
     destroyed in a moment
And let them be blotted out of the Book of Life and not be inscribed
     together with the righteous.
Blessed art Thou, O Lord, who humblest the proud!

The malediction against the Nazarenes and Minim is thought to be the work of Samuel the Small (80–90 C.E.).

10. W. D. Davies, *The Setting of the Sermon on the Mount* (Cambridge: Cambridge University Press, 1964), 275–79.

11. Cited by Martyn, *History*, nn. 69 and 75; see also n. 81, in which he responds to D. R. A. Hare.

12. For example, R. Kimelman, "*Birkat ha-Minim* and the Lack of Evidence for an Anti-Christian Jewish Prayer in Late Antiquity," in *Jewish and Christian Self-Definition*, ed. E. P. Sanders et al. (Philadelphia: Fortress, 1981), 2:226–44; also S. T. Katz, "Issues in the Separation of Judaism and Christianity after 70 C.E.: A Reconsideration," *Journal of Biblical Literature* 103 (1984): 43–76. The near consensus at the end of the 1970s was stated well by J. T. Townsend, "The Gospel of John and the Jews: The Story of Religious Divorce," in *Anti-Semitism and the Foundations of Christianity*, ed. A. Davies (New York: Paulist Press, 1979), 72–97.

13. According to the assessment of scholarship by A. L. Nations, "Jewish Persecution of Christians in the Gospel of John" (unpublished paper read before the Fourth Gospel Section of the Society of Biblical Literature national meeting, Atlanta, November 1986).

14. D. M. Smith, "Johannine Christianity: Some Reflections on Its Character and Delineation," *New Testament Studies* 21 (1975): 222–48, esp. 233, 234. See Brown, *The Community of the Beloved Disciple*, 6, n. 5.

15. For example, R. H. Charles, *The Revelation of St. John*, International Critical Commentary (Edinburgh: T. & T. Clark, 1920), 1:56–57, 88–89.

16. On the possible relation of the conflict between Jews and Christians in Revelation to the *Birkat ha-Minim* and thus to the Gospel of John, see C. J. Hemer, *The Letters to the Seven Churches of Asia in Their Social Setting* (Sheffield, U.K.: JSOT, 1986), 4, 9, 12, 149.

17. F. F. Segovia, *Love Relationships in the Fourth Gospel: Agape/Agapan in 1 John and the Fourth Gospel* (Atlanta: Scholars Press, 1982), esp. 21–24, 217–19, argues that the final redaction of the discourse is the work of the author of 1 John or someone closely related to him in theology and ecclesiastical setting.

18. R. Bultmann, *The Gospel of John: A Commentary*, trans. G. R. Beasley-Murray et al. (Philadelphia: Fortress, 1971), 86–87. R. A. Culpepper, *Anatomy of the Fourth Gospel: A Study in Literary Design*, New Testament Foundation and Facets (Philadelphia: Fortress, 1983), 128–31, brings out the important element of truth in Bultmann's position: "Through the Jews, John explores the heart and soul of unbelief" (129). See also Ashton, "*Ioudaioi* in the Fourth Gospel," *Novum Testamentum* 27 (1985): 68.

19. Bultmann, *Theology of the New Testament*, 2:5.

20. C. H. Dodd, *The Interpretation of the Fourth Gospel* (Cambridge: Cambridge University Press, 1953), 5.

21. Ibid., 9.

22. C. K. Barrett, *The Gospel According to St. John*, 2nd ed. (Philadelphia: Fortress, 1978), 93, n. 1: "The best attempt to provide a specific *Sitz im Leben* for the Gospel is that of Martyn"; see 137–38 and *passim*. Barrett has reservations only as to whether Martyn's thesis alone does justice to the range of John's background and intention. Culpepper, *Anatomy of the Fourth Gospel*, has a different agenda and perspective, but his literary analysis achieves results that are not at all incongruous with Martyn's.

23. Brown, *The Community of the Beloved Disciple*, 93–144. This view becomes basic to his magisterial commentary, *The Epistles of John*, Anchor Bible 30 (Garden City, N.Y.: Doubleday, 1982), where he sets it out and defends it exegetically.

24. Only after having completed this paper did I become aware of the careful study and proposals put forward by N. A. Beck, *Mature Christianity: The Recognition and Repudiation of the Anti-Jewish Polemic of the New Testament* (Selinsgrove, Pa.: Susquehanna University Press, 1985), 248–74. Beck is thoroughly cognizant of historical-critical issues and literature, and should be consulted for the latter. He makes the noteworthy point that John's polemic operates at different levels (see R. E. Brown) and is not simply directed against Jews in an undifferentiated way (268–70). Whether one should drop "the Jews" in translating *Ioudaioi* and replace it with "the religious authorities" or the like, as Beck suggests, is an important and debatable question. Exactly the same issue arises from the standpoint of feminist hermeneutic in dealing with and translating allegedly sexist or paternalistic language in the Bible. My own conviction is that we cannot resolve these issues by removing offensive aspects of scripture occasioned by the concrete circumstances of historical origin. Those who want to read "Jews" will continue to do so, no matter what others say or think!

Chapter 11 _____

Purifying the Pulpit
Atoning for Anti-Judaism in Christian Preaching

William Willimon _____

During the summer of 1991, I preached in a rather sad Baptist congregation in the Rühr Valley, in a forlorn German rust belt city. The church was one of those postwar, concrete, gray, sad sort of German churches. I and my sermon were received warmly on that cold, rainy Sunday morning, despite my lousy German. After service, I was shown the congregational archive where a small collection of artifacts was lovingly preserved.

"That was our beautiful church," an old lady told me, pointing to a photograph of an impressive Neo-gothic church. "We had one of the greatest organs in the area. It was a wonderful church. One night, in 1945, it was all destroyed. An Allied bombing raid. American bombs, I think."

I stood there for a long, awkward moment before we were rescued by a summons to lunch. Leaving the congregation that afternoon, I was filled with a great sense of sorrow for a destructive past.

At the end of the next week, the very next week, I was leafing through files of the *Kirchenkampf* (the "church battle") archives near Münster. To my surprise, I came across a collection of sermons and church newsletters of the 1940s from the very congregation I had visited the week before. The mimeographed church newsletters all had a drawing of the big, Neo-gothic church in the upper corner. The newsletters reminded me of the typical church newsletter here in North America — reports on finances, notices of meetings, invitations to potluck suppers. In each newsletter the pastor wrote a "message to the congregation," most of them short meditations on various biblical themes.

In the spring of 1940, the pastor's weekly theme was, "Does Salvation Come from the Jews?"

His answer, "No!" Salvation is not from the backward, vindictive, culture-bound, legalistic religion of Israel. Jesus rose above such backwardness. Salvation comes through Jesus alone who was crucified by the Jews because of his prophetic condemnation of the Jewish misunderstanding of God. And so forth.

A shudder went down my spine there in the dusty confines of the archives. That newsletter became for me a metaphor of the high price that is to be paid by the church for the sin of our anti-Judaism. The rubble that results from our apostasy against Israel is all around us. I felt confirmed in my conviction that a major pastoral and homiletical task for pastors post-1940 is to lead our congregations in atonement for the sins of our fathers against the Jews.

Our anti-Jewishness is not deeply intellectual, nor is it complex and theoretical. A study of anti-Jewish preaching in Germany and in America in the twentieth century revealed the tired lack of originality in our anti-Jewishness. Furthermore, as my discovery of the church newsletter revealed, our Christian anti-Jewishness is mundane, grassroots, down home, and ordinary — as mundane and ordinary as a church newsletter. There, wedged in between reports of potluck suppers and church business meetings, is our sin against the Jews, our mundane, unspectacular, unoriginal contribution to the Holocaust.

It is the nature of anti-Judaism to be unspectacular in its inception, to seep in through the cracks in our theology, to squeeze into the margins of our sermons, to peek through our proclamation of Christ in ways we may not have meant, but ways that are no less insidious because of our lack of intent. Over the years — since that summer of 1991 to be exact — I have attempted to note and to remember outright or potentially anti-Jewish comments in sermons. These comments were overheard in sermons by mainline, liberal Protestant pastors:

- "Israel sat in a four-thousand-year darkness. Then the light of Christ came into the world and all was light."

- "It wasn't that God changed [with the advent of Jesus]; it was rather that we, that is, our perception of God changed. We saw what an error it was to regard God as vindictive and full of wrath. We at last saw what the patriarchs like Abraham failed to see. God is love."

- "Here was the religion where orthodox males prayed each day, 'God, I thank you that I was not born to be a woman.'"

- "The Old Testament is full of war and violence. The land of Israel still is today. This violence is a reminder of how radically different was the way of Jesus."

- "Progressive revelation! God is so large, so great, it takes centuries to get the point. The history of Judaism, and even Christianity, is a long story of a gradual, progressive realization of the full nature of God."

Supersessionism is a hard habit to break. It is the nature of modernity to be arrogant, to see history as gradual progression toward enlightenment. (How anyone could be dumb enough to believe this at the end of the world's bloodiest century, I don't know.) A favorite anti-Jewish libel has been that the faith of Israel is outmoded, primitive, something overcome by Christianity, or the Enlightenment, or some other ideology that now makes Jews superfluous. Therefore, Christian preachers must constantly critique the limits of modernity and what it has done to the Jews.[1] Moreover, we must constantly reiterate the special relationship, the peculiar indebtedness that the Christian faith has with God's people, the Jews. Our preaching must be an act of atonement for our continuing sin against Jews. We atone through repentance, by knowledge of and acknowledgment of, our sin. Atonement is a gift of a God who loves to forgive sinners, but it is also a gift of sinners who own their sin and claim their forgiveness through changed lives.

After Auschwitz, Christian preachers are compelled to consider the ways in which our preaching, in sometimes subtle but nevertheless tragic ways, fosters contempt for God's people, the Jews. The roots of anti-Jewish preaching lie in the New Testament itself, or rather in our misinterpretations of the New Testament. Even the designations "New Testament" and "Old Testament" imply that one has superseded or negated the other, as if God has now superseded Israel and nullified the covenant with Israel by a new covenant with the church.

In many places within the Christian scriptures, we are overhearing a painful, fierce family debate within Israel about the significance of Jesus. In some instances, we are overhearing a minority movement within Israel (the church) arguing with the religious majority (the synagogue) over who is truly faithful to Torah. It is an interpretive perversion for contemporary Christians, in our majority position, with two thousand years of Christian persecution of the Jews in our past, to align ourselves with New Testament critics of "the Jews" as if the New Testament were taking a superior attitude to Jesus' own people. It is tragic for contemporary Christian preachers to interpret the numerous prophetic rebukes of Israel, all examples of the marvelous self-critical ability of Israel, as if these rebukes were addressed to "the Jews" and not to us.

Some Jews looked at Jesus and saw the Messiah; others did not. Jesus was rejected by a variety of critics, some of whom were Jews. For contemporary Christian preachers to blame all Jews throughout history for the actions of a few of Israel's leaders at the time of Jesus is a sad misreading of history. The Jews did not kill Jesus; crucifixion was a vicious form of Roman punishment used quite often against Jewish insurrectionists. Jesus was one of the many Jews whom the Romans martyred for their faith. For later generations of Christian preachers to somehow implicate all Jews throughout history in the death of Jesus, for the church to turn on and to persecute Jesus' own people is a terrible act of Christian apostasy and sin against the people who taught the world to look for the Messiah and gave us God's word to show us the way.

Few Christian preachers would intentionally preach in a way that would hurt the Jews. However, there are many ways in which we are guilty of presenting Judaism in a false light:

1. Preachers will sometimes caricature the Hebrew scriptures, saying that "the Old Testament was full of judgment and wrath; the New Testament is full of love and grace." The God depicted in the Old Testament is the same God rendered by the Christian scriptures. The Hebrew scriptures were the only scriptures Jesus or Paul knew. There is good news in the Hebrew scriptures as well as judgment in Christian Gospels.

2. Judaism is sometimes falsely depicted as cold, dead, and legalistic. Jesus' criticism of some Pharisees in his day is interpreted as blanket condemnation of all Jews in every age. The gospel is said to have entered a religious and moral vacuum, or inflamed an otherwise dead religion. These are unfair depictions of Judaism in Jesus' day or ours.

3. The myth that "the Jews killed Jesus" is perpetuated when contemporary Christian preachers uncritically apply biblical passages about "the Jews" to present situations. Rather than say "the Jews" plotted against Jesus, it is more accurate to say "some of the authorities plotted against Jesus." Rather than say "a group of Jews rioted against Paul's preaching," it is better to say "Paul faced opposition from some of his fellow Jews at this synagogue."

Even though recent biblical scholarship has uncovered the true "Jewishness" of the rabbi named Jesus, the Jew of Tarsus named Paul, and indeed the close dependence of the Christian scriptures on the faith of Israel, Christians do have major theological differences with the Jews. Those differences do not lie in our superior moral or spiritual relation to the Jews, but rather in our differences concerning Jesus. Yet after Auschwitz, after the bitter fruit of centuries of Christian anti-Jewish rhetoric, Christian complicity in the persecution of Jews, and the comparative Christian silence during the Holocaust, faithful, biblical Christian preachers must examine the depictions and renderings of Jews and Israel in our preaching, must ask the God of Israel and Jesus to purify us of our anti-Jewish past, and enable us so to proclaim the gospel in our day that our brothers and sisters in Israel see in us a better reflection of the faith of Jesus, the Jew from Nazareth.

In a few Sundays, I will be preaching on Luke 4, Jesus' visit to his hometown synagogue in Nazareth. For the contemporary preacher to stand beside Jesus in the pulpit at Nazareth, lashing out against these conservative Jews (I've heard this text preached in just this way) would be interpretive perversion. We are not to find our place with Jesus in the pulpit, attacking the synagogue attendees in Nazareth. Rather, we are to find ourselves in the congregation that day, with those good synagogue-going folk who are challenged by Jesus. His challenge that day was not solely against Israel, but rather against any group (like today's church) that attempts to make the living God into our tame, housebroken pet.

A few Sundays later, I will preach on the Transfiguration. Today's preacher need not interpret this story solely in terms of Jesus superseding Moses and Elijah (for the story does not claim such supersession). Rather, we can preach this story as part of the faith in God that we Christians have received from Israel, faith in a God who comes to us, speaks to us, and comforts us along our journey.

Jesus told the story of the Waiting Father (the Prodigal Son), which we shall also tell about a month after Transfiguration. Reading our relationship with Jews into this story, we Gentile Johnny-come-latelies into faith in the God of Israel might see ourselves as the younger brother, the younger brother who came in from the "far country" and was invited into the party. As Gentiles, we had no claim upon the promises of the God of Israel. Yet through an amazing act of God's grace, we were invited into those promises. The Father's party, which by rights was for the older brothers and sisters in Israel, became a party also for us.

In an act of singular theological perversion, this story took a strange turn in our day. The younger brother, we Gentiles, joined the party and attempted to lock the older brother out of the party, claiming that God's grace was meant only for us. We Gentile Christians acted as if our older brothers and sisters in the faith were no longer in God's family.

Yet the story reminds us: when we shut out the older brother, we also alienate ourselves from the Father. The story of the Prodigal Son ends with the younger brother in the Father's house, enjoying the party. Yet out in the darkness, standing beside the older brother, was the Father. In excluding our older Brother, we had excluded the Father as well.

Notes

1. Among the books that I have found most helpful on the subject of removing anti-Judaism from the pulpit are R. Ruether, *Faith and Fratricide: The Theological Roots of Anti-Semitism* (New York: Seabury Press, 1974); C. M. Williamson, *Has God Rejected His People? Anti-Judaism in the Christian Church* (Nashville: Abingdon, 1982); C. M. Williamson and R. J. Allen, *Interpreting Difficult Texts: Anti-Judaism and Christian Preaching* (London: SCM Press, 1989).

Chapter 12

Reimaging the Christian–Jewish Relationship

The Next Stage in the Dialogue

John T. Pawlikowski

Using the Second Vatican Council's document *Nostra Aetate* as a benchmark, we are now four decades into the contemporary Christian-Jewish encounter. In actual fact the roots of the dialogue go back somewhat earlier as a pioneering generation of biblical scholars, educational researchers, and ecumenists laid the groundwork for that historic document as well as for similar statements from other Christian denominations. As we look back over these four decades, we can discern three important phases of the dialogue generated by the Catholic and Protestant documents. These phases are not entirely sequential in nature. Though we now stand in the first part of phase 3, not all the crucial work of the first two phases has yet been completed. In fact, some parts of the world are still experiencing the dialogue's early phases.

Phase 1 can best be described as the "cleansing" phase. It has primarily affected Christian education. Made possible by initial textbook studies on Protestant and Catholic materials at Yale and St. Louis universities respectively and subsequent surveys by Eugene J. Fisher, Philip Cunningham, and others, this phase has involved the removal from mainline Christian educational texts of the charge that Jews collectively were responsible for the death of Jesus, that the Pharisees were the archenemies of Jesus and spiritually soulless, and that Jews had been displaced in their covenantal relationship with God as a result of their refusal to accept Jesus as the Messiah, that the "Old Testament" was totally inferior to the New, and that Jewish faith was rooted in legalism while the Christian religion was based on grace. This phase is substantially complete as far as it goes in most of the mainline Christian churches in Western Europe and North America.

The second phase of the contemporary encounter between Jews and Christians dates back in some ways even further than the textbook studies. It is rooted in the new approach to the study of the Hebrew scriptures and the New Testament that began with several key individuals prior to World War II. Clearly a major shift of emphasis is under way in Christianity relative to the Hebrew scriptures. Increasingly, respected Christian scholars are recognizing the spiritual values of the books of the Hebrew scriptures in their own right and not merely as a backdrop for New Testament teaching. Research resulting from the contemporary Christian-Jewish encounter has begun to impact even more profoundly on New Testament interpretation, both with respect to the teachings and person of Jesus and the pastoral journeys of St. Paul. Recent years have seen a profound shift in New Testament exegesis with an increasing number of scholars emphasizing that Jesus must be returned to his essentially Jewish context if the church is to understand his message properly.

The third phase of the dialogue is only in its beginning stages. A number of Christian theologians, and a few Jewish religious scholars, have attempted to rethink the relationship between the church and the Jewish people in fundamentally new ways. And a few significant documents have appeared such as the Jewish document on Christianity *Dabru Emet,* a statement from the Catholic Pontifical Biblical Commission on the Jews and their scriptures, *A Sacred Obligation* from a group of Protestant and Catholic scholars who have been jointly studying the Christian-Jewish relationship since 1969, and the declaration *Church and Israel* from the important Leuenberg Church Fellowship of Reformation Churches in Europe. Finally, a study document coming from an ongoing Christian-Jewish dialogue co-sponsored by the National Council of Synagogues and the Secretariat for Ecumenical and Interreligious Affairs of the United States Conference of Catholic Bishops called *Reflections on Covenant and Mission* has stirred considerable discussion regarding its claim that Jews need not be the subject of Christian evangelization.

Neither the earlier documents nor the more recent ones have yet had a decided impact on mainstream Christian and Jewish theology. A few breakthroughs have been made, but on the whole the documents and scholarly studies on the Christian-Jewish relationship remain rather marginal in both faith communities. And little has been done to bring the new theological vision to bear on the shape of Christian worship. But these documents may be beginning to exercise some impact. The potential exists for a major transformation of Christian theology in particular, but only time will tell whether this potential will be realized.

In the following pages I will summarize some of the significant developments in the scriptural area and how they impact our image of the Jewish-Christian relationship. I will then evaluate some of the proposed new models and their impact on Christological understanding within the churches and the related question of evangelization of the Jews.

Developments in Scripture Studies

The contemporary dialogue with Jews and Judaism has begun to demonstrate an impact on the understanding of the New Testament and early Christianity in both Christian and Jewish circles. We are witnessing a genuine revolution in New Testament and early Christian scholarship, as well as parallel scholarship on the Judaism of the period. Within Christian biblical scholarship we are experiencing a rapid end to the dominance of the early *Religionsgeschichte,* which emphasized the almost totally Hellenistic background of Pauline Christianity, as well as its later, somewhat modified manifestation in the writings of Rudolf Bultmann and some of his disciples such as Ernst Käsemann and Helmut Koester. These exegetical approaches to the New Testament seriously eroded Jesus' concrete ties to, and dependence upon, biblical and Second Temple Judaism. This in turn tended to produce an excessively universalistic interpretation of Jesus' message which harbored the seeds of theological anti-Judaism.

There have been a number of leading biblical scholars, some with a continuing transcontinental influence, who have contributed to the de-Judaization of Christian faith. One of the most prominent has been Gerhard Kittel, the original editor of the widely used *Theological Dictionary of the New Testament.*[1] Kittel viewed postbiblical Judaism as largely a community in dispersion. "Authentic Judaism," he wrote, "abides by the symbol of the stranger wandering restless and homeless on the face of the earth."[2] And the prominent exegete Martin Noth, whose *History of Israel* became a standard reference for students and professors alike, described Israel as a strictly "religious community," which died a slow, agonizing death in the first century C.E. For Noth, Jewish history reached its culmination in the arrival of Jesus. His words are concise and to the point in this regard:

Jesus himself . . . no longer formed part of the history of Israel. In him the history of Israel had come, rather, to its real end. What did belong to the history of Israel was the process of his rejection and condemnation by the Jerusalem religious community. . . .

Hereafter the history of Israel moved quickly to its end.[3]

A third example is Rudolf Bultmann, who exercised a decisive influence over Christian biblical interpretation for decades. Unlike Kittel, who was removed from his teaching post at Tübingen in 1945 because of his explicit pro-Nazi sympathies, Bultmann's exegesis did not carry over into politics. But theologically speaking, his understanding of the Christ Event also left Jews and Judaism with little or no meaning after the coming of Jesus. In his *Theology of the New Testament* he held to a view similar to that of Martin Noth.[4] For Bultmann a Jewish people cannot be said to exist with the emergence of Christianity. For him Jewish law, ritual, and piety removed God to a distant realm. In contrast, the continued presence of Jesus in prayer and worship enabled each individual Christian to come ever closer to God. Bultmann's understanding of Judaism in Jesus' day was based on totally inadequate sources in terms of Second Temple Judaism and Jesus' relationship to its teachings and spirit.

This deep-seated tradition of separating Jesus from Judaism has continued to manifest itself in more recent biblical scholarship. Scholars such as Norman Perrin and John Dominic Crossan often interpreted Jesus' parables in a way that made them anti-Judaic in tone. This incidentally is where Clemens Thoma's lifelong work on the parables has made such an important contribution as a counterforce to this continuing Bultmannian tendency. The Bultmannian/Noth perspective has also surfaced in some of the liberation theologians, whose work is deeply rooted in the biblical tradition. The writings of Gustavo Gutiérrez and Jon Sobrino offer us two important examples of the continuing impact of the Bultmannian shadow. Gutiérrez, for example, has written that since "the infidelities of the Jewish people made the Old Covenant invalid, the Promise was incarnated both in the proclamation of a New Covenant, which was awaited and sustained by 'the remnant,' as well as in the promises which prepared and accompanied its advent."[5] And Clark Williamson, in a detailed study of Jon Sobrino's *Christology at the Crossroads*, has concluded that "each aspect of this anti-Judaic model is to be found in Sobrino's *Christology at the Crossroads*. Each theme can be documented in his text."[6]

In the last several decades we have seen a dramatic shift away from the predominance of the anti-Judaic understanding of the New Testament promoted by the likes of Kittel, Noth, and Bultmann. Led by scholars such as W. D. Davies, E. P. Sanders, Douglas Hare, Daniel Harrington, Robin Scroggs, and Clemens Thoma, the list of those repudiating what Arthur J. Droge has termed the "Bultmannian captivity" of New Testament exegesis continues to grow.

One important area in this regard is Pauline scholarship, which has proved to be so influential over the centuries in defining Christian self-identity over against Judaism. Certain Jewish scholars have intensified the anti-Judaic picture of Paul by arguing that while Jesus may have been a maverick in terms of the Jewish tradition, he clearly remained tied to the community of Israel. Paul, on the other hand, was responsible for the split between church and synagogue. Retired Bishop Krister Stendahl began the rethinking process regarding Paul and Judaism several decades ago.[7] E. P. Sanders, Peter Tomson, James D. G. Dunn, Daniel Harrington, and Lloyd Gaston have followed Stendahl's lead. They have been joined of late by several Jewish scholars, most notably, Alan Segal.

What is beginning to emerge from this new Pauline scholarship is a picture of Paul as still very much a Jew, still quite appreciative of the Torah (he may well have assumed its continued validity for Jewish Christians), and still struggling toward the end of his ministry to balance his understanding of the newness implied in the Christ Event with the continuity of the Jewish Covenant, something quite apparent in the famous chapters 9–11 of Romans on which Vatican II built its revolutionary understanding of the church's relationship to the Jewish people. It is also possible that some of the Pauline writings, especially those that have served as the basis for later Christological thinking, may have their roots in Paul's personal contact with the Jewish mysticism of his time, though Paul would have added his distinctive interpretation.[8]

Jesus and Judaism

We have also seen, both in official church statements and among New Testament scholars, a growing appreciation of Jesus' rootage in the progressive Judaism of his day. James Charlesworth and Cardinal Carlo Martini, S.J., the retired archbishop of Milan, are two prime examples of such new interpretation. Cardinal Martini has written that "without a sincere feeling for the Jewish world, and a direct experience of it, one cannot fully understand Christianity. Jesus is fully

Jewish, the apostles are Jewish, and one cannot doubt their attachment to the traditions of their forefathers."[9] And the 1985 Vatican *Notes* on preaching and teaching about Jews and Judaism declares that "Jesus was and always remained a Jew.... Jesus is a man of his time, and his environment — the Jewish Palestinian one of the 1st century, the anxieties and hope of which he shared."[10] In other words both recent scholarship as well as official Catholic teaching are saying that any portrayal of Jesus that separates him from the Judaism of his time in the manner of Bultmann represents a truncated and distorted presentation of his message and mission. For Jesus there was no "Old Testament." There were only "the scriptures," which he deeply integrated into a constructive way in his preaching.

One of the best summaries of where we are today in terms of Jesus' relationship to the Judaism of his time and the implications it has for understanding the church-synagogue relationship has come from the biblical scholar Robin Scroggs. His view has been endorsed by the late Cardinal Joseph Bernardin of Chicago, a leader in promoting Jewish-Catholic reconciliation in his own writings.[11] Scroggs emphasizes the following points: (1) The movement begun by Jesus and continued after his death in Palestine can best be described as a reform movement within Judaism. There is little evidence during this period that Christians had a separate identity from Jews. (2) The Pauline missionary movement as Paul understood it was a Jewish mission that focused on Gentiles as the proper object of God's call to his people. (3) Prior to the end of the Jewish war with the Romans in 70 c.e., there is no such reality as Christianity. Followers of Jesus did not have a self-understanding of themselves as a religion over against Judaism. A distinctive Christian identity began to emerge only after the Jewish-Roman war. And (4) the later portions of the New Testament all show some signs of a movement toward separation, but they also generally retain some contact with their Jewish matrix.

While not every New Testament scholar may subscribe to each and every precise point made by Scroggs, the consensus is growing that the picture he lays is basically accurate. Such a picture clearly contradicts the classical depictions of Christian-Jewish separation held by most people in each faith tradition.

As biblical scholars and theologians have begun to probe the implications of this new vision of Jesus as profoundly intertwined with the Jewish community of his time, two initial approaches have come to the fore in terms of understanding his and the early Christian community's relationship with the people of Israel. While within each approach different nuances appear as we move from scholar to scholar, we can generally characterize the two trends as "single covenant" and "double covenant" perspectives, with a few scholars such as Rosemary Radford Ruether and Paul Knitter arguing for multiple covenants.

Covenantal Theologies

The first approach is generally called the "single covenant" theory. It holds that Jews and Christians basically belong to one covenantal tradition that began at Sinai. In this perspective, the Christ Event represented the decisive moment when the Gentiles were able to enter fully into the special relationship with God that Jews already enjoyed and in which they continued. Some holding this viewpoint maintain that the decisive features of the Christ Event have universal application, including to the Jews. The statement on the Jewish Bible released in late 2001 by the Vatican's Pontifical Biblical Commission appears to argue that within historical time Jews await the Messiah through their own covenant. There is no need for Jews to convert to Christianity. But, when the Jewish Messiah eventually arrives, he will have some of the characteristics integral to Jesus' messiahship. Thus Jesus' messiahship retains universal implications. Other scholars in this continuing discussion are more inclined to argue that the Christian appropriation and reinterpretation of the original covenantal traditions, in and through Jesus, apply primarily to non-Jews.

The "double covenant" theory, which I have personally favored, begins at the same point as its single covenant counterpart, namely, with a strong affirmation of the continuing bonds between Christians and Jews. But then it prefers to underline the distinctiveness of the two traditions and communities, particularly in terms of their experiences after the final separation of church and synagogue. Christians associated with the perspective insist on maintaining the view that through the ministry, teachings, and person of Jesus a vision of God emerged that was distinctively new in terms of its central features. Even though there may well have been important groundwork laid for the emergence in Second Temple or Middle Judaism, what came to be understood regarding the divine-human relationship as a result of Jesus has to be regarded as a quantum leap.

It is very likely that discussions regarding the best way to reformulate a Christian covenantal theology will continue in earnest for the foreseeable future. Cardinal Walter Kasper, the president of the Holy See's Commission for Religious Relations with the Jews, has attempted such reformulation in addresses to the meeting of the International Vatican-Jewish Dialogue in New York in May 2001 and to the Annual Meeting of the International Council of Christians and Jews in Montevideo, Uruguay, in July 2001.[12] Many scholars now feel dissatisfied with both the single and the double covenantal options. This dissatisfaction stems from new research on the nature of Judaism in the first century C.E. as well as new insights into the process of church-synagogue separation.

With regard to the nature of first-century Judaism, scholars such as Jacob Neusner, Hayim Perelmuter, and Efraim Shuemli have emphasized that the Judaism of the first century was far from monolithic.[13] In fact, this was a very creative era in Jewish history. New groups were emerging that challenged the viewpoints of traditional Judaism. What Ellis Rivkin has termed "the Pharisaic Revolution," a revolution that clearly seeded the perspectives of Jesus and early Christianity, was challenging established Jewish perspectives in many areas, Neusner and Shmueli prefer to speak of "Judaisms" rather than "Judaism." Since Christian interpretations of the single covenantal perspective are often rooted in an ongoing, linear understanding of Judaism, their claim about "Judaisms" as the authentic picture of the Jewish belief in the first century poses a genuine challenge for a single covenantal model, which remains based in a far more uniform and linear understanding of the Jewish tradition. It also has to be said that a single covenantal theory can often mask a continued understanding of Christianity as the fulfillment of Judaism along classical Christian lines. Such theologies of fulfillment, even if they contain a positive view of the Jewish biblical tradition and argue for Jewish covenantal retention after Christ, have difficulty answering the question concerning to which of the Judaisms Christianity is linked and which it might complete. Most advocates of a single covenantal theory have not really dealt with this new, complex picture of the Jewish tradition.

Separation of Church and Synagogue

The other dimension of recent scholarship has to do with the view of how and when the separation of church and the synagogue took place. Most Christians were weaned on the idea that the church was basically established as a distinct religious entity by the time Jesus died on Calvary. On the Jewish side, the prevailing position was that, while Jesus obviously retained ties with the Jewish community, it was Paul, through his mission to the Gentiles, that really brought about the total separation between Christianity and Judaism. Both perspectives now appear quite simplistic. Even if we factor in the supposed decisions made on the Christian side at the so-called Council of Jerusalem spoken of in the book of Acts and on the Jewish side at the Synod of Jabneh, which supposedly placed Christians outside the parameters of the Jewish community, we now know that neither the council nor the synod gave final closure to the issue of whether Christians are merely followers of the Way of the Jew Jesus or a distinctively new religious community whose views have definitely broken any initial ties to Judaism.

Important Christian and Jewish scholars are now arguing that the actual separation between the church and the synagogue, while well advanced by 100 c.e., was not completed for several centuries after that. These scholars, such as Robert Wilken, Wayne Meeks, Alan Segal, and Anthony Saldarini, have uncovered continued ties between certain Jewish and Christian communities, particularly in the East.[14] Evidence of such ties is apparent in the second, third, and, in a few places, even the fourth centuries. And the ties were not just on the level of religious self-identity. They also affected popular practice. John Chrysostom, for example, launched a harsh critique of Judaism partly out of frustration that Christians in his area were continuing to participate in synagogue services on a regular basis. What sort of role these Christian synagogue attendees played is unknown and likely will remain so unless someone discovers a new cache of documents in a cave. It obviously would be terribly illuminating to have such information. But short of this, we can say that on the Christian side some people believed that their acceptance of Jesus did not undercut the importance of participating in Jewish ritual. On the Jewish side there certainly had to be some recognition that the Christians authentically "belonged" to the community since no evidence exists that they had to fight their way into the synagogue for Shabbat services.

As a result of this new scholarship, a number of those who have been deeply involved in rethinking the theology of the Jewish-Christian relationship over the years have begun to feel a certain measure of dissatisfaction about presenting the relationship between Judaism and Christianity in "mother-daughter" or "elder and younger brother" language, or even in single/double covenantal terms. These models now seem inadequate. Hence a number of new models for understanding the complex relationship have begun to emerge.

New Models for Relationship

Among the newly emerging images of the Christian-Jewish relationship the following appear to hold out the most promise. The first is the notion of "siblings" advanced by Jewish scholars Alan Segal and the late Hayim Perelmuter. This image argues that two new communities resulted from the revolution taking place in Second Temple Judaism. The first was rabbinic Judaism and the second the Christian church. Both went beyond former incarnations of Judaism in their basic message. While they had some early connections they eventually split into distinct and separate religious communities. This model has the advantage of stressing continued bonding ("siblings" remain connected no matter how distinctive they become) while also allowing for recognition that Christianity is far more than Judaism for the Gentiles.

Another image along the same lines is put forth by Mary Boys in her important volume *Has God Only One Blessing?*[15] She depicts Jews and Christians as "fraternal twins." This image has the same advantages as "siblings," although she appears to posit a somewhat deeper connection between Jews and Christians than even the "siblings" model. Her model may in fact tilt a bit too much for the connected rather than the disconnected side of the relationship. I believe it is necessary to stress that Judaism and Christianity over the centuries have become distinctive religious communities. While their bondedness needs emphasis and Christianity needs to recover its Jewish roots, postbiblical Judaism and Christianity differ in significant ways in their approach to religious understanding, and we should not gloss over this.

The theologian Clark Williamson, who has written important works on the Christian-Jewish relationship such as *A Guest in the House of Israel*[16] and been an active participant for many years in the ongoing Christian Scholars Group on Christian-Jewish Relations, argues for a basic relationship model of "partners in waiting." This is a more open-ended image. It lacks the emphasis on inherent bonding contained in the "siblings" and "fraternal twins" models. "Partners," after all, have no basic familial ties, but it does imply some linkage in terms of future hope. There is also a sense of common witness to the world implicit in Williamson's model.

The final model is in the process of being developed by University of California scholar Daniel Boyarin. In a series of addresses at the University of Chicago and the Catholic Theological Union in Chicago he has proposed the thesis that what finally resulted from the complex social and religious revolution in Second Temple Judaism were two new distinct religious communities known as rabbinic Judaism and Christianity. Thus for Boyarin we should image the Christian-Jewish relationship in terms of "co-emergent religious communities." His perspective accounts fairly well for the historical evidence now at hand in terms of that multiplicity of "Judaisms" at the time of Jesus and for the gradual process of separation outlined above. But it is weaker than the other images in stressing the continued bonding between church and synagogue.

We are still in the early stages of the contemporary rethinking of the Christian-Jewish relationship. Note that the newly emerging images are all more parallel than linear in their understanding of the relationship, unlike the earlier images of "single covenant," "mother-daughter," and "elder and younger brother." It would be the argument of all the scholars involved in this thinking that no simple straight lines can be seen from biblical Judaism to rabbinic Judaism and Christianity. Certainly a connection remains, but it is not as linear as once believed. We need now to continue the reflection process. New models may appear that will capture the complexity of the relationship even better than those we have just briefly examined. For now, my preference is for the "siblings" model. I believe it takes into account the pioneering work of Daniel Boyarin but leaves us with a better and clearer balance in terms of similarity/distinctiveness.

Implications for Christology

The new biblical scholarship raises important questions for theological understanding within Christianity, especially with regard to Christology. Traditional Christological approaches rooted in the belief that the Christ Event brought about the fulfillment of Judaism and the inauguration, in Jesus' lifetime, of a totally new religious community called the church to replace the "old Israel" no longer seem to meet the test of historical accuracy. So Christology needs serious rethinking, as the statement from the Christian Scholars Group on Christian-Jewish Relations *A Sacred Obligation* makes clear: "Affirming God's Enduring Covenant with the Jewish People has consequences for Christian Understandings of Salvation."[17]

Because Christology stands at the very nerve center of Christian faith, reevaluations of Christological affirmations cannot be done superficially. There is a trend found in some sectors of Christianity, especially in those most open to general interreligious understanding, that tends to depict the Christ Event as one of several authentic revelations with no particular universal aspect. Such a starting point is not acceptable to myself nor to people who have called for a significant rethinking of the church's theology of the Jewish people such as Cardinal Walter Kasper of the Vatican or the scholars associated with *A Sacred Obligation.* We must maintain from the Christian side some understanding that the Christ Event has universal salvific implications. As I have expressed in my major writings on the topic, for me Incarnation Christology has the best possibility for preserving such universalistic dimensions of the Christ Event while opining "authentic theological space for Judaism," as the late pioneer in Christian-Jewish relations Cardinal Joseph Bernardin of Chicago termed it.[18] I would now add that several of the affirmations in the new Pontifical Biblical Commission document on the Jewish scriptures also open up important possibilities in this regard.[19] I am thinking in particular of the document's claim that Jewish messianic expectations are not in vain and, even more, the affirmation that when the Jewish Messiah comes he will have some of the traits associated with Christ. The latter is a crucial claim because it seems to provide some room for a distinction between Christ and the Jewish Messiah.

The Pontifical Biblical Commission document is a study rooted in biblical exegesis, not a work of systematic theology. Hence it did not amplify this theological *kernel.* That remains a task for contemporary theologians in the church. But the affirmation opens the door for the possibility of exploring whether one can speak about the universal significance of the Christ Event in a way that allows for its articulation through religious symbols not directly connected with Christology, such as Jewish religious symbols. This may prove the most fruitful way of developing a Christology that remains open to religious pluralism, particularly with respect to Jews who are acknowledged to have authentic revelation from the Christian theological perspective, as Cardinal Walter Kasper has insisted in a number of recent presentations.[20]

At this point let me add that while I feel the Pontifical Biblical Commission document opens some new possibilities for dealing with Christological affirmation in the churches in a way that can leave a positive role for Judaism in the humanity's salvific process, there are troubling aspects to parts of the documents, as both Jewish and Christian scholars such as Michael Singer, Lawrence Frizzell, and Elias Mellon have underscored. This is especially the case with the document's portrayal of postbiblical Judaism, which regrettably seems to fall back on classical Christian stereotypes.

Another dimension of the Christological perspectives emerging from reflection on the new biblical scholarship may be the willingness to acknowledge that, while Christology remains central to the process of human salvation from the Christian theological perspective, there may be features in other religious revelations that also are central to this process without coming down on which is the most central. I have argued this viewpoint previously in my own writings regarding the role of the Jewish covenantal tradition, and I would reaffirm it again at this point.[21]

For the sake of completeness, I should mention one other possibility now under discussion. It is the perspective offered by Cardinal Joseph Ratzinger in several of his recent publications.[22] Ratzinger would maintain that Jews are a special case in terms of salvation. It would seem that he would exempt them from the framework presented in the controversial document *Dominus Iesus* issued from his Vatican congregation.[23] According to Cardinal Ratzinger the Jewish community would move to final salvation through obedience to its revealed covenantal tradition. But at the end time Christ's Second Coming would confirm their ultimate salvation. It is not clear whether Cardinal Ratzinger would demand explicit recognition of Christ as the Messiah from Jews as a requirement for their salvific confirmation, as is the case with some evangelical Christians who espouse similar views.

In my judgment this "delayed" messianism of the Christ Event in terms of the Jewish people is not as productive a starting point for rethinking Christological understanding today as is the direction found in the Pontifical Biblical Commission document. It would be interesting to know whether Cardinal Ratzinger would wish to adapt his position in light of the recent Pontifical Biblical Commission document for which he wrote a supportive introduction.

In rethinking Christology in light of the Christian-Jewish dialogue we will also need to include the reflections that have emerged regarding God's relationship to humanity after the experience of the Holocaust. Both Christian and Jewish scholars have addressed this issue.[24] Obviously, any alteration of our understanding with respect to God in light of the Holocaust will necessarily impact on Christianity's understanding of the Christ Event. We may have to move much more in the direction of a narrative Christology and to an emphasis on Jesus' ministry as a prime example of what Vytautas Kavolis has termed the "humanization of morality."[25]

In such a Christological vision the saving power of Christ is manifested in the lives of those who stand up for victims in the midst of social oppression. The rescuers during the Holocaust period are one important example of such witness. Writing in this vein James Moore argues that any "redemptive" emphasis in Christology must always "be tied to the historical reality of any point in time, dismissing all efforts to thoroughly spiritualize the notion of redemption."[26]

We remain at a very early stage in the process of rethinking the Christian theological understanding of Judaism and the impact of this rethinking on Christological understanding. As Christians we will likely never come to a point where our Christological affirmations will lead us to a theology of religious pluralism that squares totally with the basic faith affirmations of Judaism and other religions. Nor will the development of new thinking about Christianity exemplified in the Jewish document on Christianity *Dabru Emet* and its companion volume resolve all Jewish theological concerns about church teaching.[27] But in our globalized world in which interreligious understanding is not merely confined to the realm of theological ideas but directly impacts people's life together in the human community we can ill afford to shrink from this task.

Notes

1. Gerhard Kittel and Gerhard Friedrich, eds., *Theological Dictionary of the New Testament* (Grand Rapids, Mich.: Eerdmans, 1985).

2. Gerhard Kittel, *Die Judenfrage* (Stuttgart: Kohlhammer, 1933), 73.

3. Martin Noth, *The Laws in the Pentateuch and Other Studies* (Edinburgh: Oliver and Boyd, 1966).

4. Rudolf Bultmann, *Theology of the New Testament* (New York: Scribner's, 1951).

5. Gustavo Gutiérrez, *A Theology of Liberation* (Maryknoll, N.Y.: Orbis, 1973), 61.

6. Clark Williamson, "Christ against the Jews: A Review of Jon Sobrino's Christology," in *Christianity and Judaism: The Deepening Dialogue*, ed. Richard W. Rousseau, S.J. (Scranton, Pa.: Ridge Row Press, 1983), 148.

7. Krister Stendahl, "The Apostle Paul and the Introspective Conscience of the West," *Harvard Theological Review* 56 (1963): 199–216.

8. Hayim Perelmuter and Wilhelm Wuellner, eds., *Proceedings: Conference on the Questions of the Letters of Paul Viewed from the Perspective of the Jewish Response Mode* (Chicago: Catholic Theological Union, 1991), 15–18.

9. Carlo Maria Martini, S.J., "Christianity and Judaism: A Historical and Theological Overview," in *Jews and Christians: Exploring the Past, Present, and Future*, ed. James H. Charlesworth (New York: Crossroad, 1990), 19.

10. Helga Croner, ed., *More Stepping Stones to Jewish-Christian Relations: An Unabridged Collection of Christian Documents 1975–1983* (New York and Mahwah, N.J.: Paulist Press, 1985).

11. Cardinal Joseph L. Bernardin, *A Blessing to Each Other: Cardinal Joseph Bernardin and the Jewish-Catholic Dialogue* (Chicago: Liturgy Training Publications, 1996), 78–79.

12. Cardinal Walter Kasper, "The Good Olive Tree," *America* 185, no. 7 (September 17, 2001): 2–14.

13. See Jacob Neusner, *Death and Birth of Judaism: The Impact of Christianity, Secularism and the Holocaust on Jewish Faith* (New York: Basic Books, 1987); Efraim Smueli, *Seven Jewish Cultures: A Reinterpretation of Jewish History and Thought* (New York: Cambridge University Press, 1990); and Hayim Goren Perelmuter, *Siblings: Rabbinic Judaism and Early Christianity at Their Beginnings* (New York: Paulist Press, 1989).

14. See Wayne A. Meeks and Robert Wilken, *Jews and Christians in Antioch in the First Four Centuries* (Missoula, Mont.: Scholars Press, 1978); Robert Wilken, *John Chrysostom and the Jews: Rhetoric and Reality in the Late 4th Century* (Berkeley: University of California Press, 1983); Anthonly J. Saldarini, "Jews and Christians in the First Two Centuries: The Changing Paradigm," *Shofar* 10 (1992); and Robin Scroggs, "The Judaizing of the New Testament," *Chicago Theological Seminary Register* 75, no. 1 (Winter 1986).

15. Mary Boys, *Has God Only One Blessing? Judaism as a Source of Christian Self-Understanding* (New York and Mahwah, N.J.: Paulist Press, 2000).

16. Clark Williamson, *A Guest in the House of Israel: Post-Holocaust Christian Theology* (Louisville: Westminster/John Knox, 1993).

17. See *A Sacred Obligation: Rethinking Faith in Relation to Judaism and the Jewish People: A Statement by the Christian Scholars Group on Christian-Jewish Relations* (Boston: Boston College, 2002).

18. See John Pawlikowski, *Christ in the Light of the Christian-Jewish Dialogue* (New York and Ramsey, N.J.: Paulist Press, 1982); John Pawlikowski, *Jesus and the Theology of Israel* (Wilmington, Del.: Michel Glazier, 1989); and John Pawlikowski, "Christology, Anti-Semitism, and Christian-Jewish Bonding," in *Reconstructing Christian Theology*, ed. Rebecca S. Chopp and Mark Lewis Taylor (Minneapolis: Fortress, 1994). On Cardinal Bernardin's thinking, see Joseph Cardinal Bernardin, *A Blessing to Each Other: Cardinal Bernardin and the Jewish-Catholic Dialogue* (Chicago: Liturgy Training Publications, 1996), 78–79.

19. The Pontifical Biblical Commission, *The Jewish People and Their Sacred Scriptures in the Christian Bible* (Vatican City: Libreria Editrice Vaticana, 2002).

20. Kasper, "The Good Olive Tree," 12–14; Cardinal Walter Kasper, "Spiritual and Ethical Commitment in Jewish-Christian Dialogue," in *From the Martin Buber House*, ed. Ruth Weyl, 30 (Summer 2002): 12–20. Cardinal Kasper has also delivered important addresses on this topic in Jerusalem, Chicago, Boston, and Connecticut.

21. See n. 18; also see John Pawlikowski, "Christology after the Holocaust," in *The Myriad Christ: Plurality and the Quest for Unity in Contemporary Christology*, ed. T. Merrigan and J. Haers (Leuven, Paris, and Sterling, Calif.: Leuven University Press and Uitgeveru Peeters, 2000), 381–97.

22. Cardinal Joseph Ratzinger, "The Heritage of Abraham: The Gift of Christmas," *L'Osservatore Romano* 29 (December 2000); Cardinal Joseph Ratzinger, *Many Religions — One Covenant* (San Francisco: Ignatius Press, 2000); and Cardinal Joseph Ratzinger, *God and the World: Believing and Living in Our Time* (San Francisco: Ignatius Press, 2002).

23. The text of *Dominus Iesus* can be found in *Origins* 30, no. 14 (September 14, 2000): 209–19; for a discussion of *Dominus Iesus,* see John Pawlikowski, Paul Griffiths, Francis X. Clooney, Robert A. Cathey, and Mary C. Boys, *"Dominus Iesus:* A Panel Discussion," *Proceedings of the Fifty-sixth Annual Conference of the Catholic Theological Society of America,* 56, ed. Richard C. Sparks (2002): 97–116; for a Jewish perspective, see David Berger, *"Dominus Iesus* and the Jews," *America* 185, no. 7 (September 17, 2001): 7–11.

24. See *From the Unthinkable to the Unavoidable: American Christian and Jewish Scholars Encounter the Holocaust,* ed. Carol Rittner and John K. Roth (Westport, Conn.: Praeger, 1997); and *Contemporary Jewish Religious Responses to the Shoah,* Studies in the Shoah V, ed. Steven Jacobs (Lanham, Md.: University Press of America).

25. See Vytautas Kavolis, *Moralizing Cultures* (Lanham, Md.: University Press of America, 1993).

26. See James F. Moore, *Christian Theology after the Shoah,* Studies in the Shoah 7 (Lanham, Md.: University Press of America, 1993).

27. See *Christianity in Jewish Terms,* ed. Tikva Frymer-Kensky, David Novak, Peter Ochs, David Fox Sandmel, and Michael Signer (Boulder, Colo.: Westview, 2000); and John T. Pawlikowski, "Christianity in Jewish Terms: Re-visioning Our Self-Understanding," *Living Light* 38, no. 1 (Fall 2001): 66–72.

Afterword

Ed Satell _____

It is an honor to have the opportunity to reflect on this fine collection of essays by the brilliant and dedicated Christian scholars represented in this book.

As a Jew, privileged to be born in America the same year Joe DiMaggio joined the New York Yankees, I have known two sides of Christianity, one positive and one negative. One side produced remarkable contributions and the second disastrous outcomes.

The positive side created many noble traditions built on a concept of mutual respect and resulted in remarkable humanistic contributions. These include:

1. Democracy — to the greatest extent realized in history. While not a Christian idea, the implementation of democracy giving greater liberty than ever before has taken place in modern societies dominated by Christians who passionately rejected the tyrannical, anti-democratic practices in established societies dominated by other Christians. Beginning with the American Revolution, political leaders increasingly extended the full weight of their moral prestige to equal rights. These largely Christian societies produced people with the political power and influence in their states to develop rules and institutions facilitating:

   - the free exercise of religion according to one's conscience and beliefs;

   - the separation of church and state;

   - the idea that all people be treated with dignity and given a voice.

2. Unparalleled progress — in notable areas. In these democratic states there have been unparalleled advances in education, medicine, the average standard of living, and — most importantly — liberty.

3. Human rights — to the greatest degree in history. The well-being and security of our modern, free society rests on the foundation of equal rights and personal liberties for all, without regard to one's religious beliefs, race, ethnicity, or gender.

4. Tolerance — at the highest level ever. This is based on the concept that each person's duty to God is founded on the idea that we are all God's children created in the image of God. Thus, there must be a fundamental respect for the equal rights of others protected by law.

Unfortunately, side-by-side with these remarkable contributions is a paradoxical historical dark side. The record shows that tolerance has been a difficult issue for Christians over many centuries.

Christian societies, with their clerical and lay leadership in charge of political systems, believed that theirs was the only true and complete religion. This troubling view was based on the religious conviction that they alone knew God's true message and that it was their duty to bring it to *all* humankind. This duty frequently extended to coercing people to accept Christian religious beliefs and practices rather than follow their own beliefs and traditions. Such practices often ran unchecked, resulting in deprivation, destruction, and, death in almost every century, affecting literally millions of people. People were treated differently and accorded fewer rights, not because of skill, knowledge, performance, or competence, but solely because they had a different religious faith. A social justice system was abandoned for a religious belief system.

This part of history, generally accepted today by Christian scholars, was more than a clash of civilizations. It was a moral and political outrage. In these dark periods of history, the credo was: "If you don't believe as we believe, you are not entitled to social justice or human rights." Simply put, rights and tolerance flowed from religious beliefs, and that meant only Christianity. As James Carroll, prize-winning Catholic author chronicled in *Constantine's Sword,* the result was often savagery, injustice, and death for many.

Today Life Is Different

Today, in the United States, life is much different. More than ever, much of the Christian community has accepted religious diversity and rallied to a more positive concept of tolerance — one that Cardinal Archbishop Franz Koenig refers to as "one of mutual respect."

This is consistent with the view that the dialogue be characterized by common respect, not demonization.

I was fortunate to have been born in an era when some of the most influential Christian religious leaders, steadfastly and passionately, reversed centuries of religious dogma that were leading sources of hatred. How thrilling it is to be part of the generation that witnessed dramatic changes, as evidenced by:

- The Catholic document *Reflections on Covenant and Mission*, which describes the growing respect for Jewish tradition that has unfolded since the Second Vatican Council. The document states that "a deepening Catholic appreciation of the eternal covenant between God and the Jewish people, together with the divinely given mission of Jews to witness to God's faithful love, lead to the conclusion that campaigns that target Jews from conversion to Christianity are no longer theologically acceptable in the Catholic Church" (as noted in Edward Idris Cardinal Cassidy's chapter, p. 31).

- Pope John Paul II's words at Yad Vashem in March 2000: "I assure the Jewish people that the Catholic Church, motivated by the gospel law of truth and love and by no other consideration, is deeply saddened by the hatred, acts of persecution and displays of anti-Semitism directed against Jews by Christians at any time and in any place. . . . Let us build a new future in which there will be no more anti-Jewish feeling among Christians" (as noted in Eugene J. Fisher's chapter, p. 90).

- Statements made on the 450th anniversary of the death of Martin Luther by the World Lutheran Federation and the Evangelical Lutheran Church in America. These statements disassociated "the Lutheran Church today from the anti-Jewish writings that marred Luther's later days. The president of the Council of Protestant Churches in Germany, Klaus Engelhardt, in a Brotherhood Week Statement in March 1996, warned strongly against any attempts to explain or justify Luther's anti-Judaism on theological grounds" (as noted in Dr. Eugene J. Fisher's chapter, p. 81).

These views, while not fully accepted by everyone, are beautifully demonstrated in these essays and generally supported by the vast majority of Christians in the United States. These writings tend to embrace what Judaism and most of the religions of Asia affirm — that human beings may use different religions to speak to God just as they use different languages to speak to each other.

In other words, we now live in a society that supports religious pluralism, sharing a common vision of peace and cooperation among all people along with acceptance and tolerance of different religious beliefs and practices.

Advances in Acceptance:
A Family History

My family history going back just five generations illustrates the advances made in acceptance of religious diversity.

For me, life was better than it was for my father. I grew up in an era with greatly reduced visible and invisible "no Jews allowed" signs. There were still a few housing communities, jobs, and promotions restricted for me — meaning areas in which I wasn't allowed to buy a home and a number of fraternities at college and business clubs after college that I couldn't join. Generally however, I did enjoy most of the liberties available to Christian society. I could go to the college of my choice based on honest competition and, largely, had equal economic opportunities. While certain social institutions were still segregated, much of my life was one of assimilation with shared human rights and equal societal rights.

For my father, life offered more opportunities than it had for his father. Born in Russia, he immigrated to the United States at the age of two. Freed from tyranny and persecution, he was able to experience greater liberty and opportunity. Yet he often had to avoid stone-throwing on the way to school, and some limitations on job opportunities led him to change his name and keep silent about his heritage. Nevertheless, because his father immigrated to America, he survived the Holocaust that killed six million Jews mostly from countries dominated by Christians. Many other relatives did not.

My grandfather had it better than his father. He survived the pogroms where about one-third of all Jews living in Russia were murdered, largely by Christians, simple because they were Jewish. He somehow walked over a thousand miles to board a ship to come to America. Once here, he worked hard to earn the necessary sums to send for his family so they too, could join a society that, though segregated and intolerant in many ways, offered basic liberties and genuine hope for his children's future.

My children have it better than I did. My youngest children have no experience with religious intolerance. In response to historical issues, they have little sensitivity saying, "That was then, this is now." Their experience is largely that such problems of intolerance don't exist anymore. What great times we live in and what a great country. God bless America. We live in the best of times.

Today I'm the principal owner of a company that employs over six hundred people. These employees represent many faiths, races, and ethnic backgrounds. No one in our leadership judges people based on his or her church affiliation — that is fully accepted as a private and personal matter. Our concerns are solely about competence in its many forms, to serve our customers with excellence, and to be a workplace that fairly balances the needs of our employees and the company. That, we believe, serves the long-term interests of us all.

It is a thrill to be both involved in and supportive of this educational project. It offers great promise for increased understanding and allows for personal acceptance of a higher power as we each know it. That should lead to a better society for all inhabitants.

Contributors

Norman A. Beck is the Poehlmann Professor of Theology and Classical Languages and the Chairman of the Department of Theology, Philosophy, and Classical Languages at Texas Lutheran University. In addition to teaching full-time he serves as the contract pastor of St. John's Lutheran Church in Denhawken, Texas. His academic degrees include those from Princeton Theological Seminary, Trinity Lutheran Seminary, Capital University, and an honorary D.D. from Trinity Lutheran Seminary.

Irvin J. Borowsky is the founder/chairman of the American Interfaith Institute. For over two decades, the Institute has been a leader in building relationships among Americans of all faiths and defusing bigotry within a framework of research, international symposia, and educational initiatives. Mr. Borowsky has been at the cutting edge of removing anti-Semitism from the pulpit and the Bible. He has edited and published eighteen books and thirty-one special reports for professors teaching the next generation of priests, ministers, and rabbis. Mr. Borowsky is, in addition, the founder/chairman of the National Liberty Museum in Philadelphia. The distinguished exhibitions and programs of the National Liberty Museum, which celebrate the historical and diverse perspectives of the American experience, are seen by over sixty thousand visitors annually. Mr. Borowsky's philanthropic outreach reflects a broad base of interests, creativity, and influence throughout the nation and abroad. Under his aegis, the American Interfaith Institute and the National Liberty Museum continue to develop Christian-Jewish relationships and address the nation's need for understanding and tolerance in futures to come.

Mary C. Boys is the Skinner and McAlpin Professor of Practical Theology at Union Theological Seminary, New York City. Among the seven books she has authored or edited is *Has God Only One Blessing? Judaism as a Source of Christian Self-Understanding*. She is past president of the Association of Professors and Researchers in Religious Education and a Henry Luce III Fellow in Theology. A Roman Catholic, she has been a member of the Sisters of the Holy Names of Jesus and Mary since 1965.

Edward Idris Cassidy is President of the Pontifical Council for Promoting Christian Unity and of the Commission for Religious Relations with the Jews. In 1943, he entered St. Columba's Seminary, Springwood, Australia, and a year later was promoted to St. Patrick's College, Manly. After receiving a diploma in diplomatic studies, he joined the diplomatic service of the Holy See.

Eugene J. Fisher, Associate Director of the Secretariat for Ecumenical and Interreligious Affairs of the United States Conference of Catholic Bishops (USCCB), has received from Pope John Paul II his fifth quinquennial appointment as Consultor to the Holy See's Commission for Religious Relations with the Jews. Dr. Fisher is one of ten such Consultors worldwide and the only American.

Howard Clark Kee is President of the American Interfaith Institute. He is Emeritus Professor of the New Testament at Boston University and Senior Research Fellow in Religious Studies at the University of Pennsylvania. He is the author of many books and articles in the fields of New Testament and the history of early Christianity.

Barclay M. Newman is Senior Translations Officer for the American Bible Society. He was chair of the Contemporary English Version (CEV) of the Bible. He was a member of the Old Testament Committee for the Good News Translation, also known as Today's English Version. Before joining the American Bible Society in 1986, Dr. Newman was a United Bible Societies Translation Consultant in the Far East for twenty years, living and working in the Philippines, Indonesia, Singapore, and Malaysia. He established the Department of Translation at the University of Malaysia, where he also lectured. He has written extensively on issues of translation, both religious and secular.

John T. Pawlikowski is Professor of Social Ethics and Director of the Catholic-Jewish studies program at Catholic Theological Union in Chicago. He has also served by presidential appointment on the United States Holocaust Memorial Council since its inception in 1980 and is a member of the Council's Executive Committee, Academic Committee and Committee on Conscience, and is chair of the Church Relations Subcommittee.

Petr Pokorný is Head of the Center for Biblical Studies and member of the Protestant Theological Faculty at Charles University in Prague, Czech Republic. He has written *Jesus in the Eyes of His Followers: Newly Discovered Manuscripts and Old Christian Confessions, The Genesis of Christology: Foundations for a Theology of the New Testament,*

Colossians: A Commentary, Philosophical Hermeneutics and Biblical Exegesis, as well as several German monographs and countless articles on the New Testament.

James A. Sanders has been a professor at the Claremont School of Theology, Claremont Graduate School, Colgate Rochester Divinity School, Union Theological Seminary, Columbia University, Yale University Divinity School, and Jewish Theological Seminary in New York City. He is founder and president emeritus of the Ancient Biblical Manuscript Center in Claremont, California. Under his direction the Center houses the most complete and best preserved collection of archival quality films of the Dead Sea Scrolls in the world. He oversaw the publication of *The Dead Sea Scrolls Catalogue and Index* and published a diplomatic edition of films of *Leningradensis,* the oldest complete Hebrew Bible in the world. He has authored or edited 20 books and over 250 scholarly articles. He is past president of the Society of Biblical Literature. He is the only American member of the United Bible Society's Hebrew Old Testament Text Critical Project.

D. Moody Smith is George Washington Ivey Professor Emeritus of New Testament in the Divinity School of Duke University, where he taught theological and graduate students for thirty-seven years and directed two dozen doctoral dissertations, many on some aspects of the Johannine literature. He has published numerous books and articles on the Gospel and letters of John. In 1999 he was President of the Society of Biblical Literature.

Krister Stendahl, one of the pioneers in the theory and practice of Jewish-Christian dialogue, received his Theological Doctorate from the University of Uppsala in 1954. Dean and John Lord O'Brian Professor of Divinity at Harvard Divinity School from 1968 to 1979, he was moderator of the World Council of Churches Consultation on the Church and the Jewish people from 1975 to 1985. He was Bishop of Stockholm from 1984 to 1989. Retired to Cambridge, Massachusetts, he remains a prolific author and he is a foremost authority on St. Paul.

William Willimon is a graduate of Wofford College, Yale Divinity School, and Emory University. He has served as pastor of churches in Georgia and South Carolina. For four years, beginning in 1976, he served as Assistant Professor of Liturgy and Worship at Duke Divinity School, teaching courses in liturgics and homiletics, and served as Director of the Ministerial Course of Study School at Duke and Presiding Minister in the Divinity School Chapel. In 1992 he was named as the first Distinguished Alumnus of Yale Divinity School.

Index

Steinfels, Margaret O'Brien, 82
Stendahl, Krister, 82, 161
Stern, Robert, 85
Sternberg, Sigmund, 86–87
Strabo, 64
supersessionism, 47, 55, 60 n. 2, 72, 153
supersessionistic anti-Jewish polemic, 17–18, 20
synagogue
  expulsion from, 135–38
  separation from church, 164–65

Tanenbaum Foundation, 81
technology, 59, 62 n. 28
Tertullian, 54
texts, for each minority, 45–46
Theological Dictionary of the New Testament, 159
Theology of the New Testament (Bultmann), 160
Thoma, Clemens, 160, 161
Toaff, Elio, 80
Today's English Version, 20, 22
tolerance, 174–75
Tomson, Peter, 161
Torah, debate over interpretation of, 50
Toward Greater Understanding (Cernera), 79
triumphalism, 47
Twelfth Benediction, 136–38

United States, Christian-Jewish relations in, 82–85
United States Conference of Catholic Bishops, 31, 91, 93
universalism, 41, 42, 46

University of Rome, 82
Urbach, E. E., 42
U.S. Holocaust Memorial Museum, 83, 84

Van Buren, Paul M., 86
Vatican. *See also* Roman Catholic Church
  Notes on preaching and teaching (1985), 162
  release of materials from archives, 95
Voll, Fritz, 83
Voltaire, 41, 57

Waxman, Mordecai, 84, 86, 86
Weber, Ferdinand, 57
Wellhausen, Julius, 57
Wengst, Klaus, 142
We Remember: A Reflection on the Shoah, 47, 85–86, 87, 88
Wilken, Robert, 165
Williamson, Clark, 160, 166
Winer, Mark, 81, 85, 92
Wise, Isaac Meyer, 70
Wise, Stephen, 70
Wistrich, Robert, 47
World Lutheran Federation, 81, 175
World Union of Progressive Judaism, 91
Wurzburger, Walter, 83

Yad Vashem, 26, 85, 88, 89–90, 175
Yoffie, Eric H., 27

Zaiman, Joel, 85, 87
Zegota, 80
zero-sum problem, 44, 45
Ziyadah, Muhammad, 58

Books by the
American Interfaith Institute_____

Every Day Remembrance Day
by Simon Wiesenthal, 1986

Jews and Christians: Exploring the Past, Present and Future
edited by James H. Charlesworth, 1990

Jesus' Jewishness: Exploring the Place of Jesus in Early Judaism
edited by James H. Charlesworth, 1991

Artists Confronting the Inconceivable
by Irvin J. Borowsky, 1992

The Crucified Jew: Twenty Centuries of Christian Anti-Semitism
by Dan Cohn-Sherbok, 1992

Overcoming Fear between Jews and Christians
edited by James H. Charlesworth, 1992

Faith without Prejudice: Rebuilding Christian Attitudes toward Judaism
by Eugene J. Fisher, 1993

Within Context: Essays on Jews and Judaism in the New Testament
edited by Professor David Efroymson, Dr. Eugene Fisher, and Rabbi
Leon Klenicki, 1993

*Mature Christianity in the 21st Century: The Recognition and Repudiation
of the Anti-Jewish Polemic in the New Testament*
by Norman A. Beck, 1994

*Education for Shalom: Religion Textbooks and the Enhancement of the
Catholic and Jewish Relationship*
by Philip A. Cunningham, 1995

*Friends, Colleagues and Neighbors: Jewish Contributions to American
History*
by David A. Rausch, 1996

Dead Sea Scrolls: The Rule of the Community
Photographic Multi-Language Edition
by James H. Charlesworth, 1996

Removing Anti-Judaism from the Pulpit
edited by Howard Clark Kee and Irvin J. Borowsky, 1996

Removing Anti-Judaism from the New Testament
edited by Howard Clark Kee and Irvin J. Borowsky, 1998

Voyage to Liberty through Faith
by Irvin J. Borowsky, 2000

Heroes of Liberty from Around the World
by Irvin J. Borowsky, 2003

Faith Transformed: Christian Encounters with Jews and Judaism
edited by John C. Merkle, 2003

Defining New Christian/Jewish Dialogue
edited by Irvin J. Borowsky, 2004

Write or fax for catalogue
American Interfaith Institute
321 Chestnut Street, Philadelphia, PA 19106, USA
Fax: 215-925-3800
E-mail: aii@interfaith-scholars.org

Of Related Interest

The World Spirituality Series:
An Encyclopedic History of the Religious Quest

Our *World Spirituality Series* entails a comprehensive account of the variety of spiritualities throughout human history. A multi-volume series with more than 500 contributing scholars worldwide, presenting the spiritual wisdom of the human race in its historical unfolding, from prehistoric times through the great religions to the meeting of traditions at the present. The series includes the following volumes:

Jewish Spirituality
Volume I
0-8245-0762-2, $49.50 hardcover
0-8245-0891-2, $29.95 paperback
Volume II
0-8245-0965-X, $29.95 paperback

Christian Spirituality
Volume I
0-8245-0847-5, $37.50 paperback
Volume II
0-8245-0967-6, $37.50 paperback
Volume III
0-8245-1144-1, $35.00 paperback

African Spirituality
Volume I
0-8245-0780-0, $34.95, paperback

Buddhist Spirituality
Volume I
0-8245-1452-1, $24.95 paperback
Volume II
0-8245-1595-1, $49.50 hardcover
0-8245-1596-X, $34.95 paperback

Confucian Spirituality
Volume I
0-8245-0775-4, $50.00 paperback
Volume II
0-8245-2254-0, $60.00 paperback

Hindu Spirituality
Volume I
0-8245-0755-X, $49.50 hardcover
Volume II
0-8245-1671-0, $39.95 paprback

Islamic Spirituality
Volume I
0-8245-1131-X, $37.50 paperback
Volume II
0-8245-1724-5, $29.95 paperback

South and Meso-American Native Spirituality
0-8245-1662-1, $29.95, paperback

Modern Esoteric Spirituality
0-8245-1444-0, $37.50 paperback

Spirituality and the Secular Quest
0-8245-0774-6, $29.95 paperback

crossroad

Of Related Interest

Abraham Heschel
Edited by Samuel Dresner
I ASKED FOR WONDER
A Spiritual Anthology

This revised gift edition of a spiritual classic features pearls of Rabbi Heschel's mystical vision, selected for their universal appeal and divided under such major thematic headings as God, prayer, religion, man, Bible, and holy deeds.

0-8245-0542-5, $16.95 paperback

Henri Nouwen
LIFE OF THE BELOVED
Spiritual Living in a Secular World

"Gentle and searching. This Crossroad book is a spiritual primer for anyone seeking God." — *The Other Side*

Over 200,000 copies in print! When Nouwen was asked by a secular Jewish friend to explain his faith in simple language, he responded with *Life of the Beloved,* which shows that all people, believers and nonbelievers, are beloved by God unconditionally.

Henri Nouwen, author of *The Only Necessary Thing* and *Here and Now,* is considered one of the great spiritual writers of our day. He taught at Harvard, Yale, and Notre Dame, and spent the last ten years of his life at L'Arche Daybreak community for physically and mentally challenged people in Toronto.

0-8245-1986-8, $14.95 paperback

Please support your local bookstore,
or call 1-800-707-0670 for Customer Service.

For a free catalog, write us at

THE CROSSROAD PUBLISHING COMPANY
16 Penn Plaza, 481 Eighth Avenue
New York, NY 10001

Visit our website at
www.crossroadpublishing.com
All prices subject to change.

crossroad